T0059754

Post Growth

Kennedy's words into a comprehensive distillation of our core economic foundations and presents our assumptions about growth not as laws of nature but as flawed precepts in inescapable conflict with them. *Post Growth* is part grand historical narrative, part philosophical treatise, and taken fully, an invitation for readers to explore the deeper undercurrents of what can make a just, fulfilling and sustainable society.'

Kerry Kennedy – President of Robert F. Kennedy Human Rights

'With a rare combination of incisive economic analysis and poetic imagination, Tim Jackson brilliantly exposes the flaws of our growth-addicted economies and reveals the profound truth that there will be – indeed there must be – life after capitalism. A thrilling intellectual journey towards a post growth world.'

Roman Krznaric – Author of *The Good Ancestor*

'Some call Tim Jackson's thesis about capitalism's flaws, and proposed remedies, provocative. After two decades as a successful capitalist (or so they tell me) I don't find it provocative at all, rather an existential imperative.'

Jeremy Leggett – Founder of Solarcentury and SolarAid

'Compelling in its critique of capitalism's relentless obsession with "more", forensic in its analysis of the growth myth's destruction of human flourishing and planetary wellbeing, and utterly inspiring in its vision of the better, fuller, more fulfilled lives that are possible, *Post Growth* is an urgent and eloquent plea for radical change.'

Caroline Lucas – MP, Green Party

'*Post Growth* is a short book. Which means you can afford to re-read it, hungrily and rapidly, to get what you may not have got first time around. Tim Jackson does us the courtesy of not trotting out a well-meaning diatribe about the fatal inadequacies of growth-obsessed capitalism; he seeks rather to explain why it is that the minds of so many have been entirely captured by the language of growth and by the mantra of more, even now, on a planet that is imploding in front of our eyes. It's a *tour de force*, sinuous, disruptive – and a masterpiece of measured rage and love.'

Jonathon Porritt – Author of *Hope in Hell*

'*Post Growth* is an extraordinary, powerful and beautifully written book – difficult to put down. Jackson names the beast in our midst that the coronavirus crisis has unmasked and makes a huge and timely contribution to humanity. A masterpiece!'

Mamphela Ramphele – Co-President, The Club of Rome

'Economic wisdom wrapped up in poetry – only Tim Jackson knows how to do that. A beautiful read.'

Kate Raworth – Author of *Doughnut Economics*

'Being relatively agnostic about economic growth I took on Tim Jackson's *Post Growth* with a critical eye, but his razor-sharp analysis and powerful storytelling has convinced me more than ever that the myth of never ending conventional growth is crumbling. If you want to measure true value in life and our economies, this is your guidebook.'

Johan Rockström – Director, Potsdam Institute for Climate Impact Research

'In trademark fashion, Tim Jackson offers up psychology, philosophy and economics through the lives of a series of extraordinary individuals who can guide us through the collapse of capitalism and the struggle to create something better. An expansive, wise and uplifting work that will reorient the conversation. Highly recommended.'

Juliet Schor – Author of *After the Gig*

'Jackson is the great storyteller of economics – of what economies can and should be. In this book he draws on the stories of original thinkers near and far to show that post growth – a future beyond capitalism – is not just necessary for our planet, but also to sustain our human spirit.'

Julia Steinberger – University of Lausanne

'This is an important and urgent book. Tim Jackson exposes the cult of growth which is leading us down a path of human misery and destruction of the natural world. A book of questions, interwoven with stories and philosophy: our collective challenge is to create the answers.'

Jo Swinson – Director, Partners for a New Economy

'Tim Jackson offers us a book that is both honest and hopeful. It gently lets its stark messages unfold through writing that is often more like poetry than political prose. As rich in imagery as it is grounded with examples and clear explanations of why our economy is in urgent need of recalibration, this is a book that future generations will be glad was written.'

Katherine Trebeck – Author of *The Economics of Arrival*

'It is harder and harder to deny that we in the "developed" world are collectively prisoners of an addictive delusion – the myth of constantly increasing economic growth. In this brief but weighty book, Tim Jackson exposes this myth with unambiguous clarity, and asks whether we are able to seize the opportunities for tough self-questioning prompted by the current global crisis.'

Rowan Williams – 104th Archbishop of Canterbury

'At a time when the oligarchy is striving to greenwash its ecocidal ways, Jackson's empowering and elegiac new book takes the real fight to them, elegantly but forcefully: to flourish on a living planet, humanity must plan for life after capitalism. Not only a must-read but also a highly enjoyable one!'

Yanis Varoufakis – Author of *Another Now*

Post Growth
Life after Capitalism

Tim Jackson

polity

First published in 2021 by Polity Press

20

Polity Press
65 Bridge Street
Cambridge CB2 1UR, UK

Polity Press
101 Station Landing
Suite 300
Medford, MA 02155, USA

ISBN-13: 978-1-5095-4251-2
ISBN-13: 978-1-5095-4252-9 (pb)

A catalogue record for this book is available from the British Library.

Typeset in 9.5 on 14 pt Fournier by
Servis Filmsetting Ltd, Stockport, Cheshire
Printed and bound in Great Britain by TJ Books Limited

The publisher has used its best endeavours to ensure that the URLs for external websites referred to in this book are correct and active at the time of going to press. However, the publisher has no responsibility for the websites and can make no guarantee that a site will remain live or that the content is or will remain appropriate.

For further information on Polity, visit our website: politybooks.com

Contents

For Linda

Prologue

'History, despite its wrenching pain,
Cannot be unlived, but if faced
With courage, need not be lived again.'
Maya Angelou, 1993[1]

'What's past is prologue; what to come,
In yours and my discharge'
William Shakespeare, 1610[2]

'The world starts to shake,' wrote the sociologist Peter Berger, 'in the very instant that its sustaining conversation begins to falter.' The year 2020 bore undeniable witness to this inconvenient truth. Our sustaining conversation didn't just falter. It did an abrupt about-turn and slapped us in the face. Hard. No surprise then that, even today, the world feels more than a little shaky.[3]

It had all been going so well. The sun rose resplendent over the highest town in Europe in the third week of January. Its early morning light shone magnificently on the snow-capped peaks, shimmering gold against a sky of deep Alpine blue. Nature in all her glory. The perfect backdrop to the annual congregation of privilege and power. The premiers and the billionaires. The limousines and the helicopters. The 50th World Economic Forum in Davos, Switzerland, was about to begin.

'It's a jamboree,' my host confided as he picked me up from the small train station late the night before and showed me to my temporary accommodation. A borrowed apartment set back from the town, overlooking the mountains. 'It's a jungle,' replied his companion. And we all managed to laugh.

Our leaders know the rules of this game. They understand intuitively that this ostentatious pageant is a beauty parade. The stakes are always high. The spotlights must gleam on sharp suits and slick haircuts. The cavalcades must jostle for superiority. The rhetoric must be finely tuned to the peculiar struggles of the day. The sun must shine dutifully on the righteous. The charade must leave no room for doubt. The mountains must forever seal the bargain struck in the basements of history: more begets more; power begets power; growth begets growth. To them that hath, it shall be given.

They have been jetting into this dazzling resort for five decades now, pledging allegiance to the great god Growth. Come snow or shine, foul weather or fine, their task has always been crystal clear: to bring succour to the weak, courage to the faint of heart. To slay the dragons of doubt, wherever they may arise. Economic growth is just a confidence trick. As long as we believe it, it will happen. All shall be well, and all shall be well, and all manner of things shall be well.[4]

There are invariably plenty of dragons. This year was no different. Europe was worried about the rise of populism. Australia was anxious about the fires still raging through its long 'black summer'. The US was worried about the trade war with China. Almost everyone was suddenly worried about the carbon. Climate change was the surprise beneficiary of this year's struggle for attention. The school strikes of 2019 had finally pushed the matter to the very top of the Forum's list of long-term risks to growth.

That was a first. Against the odds, a broad – though not quite unanimous – consensus emerged from Davos that something would have to be done before the floods and the bushfires – or the annoying activists who occasionally blocked the flow of limousines into and out of the town – derailed the economic bandwagon.

'The impatience of our young people is something we should tap,' Angela Merkel told the conference. She was referring of course to the extraordinary leadership shown by the young Swedish activist Greta Thunberg, who was there in town for a second time, speaking truth to power with the extraordinary clarity of a seer. A dove amongst the pigeons. This year, the simplicity of her message had drawn a whole new generation of activists into a battlefield they could barely recognize. They looked around them in defiance and awe. The German

Chancellor was not the only old-timer to find a tear of sympathy welling in her eye.[5]

Not everyone was impressed. 'Is she the chief economist or who is she? I'm confused,' joked the US Treasury Secretary, Stephen Mnuchin, in a moment he must surely have regretted almost instantly. 'After she goes and studies economics in college she can come back and explain that to us.' When you're in a hole, Stephen. Stop digging.[6]

But they couldn't, of course. Stop digging. Then US President Donald Trump was determined to place this nonsense in the wider context of an undying creed. 'To embrace the possibilities of tomorrow, we must reject the perennial prophets of doom and their predictions of the apocalypse,' he proclaimed. 'They are the heirs of yesterday's foolish fortune tellers.' Our hero gazes out across the savannah of upturned faces towards the horizon of endless opportunity. I imagine a self-satisfied speechwriter somewhere, smiling smugly. Life is just a Hollywood B-movie.[7]

Paradise is a land forged from a frontier mentality. Burn it down, dig it up, build over it. Progress is a construction site. It may look messy for now, but tomorrow's shopping malls and condominiums will be a glorious sight. Let those who doubt this vision perish. The school kids, the climate strikers, the extinction rebels: they can all go to hell. The heirs of yesterday's foolish fortune tellers be damned. Compulsory optimism is the flavour of the day. And the blindingly obvious is expunged from the discourse of power.

The snow above Davos grows thinner each year. The Alpine ski season is a month shorter than it was when Klaus Schwab first founded the Forum in 1971. The climate is changing. The ice is melting. A million species are facing extinction. We are shifting ecological balances in totally unpredictable ways. Sometimes in ways that have turned out to be deadly. The finite planet we call home is being altered, perhaps irreversibly, by the massive expansion in human activity that parades under the seductive banner of progress. But please don't bring these realities to our attention. We have worked so hard not even to acknowledge them.[8]

In another telling moment from the same Davos stage, Austria's newly elected Chancellor had used his time at the podium to call for Europe to become more innovative, more forward-looking, more dynamic. At 33 years old, Sebastian Kurz had just become the young-est head of state in the world for the second time in the space of as many years. He chastised the 'pessimism' of the older European economy and praised the dynamism of younger, 'hungrier' ones. Echoing the frontier rhetoric, he called for renewed optimism, more innovation, faster growth. Nothing new there.

But later in the discussion, Kurz acknowledged something curious. 'I had a recent discussion about various philosophies: a postgrowth society,' he told his audience. 'We were being told perhaps it could be good for a country not to grow, that it would be better to measure happiness rather than economic growth.' The delivery was engaging. A faint smile played across the young man's lips. For a moment, you were tempted to believe that a more sensible generation of politicians had arrived at last. That things would be different now. 'It all sounds wonderful and romantic,' he said. His eyes twinkled knowingly. 'But happiness doesn't pay pensions!'[9]

Kurz had introduced the postgrowth society only to dismiss it again immediately as a fluffy utopian notion, with no grounding in reality. But within weeks that easy denial seemed like yesterday's wisdom. The end of the warmest January on record held a harsh lesson in store. Few were aware of it even in privileged Davos. Some over-anxious minds may have harboured sneaking suspicions. A few unscrupulous politicians had already employed insider knowledge to shift their personal wealth away from the danger of financial collapse. But most were either ignorant or in denial. No one could quite have predicted the extent of the profound economic and social shock that was about to launch itself on an unsuspecting world. Even as Trump delivered his frontier eulogy, a young Chinese doctor, Li Wenliang, was fighting for his life in Wuhan Central Hospital.[10]

Less than a month before, Li had alerted the world to a new, unfamiliar and surprisingly virulent strain of coronavirus that had broken out in an area of the city occupied by an animal market. He had been roundly reprimanded for his pains. Two weeks later he would be dead: a heroic statistic on the alarmingly exponential curve of an escalating pandemic. Li would be the first of many, unnecessary and utterly preventable deaths, as frontline workers lost their lives caring for others.[11]

Within weeks, the global economy would be plunged into an existential crisis. Denial would turn to confusion. Confusion would turn to expediency. Expediency would overturn everything. Normalcy would evaporate more or less overnight. Businesses, homes, communities, whole countries went into lockdown. Even the preoccupation with growth would diminish momentarily in the urgency to protect people's lives. Alongside an uncomfortable reminder of what matters most in life, we were being given a history lesson in what economics looks like when growth disappears completely. And one thing became clear very rapidly: it looks nothing like anything the modern world has seen before.

Eventually we will find a better terminology to describe our world. Language sometimes situates itself a little too close to the object of its scrutiny. Happiness may or may not be the currency of tomorrow's pensions. By then our sights will have been recalibrated. Our vision will have been renewed. We will have the ability to articulate a future for our economy free from the shackles that bind our creativity to the terms of an outmoded dogma.

But for today *Post Growth* is still a necessary thought-world. Even in the midst of change, we remain obsessed with growth. *Post Growth* is a way of thinking about what might happen when that obsession is over. It invites us to explore new frontiers for social progress. It points in the direction of an uncharted terrain, an unexplored territory in which plenty isn't measured in dollars and fulfilment isn't driven by the relentless accumulation of material wealth.

Life after Capitalism had been a tentative, speculative subtitle to this book. An invitation to the reader to imagine our prevailing economic paradigm as a temporary thing; a barely surviving remnant of old ways of being; not the immovable immutable truth it presumes itself to be. In the early months of its writing, capitalism was taken apart, piece by piece, in an increasingly astonishing effort to save lives and rescue normalcy. During the year 2020, the world witnessed the most extraordinary experiment in non-capitalism that we could possibly imagine. We now know that such a thing is not only possible.

It's essential under certain circumstances. The goal of this book is to articulate the opportunities that await us in this vaguely glimpsed hinterland.[12]

Post Growth is an invitation to learn from history. An opportunity to free ourselves from the failed creed of the past. Just as the poet and civil rights activist Maya Angelou once invited the American people to do in the poem with which this prologue began. Its job right now is to help us reflect honestly on the situation we find ourselves in. Its deeper task is to lift our eyes from the ground of a polluted economics and glimpse a new way of seeing what human progress might mean. Soon it will not be needed. Its power for today is to free our lips from the mantra of yesterday and allow us to articulate a different kind of tomorrow.

1

The Myth of Growth

'We are in the beginning of a mass extinction. And all you can talk about is money and fairytales of eternal economic growth.'
Greta Thunberg, September 2019[1]

'Too much and for too long, we seem to have surrendered personal excellence and community values in the mere accumulation of material things.'
Robert F. Kennedy, March 1968[2]

St Patrick's Day, 17 March 1968. It was an unseasonably mild Sunday evening. The night air held the promise of an early spring as Senator Robert F. Kennedy arrived in Kansas from New York. He had just that day declared his candidacy for the 1968 Presidential race. To run, he would have to stand against the incumbent President, Lyndon B. Johnson. Senator against President; Democrat against Democrat: it looked like a tough fight ahead and Kennedy was by no means convinced of success.[3]

But as he stepped down onto the Kansas City tarmac, he and his wife Ethel were besieged by a couple of thousand supporters who broke a police cordon and charged across the runway, shouting 'Go Bobby Go!' and demanding a speech. Nothing had been arranged and there was no loudhailer. So Kennedy sportingly threw a few remarks into the wind, before realizing he was barely audible. 'That was my very first campaign speech,' he said. 'Now let's all clap.' He clapped his hands, the audience clapped theirs, and everyone laughed. It seemed like an auspicious start to a Presidential campaign.

The Senator was still noticeably nervous the next morning when he arrived at Kansas State University (KSU) for the first formal speech of the campaign. It had been scripted carefully for the occasion by his speechwriter, Adam Walinsky. First impressions matter. None of the campaign team could predict its impact. Kansas was one of the most conservative states in the country, loyal to the establishment and the American flag. It was perhaps the last place that could be expected to show sympathy for Bobby Kennedy's anti-war message.

He opened, cleverly, with a quote from William Allen White, the former editor of a Kansas newspaper. 'If our colleges and universities do not breed [students] who riot, who rebel, who attack life with all the youthful vision and vigor, then there is something wrong with our colleges,' he said. 'The more riots that come out of our college campuses, the better the world for tomorrow.' It was a candid appeal to the generation who had brought the anti-Vietnam protest movement out of the ghettos and onto the campuses of liberal, middle-class universities across America. The students loved it. Kennedy's opening salvo was met with a 'happy roar'.[4]

The excitement was palpable. The students in the hall – some of them perched on the rafters – cheered wildly at his all-out attack on the Vietnam war, his disdain for the Johnson administration and his outrage at the base morality of contemporary US policies at home and overseas. This was no cautious opening foray in a careful Presidential campaign. It was dynamite. The reception was better than anyone had dared to hope for. Eyewitnesses describe how one journalist, the *Look Magazine* photographer Stanley Tettrick, found himself hemmed in by a crowd of students, trying to stay upright in the pandemonium, while shouting to no one in particular: 'This is Kansas, fucking Kansas! He's going all the way!'[5]

Bobby Kennedy was not, as history would have it, 'going all the way'. But no one knew this, on the opening day of that fateful Presidential campaign. The team were ecstatic. The campaign was launched. The journalists had their story; and the media coverage would do their candidate no harm whatsoever. There was a palpable sense of relief as the entourage made their way to the second speech of the day at KSU's great sporting rival, the University of Kansas.

Walinsky spent the short journey re-drafting the speech he'd prepared for the second event. It had been intended as a calmer and more considered lecture, showing a more reflective, intellectual side to the

Senator. It contained one segment of particular interest here concerning the uses and abuses of the Gross Domestic Product (GDP) – the indicator used to measure economic growth. It was an odd, slightly arcane topic for a campaign speech. A testament to the radicalism of Kennedy's political vision. It almost didn't survive the rewrite.

Surprised and delighted by the rapturous response to his morning speech, Kennedy wanted more of the same for the afternoon. So he instructed his speechwriter to ditch the sober content and give the talk a bit of the morning's edge. What emerged was something that might affectionately be called a 'mash-up': sections from earlier speeches woven together with anecdote and the occasional well-timed joke. By chance the section on the GDP remained. And that simple quirk of fate would turn out to have enormous relevance to this book – and indeed to the life of its author, who was no more than a kid when it all happened.[6]

Myth matters

Every culture, every society, clings to a myth by which it lives. Ours is the myth of growth. For as long as the economy continues to expand, we feel assured that life is getting better. We believe that we are progressing – not just as individuals but as a society. We convince ourselves that the world tomorrow will be a brighter, shinier place for our children and for their children. When the opposite happens, disillusionment beckons. Collapse threatens our stability. Darkness looms on the horizon. And these demons – real as they may be in an economy dependent so entirely on growth – are rendered even more powerful by the loss of faith in our core sustaining narrative. The myth of growth.

I am using the word 'myth' here in the kindest possible sense. Myth matters. Narratives sustain us. They create our thought-worlds and shape our social conversations. They legitimize political power and underwrite the social contract. To pledge allegiance to a myth is not inherently wrong. We all do it, in some form or another, implicitly or explicitly. But to acknowledge the power of myth is not always to condone it. Sometimes myths work for us. Sometimes they work against us.

When they abide, it is for a reason. Economic growth has brought extraordinary affluence. It has lifted millions out of poverty. For those rich enough and lucky enough, it has enabled lives of unbelievable comfort and complexity and luxury. It's delivered opportunities our ancestors couldn't possibly have imagined. It's facilitated the dream of social progress. Nutrition, medicine, shelter, mobility, flight, connectivity, entertainment: these are amongst the manifold fruits of economic growth.

But the massive explosion of economic activity has also wreaked unparalleled havoc on the natural world. We are losing species faster than at any time in human history. Forests are decimated. Habitats are lost. Agricultural land is threatened by economic expansion. Climate instability is undermining our security. Fires consume whole swathes of land. Sea levels rise. Oceans acidify. The affluence we aspire to has been purchased at an unpayable price. The myth that sustained us is in the process of undoing us.

My aim here is not to rehearse these impacts or document their damages. There are many excellent accounts already available. 'For more than thirty years, the science has been crystal clear,' as Greta Thunberg reminded the UN Climate Conference in 2019. Her words became a cultural meme. They even spawned artistic and musical interpretations that reach beyond audiences scientists ever could. The hard evidence behind them resides in countless pages of painstaking work.[7]

I intend instead to pick up on her deeper challenge. Beyond the 'fairytales of economic growth' lies a world of complexity that demands our attention. Those fairytales are coded into the guidance manual of the modern economy. They've been there for decades. They continue to distort our understanding of social progress and prevent us from thinking more deeply about the human condition.

The broad thesis of this book is that good lives do not have to cost the earth. Material progress has changed our lives – in many ways for the better. But the burden of having can obscure the joy of belonging. The obsession with producing can distort the fulfilment of making. The pressure of consuming can undermine the simple lightness of being. Recovering prosperity is not so much about denial as about opportunity.

This book addresses the conditions under which we thrive. It seeks out our potential to live better, fuller, more fulfilling and more sustainable lives. The end of growth is not the end of social progress. To dethrone material expansion is not to give up on human prosperity. Another (better) world is possible. This much has been obvious at least since Kansas.

By the time Kennedy arrived at the 'Phog' Allen Fieldhouse, home to the University of Kansas basketball team, the atmosphere was electric. Well over twenty thousand people had crowded into the arena: students and staff, journalists and commentators, spilling onto the yellow court, leaving only a tiny circle for Kennedy to stand at a wooden lectern, crammed with microphones.

He opened with what must have been a more or less spontaneous joke. 'I'm really not here to make a speech,' he quipped. 'I've come because I came from Kansas State and they want to send their love to all of you. They did. That's all they talk about over there, how much they love you.' The rivalry between the two top Kansas universities was legendary. The 'Sunflower Showdown' between the two basketball teams had played out fiercely since 1907. The arena exploded in laughter. They loved him already. Enough, apparently, for him to offer them a little macroeconomics.[8]

A little macroeconomics

In the simplest of terms, the GDP is a measure of the size of a country's economy: how much is produced, how much is earned and how much is spent across the nation. It's counted, needless to say, in monetary values: dollars, euros, yuan and yen. It is the headline measure within a complex System of National Accounts, which since 1953 has provided the international standard for measuring the economic performance of the nation. Developed during the Second World War, the accounts were motivated in part by the need to determine how much governments could afford to spend on the war effort.[9]

By 1968, the size of the GDP had become a near ubiquitous indicator of political success. The formation of the Group of Seven (G7) nations in the early 1970s and the Group of Twenty (G20) nations in the 1990s cemented its influence. This one number became the single most important policy indicator across the world. For more than half a century it has stood as an unrivalled proxy for social progress. All the more extraordinary, then, to find a critique of it on the opening day of a Presidential campaign.

When Kennedy started to talk economics, the crowd grew quieter, Walinsky told me, attentive to the content as well as the rhetoric of the Senator's vision. His argument was blindingly simple. The statistic in which we place so much faith simply counts the wrong things. It includes too many 'bads' that detract from our quality of life and excludes too many 'goods' that really matter to us. The GDP 'counts air pollution and cigarette advertising, and ambulances to clear our highways of carnage', Kennedy told the University of Kansas crowd:

> It counts special locks for our doors and the jails for the people who break them. It counts the destruction of the redwood and the loss of our natural wonder in chaotic sprawl. It counts napalm and counts nuclear warheads and armored cars for the police to fight the riots in our cities. It counts Whitman's rifle and Speck's knife, and the television programs which glorify violence in order to sell toys to our children.[10]

And even as it erroneously includes all these things as benefits to us, there are numerous aspects of our lives that simply go missing from the tally. The inequality in our society. The contributions of those who are unpaid. The labour of those who care for the young and the elderly at home. It fails to measure 'the health of our children, the quality of their education or the joy of their play'. It misses 'the beauty of our poetry . . . the intelligence of our public debate . . . the integrity of our public officials'.

It would be rare to find a politician speaking in such terms today. We've become ever more captured by the language of growth. Our politics has become increasingly distanced from decency, integrity and public value. Our obsession with the GDP bears some of the responsibility for this. That single number 'measures neither our wit

nor our courage, neither our wisdom nor our learning, neither our
compassion nor our devotion to our country', concluded Kennedy.
'It measures everything in short, except that which makes life worthwhile.' At the end of his critique, he paused momentarily. The audience began to applaud. Not with the wildness of the earlier cheering,
Walinsky recalled. 'Now their applause was serious, thoughtful. But it
seemed like it might go on all day,' he said.

It's hard to convey how extraordinary Kennedy's remarks that day
were. In the late 1960s, the US economy was growing at around 5%
each year. It was assumed that those levels of growth would continue
indefinitely. Economics itself was built around the assumption that
they would do so forever. Yet here was a politician, not just any
politician, but one aspiring to be President of the largest economy on
the planet, casting doubt on capitalism's most sacred shibboleth: the
relentless accumulation of wealth.[11]

Measuring the 'busyness' of the economy and calling that progress
never was and never will be the route to a lasting prosperity. That was
the blunt message conveyed so eloquently in RFK's address to the
Kansas students. It was destined to become the poster-speech for a
critique of the GDP which has lasted to this day.[12]

Backstory

I've long been fascinated by that day in Kansas, particularly after a
live recording of the University of Kansas speech was unearthed from
a basement some twenty years ago. It elicited a frisson of historical
excitement in what was still a marginalized debate. In the intervening
years, I began to take its existence for granted. RFK's words became
just a part of the everyday vocabulary used by those critical of economic growth or of the instruments we use to measure it.

Increasingly, though, I found myself wondering about the source of
his ideas. How did a postgrowth critique find its way into a Presidential
campaign speech at that time and in that place? What motivated that
man in that moment to take such a counter-cultural position in what
must have seemed quite an arcane debate? Perhaps in finding out, I
would begin to understand why it has taken more than half a century

for the ideas themselves to be taken even remotely seriously. And why they are still for the most part neglected.

In an event marking the fiftieth anniversary of the speech, I happened to share a conference platform with Kerry Kennedy, the founder of the RFK Human Rights Foundation and Bobby Kennedy's daughter. I was keen to find out if she knew anything more about the origins of his concern over economic growth than I did. But she'd just been a child when her father was in Kansas. And though her life's work had continued his legacy, campaigning for human rights, the particularities of the GDP were an unfamiliar terrain. She hadn't known of the significance of that speech until our event together, she told me.

Crucially, though, our conversation led me to the testimony of Adam Walinsky, who was immediately receptive to my hunger for more insight. He was also quite clear that he personally wasn't the source of the ideas. The content always came from the man himself. 'I wrote them, I picked the words,' he said. 'But it was RFK who picked all the examples: they were issues he had been talking about since we got to the Senate. So the entire speech is really about the country he wanted us to be. It was about his vision of America and of what we should aspire to be.'

A little further investigation uncovered two critical links in the intellectual backstory. One was to the mid-twentieth-century American liberalism that was beginning to explore the discontents of a society built on consumerism. The other was to the astonishing impact achieved by Rachel Carson's *Silent Spring*. Published in 1962, that one book has long been credited with single-handedly kickstarting the modern environmental movement. It certainly influenced the Kennedys. Bobby's brother President John F. Kennedy had supported Carson throughout the writing of the book and publicly endorsed her work against fierce opposition from industry when it first appeared in public.

The 'burgeoning environmentalism' of JFK's administration was firmly established in a speech made by one of his close advisers during the successful 1960 election campaign, the Supreme Court Justice William O. Douglas. Bobby Kennedy and Douglas had been friends since the 1950s. They had hiked together in the wilderness. RFK's love of nature was born in part at least from his familiarity with it. Douglas was a willing ally in the struggle to build a more ecological polity. 'The preservation of values which technology will destroy . . . is indeed the new frontier,' he declared at a Wilderness Conference in San Francisco.[13]

That sentiment was echoed by the American liberals. Two intellectual figures towered over others in the emerging debate. (One of them quite literally: the economist John Kenneth Galbraith was 6 foot 9 inches tall.) Galbraith had written scathingly about the dubious rewards of consumerism. In the most widely cited passage in his bestseller book on *The Affluent Society* (1958), he wrote:

> The family which takes its mauve and cerise, air-conditioned, power-steered, and power-braked automobile out for a tour passes through cities that are badly paved, made hideous by litter, blighted buildings, billboards, and posts for wire that should long since have been put underground.[14]

His Harvard colleague and one-time neighbour Arthur Schlesinger had written in a very similar vein about the obscenity of conspicuous wealth amidst rising public squalor. In a pamphlet on *The Future of Liberalism* written in 1956, he complained that:

> Consumer goods of ever-increasing ingenuity and luxuriance pour out of our ears, but our schools become more crowded and dilapidated, our teachers more weary and underpaid, our playgrounds more crowded, our cities dirtier, our roads more teeming and filthy, our national parks more unkempt, our law enforcement more overworked and inadequate.[15]

Both men became advisers to the Kennedys during JFK's administration. The groundwork for a critique of the GDP had been laid by two important cultural conversations of the time, both of them critical of the American dream, one for social and the other for environmental reasons. But at the end of the day, the inspiration for Bobby

Kennedy's speech at the University of Kansas remains a product of one man's experience, insight and sentiment. Perhaps it stands no more in need of explanation than that.

'Everything is not fine'

Almost as curious as the backstory to the Kansas address is its abiding legacy. There was plenty there of immediate topical relevance. There was much that spoke to a deeper, more philosophical engagement with the nature of human progress. But what proved persistent over the ensuing decades was a less philosophical, more technical aspect of the speech. Beyond the rhetoric lay a clearly definable measurement problem. The principal indicator of economic success used by governments is flawed.

Measurement is a gloriously technical issue. Is the measure we're using fit for purpose or not? Do its limitations matter? Can they be addressed? How could we adjust things to make them work better? Here was something more readily fixable than our fixation on growth itself. Here was a space safe enough to permit even the cautious to flirt with Bobby Kennedy's insights without necessarily confronting the deeper challenge they posed. It took a little time for them to show up at the party, it has to be admitted. But eventually some unexpected guests arrived.

The European Commission's Beyond GDP programme in 2007 and the OECD's High-Level Group on the Measurement of Economic Performance and Social Progress in 2014 were testament to our appetite for the technicalities of measurement. Even the World Economic Forum has been able to talk in positive terms about alternatives to the GDP. Along the way, somehow, Kennedy's words themselves became iconic. They've been cited over and over again – not just by 'lunatics, idealists and revolutionaries' but even, occasionally, by latter-day Presidential candidates and conservative Prime Ministers.[16]

Discussions about measurement constitute a space of genuine policy innovation in a debate still struggling to throw off the ideological mantle of growth. Countries as varied as Bhutan, New Zealand, Finland and Scotland have begun (only recently in most cases) to develop new ways of measuring progress. Some of these initiatives provide what are sometimes called 'satellite accounts', never quite challenging the dominion of the GDP. Others make a genuine attempt to integrate the alternatives into economic policy and budgetary decisions.[17]

These conversations matter. Measurement matters. 'If we measure the wrong thing, we will do the wrong thing,' argued the Nobel Prize-winning economist Joseph Stiglitz, who co-chaired the OECD group. 'If our measures tell us everything is fine when it really isn't, we will be complacent,' he said recently. 'And it should be clear that, in spite of the increases in GDP, in spite of the 2008 crisis being well behind us, everything is *not* fine.'[18]

And yet the critique of growth itself, the genuine postgrowth refrain that runs through the Kennedy speech, is far less well rehearsed. It was virtually ignored for decades by the prevailing politics. With the help of youthful activism, it has achieved more visibility. But even now it's mainly cast as a curious anomaly, clearly at odds with the mainstream discourse. Kurz's Davos smile spoke volumes. First, they ignore you. Then they laugh. Until suddenly the need to face reality is thrust upon us.

The stationary state

Even as Kennedy was talking in Kansas, a young agricultural economist named Herman Daly was about to publish his first mainstream paper. He had been working on it since 1965. The principal argument in 'Economics as a Life Science' was that ultimately economics and biology were both engaged in the study of one and the same thing: the life process itself.

It's a sentiment that runs to the core of the arguments I want to develop in this book. An appeal to economists to understand that the economy is not a separate or even separable part of the natural world, but a 'wholly owned subsidiary' of the environment. Daly was in Brazil when he submitted the paper to the prestigious *Journal of Political Economy*, without access to sophisticated office equipment. So the manuscript was in rough copy with handwritten corrections on it. To his surprise it was accepted immediately. It appeared in print in May 1968, just a couple of months after Kennedy's critique of the GDP.[19]

The timing was such an odd coincidence that I couldn't help wondering if Daly had known about the Kennedy speech or had any connection to it. He'd only become aware of it much later, he told me. But the two direct influences on Kennedy – Carson's *Silent Spring* and the writing of the American liberals – were of course familiar to him. Galbraith's *The Affluent Society* in particular had had a profound impact on him as a young economics undergraduate.[20]

In the years that followed the publication of 'Economics as a Life Science', Daly began to flesh out more and more of the science that became known as ecological economics. At the centre of his inquiry was the question of scale. How could the human economy simply keep on growing when the dimensions of the planet were irredeemably finite? Ultimately, argued Daly, it couldn't. In the early 1970s, he published the foundations for what he began to call the 'steady state' economy – defined as one with a constant stock of capital and a constant population. Crucially, the size of this constant stock had to be small enough that the flow of material and energy needed to maintain it lay within the carrying capacity of the planet. Otherwise it would eventually collapse. It was 'an extension of the demographers' model of a stationary population to include the populations of physical artifacts', he wrote in 1974. The same fundamental idea 'is found in [the economist] John Stuart Mill's discussion of the stationary state of classical economics'.[21]

Here we arrive at one of the most curious aspects of cultural myth. Each culture is blind to its own mythical nature. We are consigned to live inside the bubble. Like Jim Carrey's character Truman Burbank in Peter Weir's movie *The Truman Show*, everything appears to be real. The routines of our life and the boundaries of our world seem immutable. From inside the bubble, growth is the irreducible norm and the concept of the stationary state looks like an insane aberration. Zoom out for a second and the roles are completely reversed. One of the founding fathers of the science of economics had written about the postgrowth economy two and a half centuries ago.

John Stuart Mill professed to a profound dislike of the society springing up around him at the height of the industrial revolution. 'I am not charmed with the ideal of life held out by those who think that the normal state of human beings is that of struggling to get on, that the trampling, crushing, elbowing, and treading on each other's heels, which form the existing type of social life, are the most desirable lot of human kind,' he wrote in his *Principles of Political Economy*, published in 1848. Of the stationary state itself he admitted: 'I cannot regard it with the unaffected aversion so generally manifested toward it by political economists of the old school.' On the contrary, he said, 'I am inclined to believe that it would be, on the whole, a very considerable improvement on our present condition.'[22]

In other words, the great classical economist was saying this: a postgrowth world may be a richer, not a poorer, place for all of us. And it's that vision of a richer, more equitable, more fulfilling world – glimpsed by Mill and demanded by Kennedy and developed by Daly – which provides the inspiration for the arguments in this book.

The journey of this book

Our prevailing vision of social progress is fatally dependent on a false promise: that there will always be more and more for everyone. Forged in the crucible of capitalism, this foundational myth has come dangerously unravelled. The relentless pursuit of eternal growth has delivered ecological destruction, financial fragility and social instability.

Was the myth ever really fit for purpose? It isn't entirely clear. Its fatal misconception lies in assuming that 'more' is always 'better'. Where there is still an insufficiency, this assertion stands – conditionally at least. Where there is already excess, it categorically doesn't. One of two critical flaws at the heart of capitalism is its inability to know where this point is. The other is not knowing how to stop when we get there.

These flaws are so deeply engrained that escaping them isn't simple. There's no convenient magic trick to spring ourselves from the trap, without shaking the foundations of our own cultural beliefs. The goal of this book is to engage in that task. By pulling apart the assumptions coded in capitalism and reframing the underlying propositions, I aim to reconstruct the foundations for a postgrowth narrative.

The journey itself is entangled in the history of thought. That history was created by some extraordinary people. Their lives and struggles provide a way of grounding theory in story. Listened to with respect, they become our guides. In this chapter, self-evidently, our principal guide was Robert F. Kennedy, former US Attorney General and aspiring Presidential candidate in the 1968 campaign. As the book unfolds, the cast begins to multiply.

I am not entirely sure whether I chose these characters or whether they chose me. Nor could I reliably say that I guided the direction of their narrative. As I wrote, their voices teased me relentlessly away from my original, more simplistic aims and forced me into complexities I hadn't intended to address. These women and men became my intellectual companions. I would lose myself over and again in their lives and their struggles. Not too much, I hope. But enough to arrive occasionally in that liminal space where something unexpected can happen. More often than not it did.

But I was also very aware that the performance of this particular journey has a potential cast of thousands. That there were others I could have chosen is blindingly obvious. That there are voices who are missing is inevitable. This is not ultimately a book of answers. It's a book of questions. With some tentative suggestions that happen to emerge from it. Another book, written on another day (or in a different year), might have had a very different cast list. I dare to imagine it might nonetheless have arrived at a similar destination.

We are trapped in an iron cage of consumerism. But the cage is of our own making. We are locked in the myth of growth. But the key was forged in our own minds. There are physical, material limits to our existence. But there is a creativity in our souls that can free us to live meaningfully and thrive together. These were the principal insights that have emerged for me, through endless conversation with my intellectual guides. For different readers, something different may emerge. If it does, I will consider my assignment a success.

'Too much and for too long'

Only a few short minutes of Kennedy's speech in Kansas were about the measurement problem of the GDP. Some of it was a visceral reaction to the rhetoric of war. 'I don't want to be part of a government, I don't want to be part of the United States, I don't want to be part of the American people,' he said, 'and have them write of us as they wrote of Rome: "They made a desert and they called it peace."'

The underlying core of RFK's political vision was a burning concern for social justice. He spoke passionately about the grinding poverty he had seen around him, corrupting the very heart of America. He spoke of children in Mississippi with distended stomachs, of Black ghettos with dismal schooling, of the long-term unemployed in the ex-mining communities of Appalachia, of rising suicide amongst indigenous people. 'I don't think that's acceptable,' he declared, 'and I think the United States of America – I think the American people, I think *we* can do much, much better. And I run for the presidency because of that.'

It was a run he was never to finish. Shortly before midnight on 4 June 1968, the day of the California Primary, Kennedy gave his last speech in the Embassy Ballroom of the Ambassador Hotel in Los Angeles. It was the end of a long day in which he'd finally taken a definitive lead over his rivals. The mood was buoyant as he thanked his supporters for their help. The result would almost certainly have guaranteed him the Democratic nomination. But as he was making his way through the kitchen to a press conference on the other side of the hotel, he was shot three times at close range.

He fell to the ground immediately. A 17-year old hotel busboy with whom he had just shaken hands dropped to his knees to protect the Senator's head against the cold concrete of the floor. Still conscious, Kennedy asked: 'Is everyone ok?' 'Yes, everyone's ok,' replied the boy. The young waiter took a rosary he'd been carrying in his pocket and wrapped it round the Senator's right hand. But it was already too late for prayers. One of the bullets had entered the skull just behind Bobby's right ear and its fragments had done irreparable damage to his brain. He died just over a day later in the Good Samaritan Hospital.[23]

'Too much and for too long,' he told his Kansas audience a few short weeks before that tragic day, 'we seem to have surrendered personal excellence and community values in the mere accumulation of material things'.

It was to be another four decades before this resounding critique of the myth of growth achieved any real purchase in politics. Strangely, what caused things to shift had as much to do with the economy itself as it did with the environmental and social limits to growth. The story of the unravelling of the myth of growth, as we shall see in the next chapter, is as much about the failings of capitalism as it is about the constraints of our finite planet.

2

Who Killed Capitalism?

'As a capitalist, I believe it's time to say out loud what we all know to be true: Capitalism, as we know it, is dead.'
Marc Benioff, 2019[1]

'Shamed, dishonoured, wading in blood and dripping with filth, thus capitalist society stands.'
Rosa Luxemburg, 1915[2]

In a curious incident, during the run-up to the 2016 Brexit Referendum in the UK, a British academic was trying to persuade a public meeting of the dangers awaiting the country if it cast itself adrift from membership of the European Union. The impact on the GDP would dwarf any savings the UK might make from its budget contributions to the EU, the expert told the crowd. 'That's your bloody GDP!' shouted a woman in the audience. 'It's not ours!'[3]

Behind this angry remark lay a host of uncomfortable truths. That almost a decade after the financial crisis, economic growth had failed to return to its pre-crisis trend. That successive years of austerity had made the lives of the poorest harsher. That faith in the expertise of economists and politicians had been severely eroded along the way. That statistics had become weaponized in the interests of elite minorities. That, in a 'post-truth' era, numbers themselves no longer held sway as immutable facts.[4]

But above all, the anger betrayed an undeniable sense of loss: a loss of faith in the myth of growth. The continual expansion of the economy – growth in the GDP – had been synonymous with the idea of social progress for as long as anyone could remember. But that cosy idea no longer reflected the reality of everyday life for ordinary people in one of the most advanced economies of the world. Beyond the fury

of the crowd lay the discernible rumbling of a cultural myth beginning
to fall apart.

Strangely, that loss of faith wasn't just confined to those left behind
by the economic system. It has appeared in the most unlikely places.
Sometimes at the heart of the establishment. A walk-on part for the
postgrowth society was not the only evidence that things were changing in Davos. One of the world's largest banks chose the 2020 World
Economic Forum to hold a week-long series of discussions under the
title 'Is Growth an Illusion?'[5]

Is growth an illusion?

It had been a bad year (indeed a difficult decade) for Deutsche Bank.
Rocked by controversy over its financial dealings with the Trump
empire and still recovering from litigation settlements which dated
from before the financial crisis, it had posted two consecutive quarters
of substantial losses immediately prior to Davos. Its $1.4 trillion
assets still placed it as the seventeenth largest bank in the world in
2020. But those assets had fallen dramatically from a pre-crisis peak
of $3.6 trillion. Growth was almost literally an illusion for the ailing
giant.[6]

It has been increasingly elusive for the advanced economies as a
whole. The 5% growth rates typical of the US economy in 1968 are
now long gone. By the start of 2020, even before the pandemic, the
average rate of growth across the OECD nations was barely 2%. If
we measure the average growth rate *per person* over these periods – a
better indicator of what economists call living standards – the decline
is even more obvious. And if we measure 'labour productivity' – the
average output generated per hour worked in the economy – then
things look worse again.[7]

In the UK, the oldest of the developed economies, the picture is
particularly striking. From a peak of around 4% in 1968, the trend
growth in labour productivity had already fallen to less than 1% before
the financial crisis in 2008. In the aftermath, its descent continued. In
the years before the coronavirus crisis, there was virtually no growth
in labour productivity at all. Sometimes – most strikingly through the

pandemic – productivity growth went into reverse. Labour productivity declined in absolute terms across the economy as a whole.[8]

These trends matter. It's only possible to squeeze GDP growth out of an economy with stationary or declining labour productivity by increasing the hours spent working there. Either more people must work or else each of them must work longer hours. Neither of these things is consistent with the promise that capitalism held out to us. Once labour productivity growth goes into reverse, in fact, we are already to all intents and purposes living in a postgrowth world. Figuring out how to survive – let alone flourish – under these circumstances is no longer trivial.

For the most part, economists don't try. They either deny the reality of these trends or else they assume we can somehow turn the ship around and return to the good old days. A sense of anxiety pervades this denial. Davos was full of it. 'Deep new rifts are tearing apart the fabric of our societies,' warned the development economist Paul Collier, because 'Capitalism's core credential of steadily rising living standards for all has been tarnished.' The very next day, it was the turn of billionaire Marc Benioff, Chair and co-CEO of Salesforce. 'Capitalism as we have known it is dead,' he lamented.[9]

The air of bemusement was palpable. Not that long ago, things were going so well. Living standards were rising; democracy was thriving; freedom – the buzzword of western liberalism – abounded. And with the fall of the Iron Curtain, political opposition to the dominant economic model seemed to have faded away. Capitalism could deliver all the progress we ever needed. The political scientist Francis Fukuyama was even persuaded to declare that we've reached 'the end of history': the pinnacle of humanity's ideological evolution.[10]

A representative state; a market economy; a consumer society: this was the recipe for social progress. Governments across the world were content to follow its rubric. And yet the formula had evidently failed. So what exactly happened? How did it all go so wrong? Who killed capitalism?

Crime scene investigation

The most obvious answer to this question is: no one. Capitalism is alive and well, thank you very much, and living the high life in New York and Dubai and London. Beijing, even. And Davos, certainly. Despite their anxiety, no one at the World Economic Forum was seriously about to give up on capitalism. The introspection was an elaborate show. In fact, the principal outcome from the surprising self-flagellation was an all-too-familiar refrain: capitalism is dead; long live capitalism!

Stakeholder capitalism; capitalism with purpose; 'woke' capitalism, as the *New York Times* amusingly called it. These were to be the new incarnations of an old regime. They were paraded almost daily by those who, sometimes by their own admission, had benefited most from the old regime. (Why should we not entirely trust them? I couldn't possibly imagine!) But beyond the sometimes distasteful rhetoric, and the unmistakable impression of power clinging on to power, lay the dawning realization that something extraordinary had happened to the foundational narrative on which social progress depends. So the question remains. Who or what was responsible?[11]

For a while now, the most convenient suspect has been the global financial crisis. I've lost count of the number of attempts I've seen to compare the average growth rate before 2008 with the average growth rate in the years that followed. It's so easy to conclude that the problems arise from the continuing 'headwinds' caused by the crisis. These commentaries miss the point completely. The decline was already happening decades before the crisis struck. The peak in labour productivity growth in most advanced economies was more than half a century ago.

Every now and then, a suspicion has caught hold that the problems are more deeply rooted. In November 2013, five years after the collapse of Lehman Brothers, the former World Bank chief economist and US Treasury Secretary Larry Summers gave a speech to the International Monetary Fund which sent something of a shock wave through the audience. The continuing uncertainties of the post-crisis years were not just temporary after-shocks. 'The underlying problem may be there forever,' he said. Low and declining growth may just be the 'new normal'.[12]

Summers was certainly not the only, or even the first, but he was certainly the most well-known economist to make such a claim. The repercussions were profound. For a while, it became acceptable to ask previously unthinkable questions. What if there just isn't so much growth to be had anymore? What if sluggish demand is here to stay? The term 'secular stagnation' – first coined in the 1930s – was revived to describe a phenomenon that was becoming too obvious to miss: an increasingly visible long-term decline in growth rates, particularly in the mature economies of the West. As the futurist Martin Ford pointed out: 'There are good reasons to believe that the economic Goldilocks period has come to an end for many developed nations.'[13]

The reputation of the economic system (and of economics itself) certainly took a pretty heavy beating during the financial crisis and has struggled to regain its mojo in the intervening decade or so since. But to attribute capitalism's woes to that time and that time alone is certainly wrong. The cracks were already visible beneath the shiny surface long before the crisis 'made them manifest'.

Fargonomics

Another common suspect is the economic shift that took place in the 1980s. The economics of 'monetarism' heralded a radical agenda of privatization and deregulation. Today's predominantly neoliberal, free market policies stem from that time. They had a profound impact on society. It's since that time in particular that inequality has risen, debt has expanded, anxiety and suicide rates have multiplied, obesity and lifestyle disease have accelerated.

'In America, the emblematic core of capitalism, half of the 1980 generation are absolutely worse off than the generation of their parents at the same age,' reveals Collier. In the intervening decades, capitalism has 'continued to deliver for some, but has passed others by'.[14]

That's a kind interpretation. Less kind is Noah Hawley's black-comedy crime series *Fargo*. In the second season of the show, set in 1979, a local family in Fargo, North Dakota, goes head to head with the infamous Kansas City Crime Family and comes off worse in the conflict. In the final episode of the season, one of the Kansas gangsters, Mike Mulligan (played by Bokeem Woodbine), arrives at the syndicate's headquarters expecting promotion for his part in the downfall of the Fargo family. He's shown to his new office in an unremarkable building and told by his manager that he'll be 'working closely with the accounting department, looking for ways to optimize revenue.' Mike is mystified. 'This is the future,' his manager explains. 'The sooner you realize there's only one business left in the world – the money business, just ones and zeros – the better off you're gonna be.'

Hawley's message is clear, right down to the time the story took place: 1979. It was the year that Ronald Reagan announced his Presidential campaign and Margaret Thatcher came to power in the UK. Monetarism announced an era in which, as the Chicago School economist Milton Friedman infamously declared: the business of business is business. Social responsibility was irrelevant. The ethics of the city became virtually indistinguishable from those of organized crime. Charles Ferguson's 2010 documentary *Inside Job* and Adam McKay's 2015 comedy-drama *The Big Short* – two films about the financial crisis – make the same point.[15]

It would all have appalled Adam Smith – the founding father of capitalism. But he wouldn't have been remotely surprised. He knew only too well that self-interest left unchecked undermines the benefits of the market. He once railed deliciously against 'an order of men whose interest is never exactly the same with that of the public, who have generally an interest to deceive and even to oppress the public, and who accordingly have, upon many occasions, both deceived and oppressed it'. The target of his attack was 'those who live by profit' – or in other words, capitalists themselves.[16]

Only the state could counter the dangers of runaway self-interest, Smith realized. Neoliberalism's fantastic conceit was to neglect this advice completely. Instead, it argued, capital should be freed from government to the greatest extent possible. What ensued was a philosophical abomination. It had nothing to do with the 'freedom' of the market and no credibility in either theory or practice. Yet over the last two decades of the twentieth century its ideas became deeply influential across the world. It is quite simply *Fargonomics*. Its ethics are gangster ethics, the law of the jungle. And it's created a form of capitalism that has worked exceptionally well for the few but continues to fail for the many.

The voices in Davos reflect a rising awareness of this failure. The assailant was known to us, they seem to imply. We made a mistake in trusting him. We understand now the lesson that Smith tried to teach us. We must reverse the damaging policies of the past and make capitalism work for everyone. Profit with purpose in Benioff's view. A strengthening of 'reciprocal obligations' in Collier's book.

These proposals are clearly important. Revolutionary even, by recent standards. They represent a call for a return to capitalism's 'golden age' – the immediate post-war period – where business was kinder, inequality was lower and the concept of social welfare mattered. But as the *Financial Times* columnist Martin Wolf has pointed out, things aren't that simple. Conditions have changed. 'The egalitarian western societies of the 1950s and 1960s had a global monopoly of industry and a social solidarity bred by shared adversity,' he wrote. 'That past is a foreign country. It can never be revisited.'[17]

It's a salutary reminder that we cannot rewind history. But perhaps, as Maya Angelou suggested, we can still learn some of its lessons. If neoliberalism was the assailant, why was it allowed to wander free over so many decades, inflicting its pain across society? Why was the damage condoned for so long? What convinced us to buy this misreading of Smith's vision of the market in the first place?

Serious money

To answer these questions, we have to rewind further. The immediate post-war period was a dry one for the ideological right, for some of the reasons that Wolf identified. The post-war consensus was forged from the harsh lessons of the Great Depression. It was dominated by the economics of John Maynard Keynes. The state has an irreducible role in the economy, said Keynes. Deficit spending by government was the only thing that saved the US economy from ruin. There was no room here for the free-marketeers.

But then came the 1970s oil crises. Against fast-rising resource prices, the West found itself ill prepared. The deficit spending of the 1930s proved ineffectual against the conditions of 'stagflation'. Worse, it gave rise to a deepening public debt which had repercussions beyond the economy itself. Here was the opportunity that the neoliberals had been waiting for. They seized their moment in the sun to precipitate a sharp shift towards the political right.[18]

The new politics offered 'freedom' as the ultimate arbiter of human affairs. The monetarists set about deregulating the economy and privatizing markets. Lowering interest rates. Loosening financial regulations. The so-called 'Big Bang' was brilliantly satirized in *Serious Money*, a 1987 play by the writer Caryl Churchill. Written in rhyming verse and played at breakneck speed, it offered 'a savage breathless indictment of high finance and its greedy, cut-throat culture'. The performance was a huge hit – even amongst those it satirized. At one point in the play, one of the most aggressive traders insists:

> We're only doing just the same
> All you bastards always done
> New Faces in your old Square Mile
> Making money with a smile
> Just as greedy, just as vile.[19]

It was a clever echo of a common justification for this new cut-throat capitalism. Money makes the world go around. Same as it ever was. Only now the culture of greed was sanctioned by a state which was trying to remove itself from the fray by privatizing everything. When the show transferred to Wyndham's Theatre in London, the newly privatized British Telecom notoriously refused to provide telephones for the production, saying: 'This is a production with which no public company would wish to be associated.' The play is now a set text for high-school exam courses.[20]

Too big to fail

A burst of 'liquidity' was just what the neoliberal economists had ordered. It worked after a fashion. Growth of a kind returned for a while. But its proceeds flowed predominantly to the rich. The reprieve – if it can be called as much – was short-lived. The 9/11 attacks in September 2001 threw another curve ball at the economy. Governments tried more of the same: more deregulation; more liquidity; and a whole new basket of complex financial instruments that no one – it turned out – really understood.[21]

The consequences were disastrous. Loose money and lax regulation ended up destabilizing financial markets. And they deepened social inequality. Protecting the interests of capital over the interests of workers inevitably favoured the rich over the poor. In a stunning reversal of almost fifty years of social progress, inequality within developed countries increased massively over the final decades of the twentieth century.[22]

The prescriptions for recovery had just made things worse. The early years of the twenty-first century turned into a 'casino' of speculative borrowing and lending. Households accumulated more and more debt. The conditions for chaos were mounting. All it took was a change in the rate of defaults on 'subprime' loans in the US housing market and in 2008 the bubble burst. The unintended consequence from half a century spent chasing after growth was the biggest crash since the 1930s.

'The question arises,' asked Summers in 2014, 'can we identify any sustained stretch during which the economy grew satisfactorily with conditions that were financially sustainable?' His answer, and the answer of an increasing number of other economists, was: no. Chasing growth through loose monetary policy in the face of challenging underlying fundamentals had led to financial bubbles which destabilized finance and culminated in crisis.[23]

Following the collapse of Lehman Brothers on 15 September 2008, western governments committed trillions of dollars to securitize risky assets, underwrite threatened savings, re-capitalize failing banks and re-stimulate the economy. No one pretended this was anything other than a short-term solution. Many even accepted that it was regressive: a temporary fix that rewarded those responsible for the crisis at the expense of the taxpayer. But it was excused on the grounds that the alternative was simply unthinkable. Collapse of the financial markets would have led to a massive and completely unpredictable global meltdown. Entire nations would have been bankrupted. Commerce would have failed *en masse*. The humanitarian costs of failing to save the banking system would have been enormous.

But government bailouts precipitated further crises. Country after country, particularly across the Eurozone, found themselves negotiating rising deficits, unwieldy sovereign debt and down-graded credit ratings. Austerity policies, brought in to control deficits and protect ratings, failed to solve the underlying issues. Worse, they created new social problems of their own. The withdrawal of social welfare compounded income inequality with something even worse: inequalities in healthcare, in longevity, in basic security, in human dignity. The injustice of bailing out the architects of the crisis at the expense of its victims became plain for all to see. 'That's your bloody GDP! It's not ours!'[24]

Ironically, none of this achieved what it was supposed to achieve. Growth rates didn't recover. Even before the Covid-19 lockdown, they were in a more or less steady decline. Austerity had left healthcare systems woefully unprepared for a global pandemic. Closing down economic activity was the only alternative. The chance of a smooth 'recovery' to the pre-crisis era remains slim. The likelihood of growth rates comparable with those in 1968, when Kennedy addressed the students in Kansas, remains virtually nonexistent. The conditions for wider social and political unrest remain palpable.

The most profound lesson from this very brief history is that the exact same policies designed to bring growth back were precisely the ones that led to its downfall. This seems to be the curious outcome from our crime scene investigation: capitalism's downfall was the result of its own obsession with growth. Perhaps this is the point to examine that obsession further. And to understand why it exists in the first place.

Moses and the prophets

First, of course, we should be clear that growth is not exclusive to capitalism. Communist countries have also routinely set growth targets for almost as long as capitalist ones have – and still do so today. There's a sense in which the myth of growth could legitimately be called meta-cultural. It sits above individual differences in ideology as a more or less universal conception of social progress. Both capitalist and socialist ideals of society have been captured by it.[25]

But there is a particularly intense relationship between capitalism and economic growth. So much so that capitalism without growth has sometimes quite explicitly been called 'bad capitalism'. Whole books have been written about this apparent 'growth imperative'. Teasing out a simple logic for it is tricky. Much depends on how capitalism itself is defined. Marx, for instance, saw capitalism as a process. And for him, that process was intrinsically about growth. 'Accumulate, accumulate! That is Moses and the prophets,' he wrote in *Das Kapital*. 'To accumulate is to conquer the world of social wealth.'[26]

The Polish-born socialist Rosa Luxemburg believed she had found a flaw in Marx's logic. In pure capitalism, she argued in *The Accumulation of Capital*, growth wouldn't actually be possible, because there wouldn't be enough income to purchase the expanded production. Her analysis led her to assume that the relentless drive for profit in capitalism (which she didn't deny) could only be satisfied by the continual exploitation of non-capitalist regions. Her most powerful writing was reserved to condemn the violent imperialism to which she believed this expansionary drive must inevitably lead.

From the perspective of 1915, a year into the First World War, when Luxemburg penned the Junius Pamphlet, this must have seemed like a very obvious conclusion. Capitalism, in the words of my second epigraph above, stood shamed and dishonoured. As we'll see in a moment, her premises weren't quite correct, even though her documentation of capitalism's culpability for inexcusable suffering was spot on. But more importantly, there's a danger of tautology in defining capitalism as a process of growth and then arguing that capitalist economies have to grow. It leaves unanswered the question of where this expansionary drive comes from.[27]

Neither is that question resolved by the most common definition of capitalism in terms of the ownership of the 'means of production' – the factories and the resources required to produce the goods and services we need: food, housing, clothing, technology. In a capitalist economy, the means of production are mostly owned by private individuals. In a non-capitalist economy, the means of production belong to 'the people' – they are owned by the state, for example, by the local community or by workers.

Consistent with this 'privatization' of the means of production, capitalism also distinguishes itself by relying mainly on the 'market' to distribute goods and services. Prices are set according to what people are prepared to pay – the 'exchange value' – on the market. In a non-capitalist economy, prices tend to be set by the state or by the community. Sometimes, of course, that price might be set at zero. In socialism, for instance, it's entirely legitimate for the state to take the position that its obligations include the universal provision of certain basic goods and services to all its citizens. Many capitalist economies also take this kind of position in relation to specific kinds of goods: healthcare, education, broadband, for instance. And quite often, market prices are either taxed or subsidized by governments of all colours and creeds.[28]

In practice, then, there's no such thing as a pure capitalist economy. Equally, most socialist or communist countries will rely to some extent on markets to distribute goods and set prices. Certainly, the most powerful communist country in the world, China, has now internalized much of the machinery of capitalism. So there's no such thing as a pure non-capitalist economy either.

As these boundaries dissolve, the precise origins of the 'growth imperative' in capitalism seem less and less obvious. The most likely candidate lies in another key ingredient alongside private ownership and market price-setting: the role of profit. At its simplest, profit is the difference between the revenues received from selling something and the costs of producing it. In principle, this difference exists both inside and outside capitalism. It doesn't particularly matter whether you are privately owned or state owned, the difference between revenues and costs is a useful way of understanding your finances.

But in the hands of capitalism, profit takes on an absolutely vital role as the primary motivation for people to invest. This is an explicit behavioural assumption in capitalism. People are only motivated to engage in production at all, in this view, by the expectation of financial reward. Capitalists expect profits. In turning over the provision of goods and services mostly to private interests, capitalism simultaneously defines profit as the primary motivation for production. The pursuit of profit becomes a powerful driving force not just for individuals but for society as a whole.

By the same token, it introduces a sharp division into society: between those who earn their living from wages, and those who earn income from profit. To make your living from profit you must own something – land or money or shares in the means of production, for instance – from which you can derive financial returns or rents. Those without such assets must earn their incomes from wages. In practice, it's possible to earn from both, of course. And the composition of the two might change at different points in our lives. But the distinction between those who earn a living from wages and those who earn income from profit or rent is clearly recognizable – particularly as it describes a fundamental difference between the richest and the poorest in society.

This division in turn creates conflict. For workers, wages are their principal source of income; for the poorest, their only way of making a living. For capitalists, wages are a cost to production, a drag on the profit that can be made from an enterprise. As the economist Richard Goodwin argued, wages and profits inevitably engage in a predator–prey relationship. The owners of capital are in constant competition with the 'owners' of wage labour. It's blindingly obvious that, under the wrong circumstances, this has the potential to lead to conflict.[29]

A little more macroeconomics

Surprisingly, perhaps, there's a key element within capitalism which can help to tame this conflict. It flows from the concept of labour productivity: the efficiency with which hours worked produce dollars of output. Since labour is a cost to production and capitalists are motivated by profit, they will tend to do whatever they can to increase labour productivity: that is, to reduce the cost of labour. The profit motive provides an in-built incentive towards labour productivity growth.

To the extent that this drive is successful, the resulting cost savings can be distributed in various directions. Some of the benefits might go to workers, through increased pay or through shorter working hours. Some could go to shareholders in the form of higher dividends. Some might be passed on to consumers in the form of lower costs for the product. Some can be used to finance investments in new technologies which further increase labour productivity in the future.

When labour productivity is increasing, all of these things are possible. Workers can be paid more. Consumers can have cheaper goods. Shareholders can enjoy more profit. And the company can afford to invest in the next generation of labour-saving technology, creating a kind of virtuous circle of continuous improvement – and continuous growth. This virtuous circle is the solution to Rosa Luxemburg's dilemma. The increase in wages is what allows for the expansion of profit. Labour productivity growth affords capitalism its biggest claim to legitimacy in the pursuit of social progress. But this inevitably only happens through growth.

When labour productivity growth stagnates, the profit motive begins to operate in a less benevolent way. The relative wage bill rises. Profit margins are squeezed. Wages, dividends, consumer prices and investment all come into competition with another. The potential for conflict between workers and investors intensifies. So does the tension between the present (consumption) and the future (investment). These too are the conditions that lead to the aggressive expansionism that Luxemburg feared.

I'm simplifying here. But this cursory understanding begins to make sense of the dysfunctional patterns of the last few decades. Behind all that we've been looking at lies the steady decline in the rate of growth of labour productivity, stemming from roughly half a century ago. The reasons for this decline are contested. Some regard it as the result of a slowing down – or a change in the structure – of consumer demand in the advanced nations. Others point to techno-logical factors that put the brake on supply.[30]

There is a disturbing possibility that the huge productivity increases that characterized the early and middle twentieth century were a one-off, something we can't just repeat at will, despite the wonders of digital technology. A fascinating – if worrying – contention is that the peak growth rates of the 1960s were only possible at all on the back of a huge and deeply destructive exploitation of dirty fossil fuels; something that can be ill afforded – even if it were available – in the era of dangerous climate change and declining resource quality.[31]

The critical question is how policy should respond to this not-so-new reality. Over the last few decades, capitalism has had a very specific response. Faced with diminishing returns, producers and shareholders have systematically protected profit by depressing the rewards to labour. Governments have encouraged this process through loose monetary policy, poor regulatory oversight and fiscal austerity. The outcome for many ordinary workers has been punitive. As social conditions deteriorated, the threat to democratic stability intensified.

The most prevalent 'rescue narrative' relies on the assumption that productivity growth will recover, primarily through new techno-logical breakthroughs. Candidate 'saviours' in these rescue narratives are various. For some, innovation will arrive from investment in the same clean, low-carbon technologies that are needed to tackle climate change and offset resource depletion. For others, innovation will come from a new digital revolution: increased automation, robotization, artificial intelligence.

We'll come back to these narratives later in the book. Each of them has important lessons for us. But for now, we're thrown back to the question of this chapter with an uncomfortable set of answers. If there is a single culprit responsible for the demise of capitalism, it is beginning to look more and more as though it's capitalism itself. At the very least, we must conclude that capitalism's inherent pursuit of growth, when growth itself was elusive, has legitimized a succession of policies which have proved nothing short of disastrous – for people, for the planet and even for the economy itself.

Dead on arrival?

The German economist Wolfgang Streeck is categorical in his prognosis. 'In my view, it is high time to think again about capitalism as a
historical phenomenon,' he writes in *How Will Capitalism End?* 'One
that has not just a beginning, but also an end.' Streeck insists that this
'end' isn't something to which we might one day reluctantly have to
look forward. It is already under way. It is happening now. Capitalism
is a social system 'in chronic disrepair', he claims. A bit like Dennis
Quaid's character in the 1988 film *D.O.A.* (Dead on Arrival), capitalism may still be talking, and just about walking, but the damage is
irreversible. The situation is irredeemably terminal. 'Nobody believes
any more in a moral revival of capitalism,' Streeck writes.[32]

If the evidence from Davos is anything to go by, this may not be
entirely true. But even as capitalism's apologists struggle to revive
the corpse, their underlying myth appears to be disintegrating. The
relentless pursuit of growth has driven us to the verge of ecological
collapse, created unprecedented financial fragility and precipitated
the terrifying spectre of social instability. Capitalism has no answers
to its own failings. It cannot pursue social justice while it continues to
prioritize profit. It cannot protect our climate while it continues to
idolize the stock market. It finds itself powerless, at the mercy of
circumstance, when the lives of millions are at stake. Capitalism's
core belief in eternal growth lies trembling in the ruins. The myth
itself is moribund.

A society that allows itself to be steered by a faulty myth risks
foundering on the shores of a harsh reality. To cling obstinately to
outdated ideas as the world proves them wrong is to court both psychological despair and cultural disaster. But when myths fail, hope
itself begins to fade. The role of cultural myth is to furnish us with
a sense of meaning and to provide a sense of continuity in our lives.
That need is a perennial one. The loss of a sustaining myth undermines our sense of meaning and threatens our collective wellbeing.

Developing new myths, better stories and clearer visions is as essential as understanding the dynamics of collapse. Perhaps more so. That
in essence is the task of this book. To look beyond the myth of growth.

To dare to see beyond capitalism itself. To revisit its most treasured assumptions. To challenge the truths that have both nourished us and damaged us. To lay the foundations for a different way of seeing and a better way of being. To develop a 'postgrowth narrative', a new foundational myth, a more robust vision to guide us into the uncertain future. It is to this task that we now turn.

3

The Limited and the Limitless

*'No experience in my life could have given me a better understanding
of the definition of the word finite. What we have out there is all we
have. There is no more.'*
Ellen MacArthur, 2015[1]

*'The world of reality has its bounds; the world of the imagination is
boundless.'*
Jean-Jacques Rousseau, 1763[2]

The oldest bridge on the Norfolk Broads dates back to the year
1385. The child King Richard, still just 17, was struggling to control
the Lords Appellant, a self-appointed group of reformists grappling
for control of his kingdom. Geoffrey Chaucer was busy conjuring up
The Canterbury Tales when its stones were first set in place. At the
time it was constructed, the bridge at Potter Heigham was a god-
send to the potters and the peat sellers making their way between
the thriving market town of North Walsham and the seaport of
Great Yarmouth, on the east coast of England. The bridge saved
them many hours of circuitous travel. It's a medieval example of
technological ingenuity overcoming the limits imposed by physical
geography.[3]

Today the area is home to a thriving tourist industry. Over 7 million
visitors arrive each year to enjoy the region's wetlands and waterways.
Nature conservation wages an uneasy battle with the profit motive
as cars, boats, people and wildlife compete for a limited space. But
the light across the flat reedy landscape is spectacular. And if you're
patient enough, towards sunset, you'll hear the haunting cry of the
bittern: the deep sonorous boom of a rare (and shy) waterfowl, as it
carries eerily over the marshes.[4]

The ancient bridge is now a screaming anachronism. No longer able to bear the volume of traffic crossing the River Thurne, its primary role has been usurped by a newer and far more practical carriageway a matter of a hundred metres or so to the north-east. The three stone arches of the original crossing offer instead a picture postcard attraction for tourists and a formidable challenge to those hoping to reach the tranquillity of the northern Broads. Only one of the arches is navigable. And then only at certain states of the tide.

For many boats, the Potter Heigham bridge is a stone-cold barrier to the navigability of the upper river. The teeming gaggle of wide-beamed motor cruisers that have increased dramatically over recent decades could wait for the lowest tide in the year. They would still have too much height and too much beam for this ancient threshold. The prospect of mishap is a constant source of amusement for canny locals. Particularly in the presence of a brisk south-westerly wind driving the unwary towards disaster. In overcoming one kind of limit, the bridge has created another.

The road to Dublin

It may seem odd to embark on the search for a new foundational narrative by raising the uncomfortable question of limits. There's an old joke about a tourist in the west of Ireland asking a local farmer the way to Dublin. 'Well, sir, I wouldn't start from here,' the farmer replies. The logic of the farmer's answer is that the route from here to Dublin may well be difficult to explain and arduous to follow. But the joke's humour stems from the fact that here, undeniably, is where we are. Here is where we must start.

People don't like being told their lives are limited. That much is clear. And when the telling is done by those whose lives appear to be much less limited, anxiety rapidly turns to resentment. The challenge of governance in a postgrowth world is profound for this very reason. Governance seems to embody an asymmetry of power between the governing and the governed. Power asymmetries are a poor place from which to introduce moral imperatives that appear to limit people's opportunities. Particularly in a culture that prizes individual freedom.

I'm going to come back to this challenge in the penultimate chapter of the book.

But the myth of growth and the denial of limits are closely related to one another. The relentless expansion of material desires at the heart of consumer capitalism is a denial of the reality of material limits. So there is a sense in which 'here' is exactly the right place to start. The rejection of limits is part and parcel of the myth of growth. It is the failure to delineate properly between what is limited and what is not that lies at the heart of capitalism's woes.

Our task, then, in getting from here to Dublin is first and foremost to articulate a meaningful relationship between the limited and the limitless. In doing so, we will discover, perhaps surprisingly, that we can reposition limits themselves as one of the most vital ingredients in human prosperity.

Prophets of despair?

In the same year that Bobby Kennedy was talking in Kansas about the failings of the GDP, a British scientist and an Italian industrialist invited a small group of people to a quiet villa in Rome to discuss what they called the 'predicament' of humankind: the problem of reconciling our restless aspirations with what we know about the limits of the natural world. Out of that meeting was born the Club of Rome, an organization of individuals who 'share a common concern for the future of humanity'. The first report published by the Club of Rome in 1972, *The Limits to Growth*, provoked a storm of controversy that continues to this day.[5]

A decade or so later, then US President Ronald Reagan proclaimed that there are 'no great limits to growth because there are no limits on the human capacity for intelligence, imagination and wonder'. It was a deliberate attempt to counter the still powerful Club of Rome narrative. But Reagan's comments are worth examining quite carefully, because they convey a partial truth. There are certainly some (almost) unlimited aspects to human existence. Intelligence, imagination and wonder may well be amongst these. And it obviously makes sense to recognize abundance wherever we may find it.[6]

Beyond this obvious fact, Reagan's pronouncement conceals two vitally important claims. The first is that human ingenuity can deliver almost endless technological innovation. The second is that these innovations will allow us to overcome any and all physical limits to economic growth. They are both familiar arguments. Economists in particular are still prone to draw on them as evidence that we can reject the idea of limits outright.

At a seminar in Whitehall, where I presented the arguments in *Prosperity without Growth*, shortly after it was first published, a government economist interrupted my presentation angrily, insisting that the very idea of limits is 'economically illiterate'. Scarcity, he would recognize. But scarcity could be reflected through price. And the market would take care of the consequences. Limits themselves are meaningless, he insisted.

In place of limits on growth itself, economists prefer to aim for what they call 'green growth': that is, a continuing expansion of the economy in ways that protect the environment; growth which doesn't trash the planet. That's a perfectly valid aspiration, of course. A lot better than growth which does trash the planet. That's for sure. But at first sight, green growth itself seems mildly contradictory. Growth means more throughput. More throughput means more impact. More impact means less planet. Endless growth – green or not – can only end up leading to no growth at all. There is no growth on a dead planet. Eternal growth precipitates the destruction of everything. As Greta Thunberg pointed out to the 2019 UN Climate Summit: it's a fairytale – with a very bad ending.[7]

To make sense of green growth, we have to understand a vital distinction that economists recognize between economic output and material throughput. The GDP is denominated in money terms rather than in quantities of physical material. So evidently economic growth is not the same as material growth. By separating out – or 'decoupling' – monetary value from its material content, so the argument goes, we can escape the dominion of finite limits, if not literally forever, then at least to any relevant degree.

This distinction leads economists to insist that their critics simply have a false conception of what economic growth actually is. 'They think of it as a crude, physical thing, a matter simply of producing more stuff,' claims the Nobel Prize-winning economist Paul Krugman. They fail to take account of 'the many choices – about what to consume, about which technologies to use – that go into producing a dollar's worth of GDP'. His conviction that these 'many choices' will allow for even the most stringent ecological goals to be achieved without ever compromising economic growth persuades him (like Trump in Davos) to denounce growth sceptics as 'prophets of despair'.[8]

Through the looking-glass

Krugman is wrong here. Growth sceptics understand perfectly the distinction between money and matter. They generally accept that there are 'many choices' in terms of technology. Many of them applaud the extraordinary power of technology – recognizing its benefits as well as its costs. It is abundantly clear that society has an enormous capacity to develop new, cleaner, lighter, greener technologies. The ingenuity so prized by Reagan is alive and well.

It's foolish to deny this, because we've seen it in action. There is abundant evidence, for example, that the carbon intensity of the global GDP has fallen by more than a third since the mid-1960s. It fell because our technological ingenuity allowed us to do things more efficiently. Greater efficiency reduced the impacts of our economic activity. Neither the existence nor the importance of this is disputed. But this kind of 'relative decoupling' alone is not sufficient to pull off the trick of eternal growth.[9]

The environment doesn't care about relative efficiency. It's not enough that the carbon content of each dollar of output is declining over time. What matters is the overall impact of human activity on the planet. To achieve a stable climate, we have to reduce global carbon emissions in absolute terms. If the GDP is growing faster than the carbon content of the GDP is declining, then overall there will be more carbon going into the atmosphere this year than there was last year. So far that's exactly what has happened.[10]

Again, the evidence confirms the obvious. Until large parts of the global economy were brought to an abrupt halt by the Covid-19 pandemic, there had been virtually no stopping the relentless rise in emissions since records began. There was no sign at all of the dramatic decline in emissions needed to stabilize the climate this century. The speed with which we're able to decouple carbon from output is nothing like what it needs to be. We're just not moving fast enough in the right direction.[11]

Even the proponents of growth will sometimes accept this point. What divides opinion, rather, is whether we can turn the ship around. Curb the precipitous environmental decline – and still hold on to growth. Proponents of green growth are convinced that we can. They pledge their allegiance to an immensely seductive creed which contains three different but interwoven articles of faith. The first (echoing Reagan) is that our unlimited ingenuity can overcome any physical limits we may face. The second is that growth itself is essential to achieve this feat. The third (auxiliary) claim is that green growth is the best way to overcome the disappointing performance of growth.[12]

Green growth, in other words, is nothing less than the saviour that capitalism has been waiting for. Green growth is better growth, in all sorts of ways, according to its advocates. Better technology, more innovation, greater efficiency. What's more, they believe, capitalism is perfectly poised to deliver these things, because of its relentless pursuit of innovation and novelty. If we are concerned about the damage economic expansion has caused, they say, we should not only endorse the path of growth, we should redouble our efforts to reach the higher ground. In short, their message is that only growth can deliver us from the mess that growth itself has landed us in.

It's a convenient and compelling narrative, driven by an underlying anxiety about what happens when growth fails us. That anxiety is real, of course. Our economies depend on growth in all sorts of ways. But this is to confuse the issue. Postgrowth ideas are useful precisely because the potential for collapse is already upon us, unless the demise of capitalism can be reversed. For green growth to play the role of saviour in this reversal, we must solve all the problems associated with the expanding scale of the economy – climate change, species loss, the pollution of rivers and oceans, the degradation of soils, the depletion of resources – whilst never for a moment letting up on the accelerator pedal of growth.

To make this work, we need more and more innovation, more and more efficiency. Efficiency must outrun scale faster than it has ever done in the past, and it must continue to do so indefinitely into the foreseeable (and unforeseeable) future. We are like the Red Queen in Lewis Carroll's novel *Alice Through the Looking Glass*, condemned to run faster and faster just so that we can stay in the same place.[13]

In a world where even staying in the same place is by no means good enough, this creed is beginning to seem wildly improbable. Blind belief in the ability to 'decouple' economic expansion from material expansion indefinitely is itself a form of denial. In this incarnation, a denial of any limits at all to technology. And this denial of limits is already leading to profoundly dystopian outcomes.

Latham's bazaar

Clustered around the Potter Heigham bridge lies a purgatory of fast food and cheap toot, centred on an enormous discount store named Lathams, which occupies four large warehouses on the banks of the river Thurne. Back in the mid-1960s, its founder, Ken Latham, set out to provide year-round local employment, supplying fishing tackle and provisions to the Broads' visitors. Somewhere along the line, it got bought out by a discount retail chain offering customers 'constantly changing quality stock at the very lowest prices'. Today, it's a mad, seething mongrel: half-stadium, half-stampede. Lathams, claims its website, has become 'an attraction in its own right'. People converge on the store from all over the country to partake in a frenzy of shopping.[14]

The logic of the situation is formidable. A century ago, tourism brought unaccustomed wealth to rural Norfolk: visitors seeking recreation; customers needing provisions; jobs for local people. It also brought competition, profit, productivity: the paraphernalia of capital, driving the sector forwards. The most accessible areas were more easily commercialized. But as the economy expanded, so did the number and size of the boats on the river. Lathams grew to cater to them; but the bridge resolutely didn't.

At some point, rumours circulated of plans to demolish the bridge, perhaps through an accident involving unexploded Second World War munitions. Fortunately, sense (of a kind) prevailed. Even the captains of commerce could see that the picturesque bridge was as much a source of Potter Heigham's wealth as it was a barrier to it. So the bridge survived to impose its own indefatigable limitations on progress. And Potter Heigham itself became the unruly locus of thwarted expansion.

This is just one tiny example. But it is a microcosm of a wider malaise. Think of New York, Beijing, Mumbai: teeming emblems of twenty-first-century progress; or chaotic communities at the boundary of restless expansion. Think of Marx's enduring maxim: accumulate, accumulate! And yet that relentless process is always and everywhere circumscribed by thresholds. Limits to our resources. Limits on our climate. Limits on financial stability. Limits to the appetite of the human soul for material excess.

Of course, we might well wish it otherwise. If wishes were horses, then beggars would ride. If it were not for the dimensions of an old stone bridge, Potter Heigham would be a different place. People would move on. Or pass through. Or reach a different compromise with its ancient threshold. Or renounce their vicarious pleasures. Or rise from the armchair of voyeurism and achieve new and wonderful feats of their own. But the intransigent stones dictate otherwise.

One small bridge in the middle of rural Norfolk is emblematic of a bigger, more intractable story. Potter Heigham is what happens when the spirit of restless expansion comes up against the physical constraints of a material world. Society's growth imperative yields a surreal, dysfunctional limbo, home to a teeming crowd of dispossessed sojourners: the luxury cruisers which can get no further; the dedicated fishermen yearning for a peace no longer there; the armchair sailors in search of other people's mishaps; the pilgrims and the pick-pockets; the vendors and the vagabonds. A trapped and tormented congregation, worshipping in the cathedral of a ruined capitalism. And the once proud 'heart and soul' of the Broads is stolen away by a glorified bazaar.

The faire chain of love

Our fierce resistance to thinking seriously about limits is a surprisingly recent tendency. Ancient wisdom often saw them in a much more positive light. 'Limitations are troublesome, but they are effective,' wrote Richard Wilhelm in his 1923 translation of the ancient Chinese book of wisdom the *I Ching*. 'In nature there are fixed limits for summer and winter, day and night, and these limits give the year its meaning,' he said.[15]

The relationship between limits and order was a familiar theme throughout the Middle Ages. In the famous, final section of *The Knight's Tale*, the first of Geoffrey Chaucer's *Canterbury Tales*, Theseus, the duke of Athens, calls on the wisdom of what he calls the First Mover – a metaphor for God, the creator – to resolve the tragic love triangle between his sister-in-law, the Princess Emelye, and the two knights Palamon and Arcite. In medieval cosmology, the First Mover creates the 'faire chain of love' or 'natural inclination' which holds the universe together. The creator knew what he was doing when he created limits, wrote Chaucer:

> For with that faire chain of love he bound
> The fire, the air, the water, and the land
> In definite bounds, from which they may not flee.[16]

Natural limits are employed in *The Knight's Tale* as a metaphor for a celestial oversight which governs the affairs of both the human and the non-human world. There is a time and a manner for human affairs just as there is for natural ones, according to this cosmology. It was an early precursor to the Newtonian worldview which, three and a half centuries later, would provide the foundations for classical physics.

It's fair to say that this vision of a precise and definable order has suffered massively since then. It was diminished under the insights of modern science. It was weakened by a decline in the power of religion. Darwin's evolution, Einstein's relativity and the irreducible uncertainty of the quantum world seemed to strip the universe of any trace of the First Mover. God is dead, declared the German philosopher Friedrich Nietzsche in one of his most famous passages of writing, before asking anxiously: 'How shall we comfort ourselves, the murderers of all murderers? Who will wipe this blood off us? What water is there to clean ourselves? What festivals of atonement, what sacred games shall we have to invent?' Cosmology itself became flattened into a broadly material domain, where meaning and purpose were relegated to the status of atoms and chance. The possibility of order didn't disappear completely, as we shall see in Chapter 5. But the task of making sense of our lives became that much harder.[17]

The art of the possible isn't so strictly ordained as it appeared to be in Chaucer's day. But the broad sense that we are living in a material world governed by physical laws survives. The conservation of energy and matter, the extension of material objects in space, their place in nature, their concentration in the biosphere, the laws that govern their motion, transformation and decay: these are the modern-day equivalents of Chaucer's 'faire chain of love'. And to reject these 'definite bounds' is tantamount to a rejection of science itself. 'For more than 30 years, the science has been crystal clear,' as Greta Thunberg reminded the delegates to the UN Climate Conference. 'How dare you continue to look away!'[18]

We are living in a material world. We rely on the bounds of its materiality every single day of our lives. The ground supports our weight as we walk on it. The air we breathe and the food we eat sustain us. We trust that seeds will grow when we plant them. We know that things will fall when we drop them. If they fall too hard, they will break. If they fall on us, it will hurt. If we burn them, they will be consumed. If they burn us, we will suffer.

The Southern Ocean

The French philosopher and Jesuit priest Pierre Teilhard de Chardin once remarked that it is our duty as human beings 'to proceed as if limits to our ability did not exist'. This commitment to the potential for an almost limitless creativity is instantly recognizable as something quintessentially human. It has clear echoes in Reagan's remarks on the human capacity for imagination and wonder. It is inherent in the creed of the green growth advocates. Our ingenuity is not just legendary, it's evolutionary. It is partly responsible for, and certainly complicit in, our enormous 'success' as a species.

But to read Teilhard as an apologist for capitalism would be a mistake. His remark was not an endorsement of our unlimited technological capability, much less an incitement to endless material affluence. It was an encouragement to reach our fullest potential as finite human beings. Life has made us 'conscious collaborators in creation', he said, 'in order to lead us, it would seem, to a goal much loftier and more distant than we imagined'.[19]

This profoundly human quality of striving to exceed our own limits matters to the inquiry in this book. Teilhard's loftier and more distant goal is beautifully exemplified by the achievements of the former round-the-world yachtswoman Ellen MacArthur. In 2001, she became the youngest person ever to circumnavigate the world, coming second in the Vendée Globe race. Two years later, she set out to break the world record for a solo circumnavigation.

In the middle of the tempestuous and unpredictable Southern Ocean, she ended up driving herself and her boat to the limits of their endurance as they strove to outrun a particularly ferocious storm. Had she failed in that task, it would almost certainly, perhaps tragically, have ended her world record attempt. But both the yacht and her skipper lived to tell their extraordinary tale. Sometimes, we can push ourselves beyond anything that seems either wise or possible. The impossible we do today; miracles take a little longer.[20]

The gung-ho, can-do attitude so beloved by certain politicians has its roots in this same desire to transcend our own limitations. The desire itself is precious. It speaks to a drive which has served us well through numerous stages of human evolution. Our restless ambition to go further, to see more, to fly higher, to achieve the unexpected, to forge a new life for our family, to collaborate in the creation of a better world: all of this is to be applauded.

This frontier mentality is often, according to the US philosopher Ken Wilber, a brutally male, testosterone-driven one. 'Men will always, to some degree, be incredibly driven to break limits, push the envelope, go all out, wildly, insanely,' he writes, noting at the same time that this tendency is not an entirely dysfunctional one, because in the process they 'bring new discoveries, new inventions, new modes into being'.

Women, by contrast, 'will always have a base of relational being', invoking a 'sturdier sense of self-esteem and autonomy' which values 'mature self, even as it continues to value relationships'. These tendencies are not, for Wilber, entirely determined by genetics. He regards our culture as having solidified difference in very particular ways, not just between the genders but across society itself. A broadly patriarchal capitalism has favoured the frontier mentality over a more relational perspective.[21]

But women too have achieved extraordinary feats of leadership, endurance and discovery. MacArthur's accomplishments are a testament to that. And men too have the capacity to value relationship. Gender stereotypes are little help to us here. But such differences may explain why it took a woman who refused to recognize her own limits to understand so clearly the limits of the natural world. MacArthur describes this realization eloquently in her 2015 TED Talk. It was the power and the beauty of the Southern Ocean that prompted her to recognize that the planet we call home is undeniably finite. It was her extraordinary ability to transcend her own limits that allowed her better to understand the limits inherent in nature. 'What we have out there is all we have,' she said. 'There is no more.'[22]

Returning from the cruel sea to the safety of home, she came to a profound realization that the global economy 'is entirely dependent on finite resources we only have once in the history of humanity'. That understanding prompted her to set out on another, entirely different, but equally challenging journey. Five years after her successful world record attempt, she surprised everyone by giving up the world of professional sailing to establish the Ellen MacArthur Foundation, an organization dedicated to the pursuit of a more sustainable 'circular economy'. The goal of the Foundation, put simply, is to adapt our vision of the economy to the constraints of the planet. Adaptation, it turns out, is the key to negotiating between the limited and the limitless.[23]

Shooting the bridge

Threading a high-masted sailing yacht through an unforgiving two-metre arch might seem like an impossible proposition. But strangely, it is achievable: through a clever combination of ingenuity, skill and blind faith. Norfolk Broads sailing yachts are designed with a hinged mast and a cleverly ratcheted winch. A complex array of shackles and stays holds the mast up when needed and guides it down when required. If the procedure is carried out correctly, you can lower the mast until it rests horizontally along the coach-roof and across a wooden crutch at the stern of the yacht. In this diminished form, the height above the waterline will be reduced to something under two metres. Just low enough to slip unscathed through the passage. If you're lucky. If you get it wrong, you'll be the entertainment.

In the days before the new bridge was built, a skilled crew would sometimes approach the old stone archway under full sail, lower mast and sail in one fell swoop and rely on tide and momentum to carry the boat through to the northern reaches of the Broads before re-hoisting everything ready to continue. It was a mark of skill and a badge of honour to de-mast and re-mast the yacht without the use of an engine or a paddle and with barely a stutter in the forward speed of the hull. Shooting the bridge, they called it.[24]

To the uninitiated, such elegance is out of reach. With the mast and sails down, the yacht is transformed from an elegant vessel into a gaggle of flailing stays and halyards atop an unwieldy hull. This mast-less state is curiously destabilizing. It involves a distinct dismantling of social identity and its reconstruction in a new and altered form. The past is no longer accessible. The future uncertain. Success seems unlikely.

Anthropologists have a word for this unsettled state of mind. They call it liminality, from the Latin word (*limen*) for a threshold. The liminal space can be a profoundly creative one. Artists and writers will sometimes seek it out in a deliberate attempt to fan the creative flames that extend the horizons of possibility. The present tense is too demanding. Disingenuously defending the structure of our lives with its illusion of normality, it ends up constraining our vision and obstructing the avenues for change. Liminality frees us from this. It breaches the fortress of the ego and breaks open the bars of social conformity. It allows us to see the world (and ourselves) as we might be, as we could be. As we still could be. Rather than through the temporary prison of the unsustainable now.

The passage itself is a curious confidence trick. The bridge is patently too low. The boat is clearly too high – even with the mast lying dormant. For a novice it is difficult even to judge the headroom, let alone feel assured of clearance. One moment you are self-evidently heading for disaster. And yet, the next, you are inexplicably slipping unscathed beneath the medieval stones. Their cold historicity grazes your outstretched fingers. Grey-green lichen shimmers on the moist archway. Its musty scent conjures the grim reality of long-forgotten lives. Liminality is populated with restless spectres from earlier transitions and uncomfortable glimpses into the immortal abyss.

And then precipitously the passage is complete. The sun dazzles you anew after the shadow of the bridge. Blue sky dances on the dappled water. Maybe it's only your imagination or maybe the wind eased a little. Twenty minutes of careful reverse engineering will see the vessel restored to functionality and ready for the northern reaches of the river Thurne, where an unaccustomed calm has taken hold.

Steam gives way to sail is the oldest rule in the book, from the smallest waterway to the widest ocean. And yet, inevitably, the lower reaches are dogged by thwarted tacks to windward and hurried avoidance strategies. To be small and reliant on wind is to be at the mercy of those who are large – and guzzling diesel. South of the bridge was all about noise and speed. Power was everything. Might was right. But here beyond the threshold, the relentless stream of over-sized launches has vanished, and the constant competition for physical space has slipped away.

Against the odds, sail has prevailed. Not through power but through restraint. Everything is quieter and more peaceful. Life will be less harried and hurried in this more spartan land. The bridge at Potter Heigham is a filter – determining who may and who may not reach the tranquillity of the northernmost Broads: the relative solitude of Martham and Hickling Broads; the other-worldly beauty of Horsey

Mere. Its physical limitations govern the rules of passage to the land beyond and set the boundaries for those who seek licence to travel there.

The affluence of limits

'The world of reality has its bounds. The world of the imagination is boundless,' wrote the French philosopher Jean-Jacques Rousseau in the eighteenth century. His response to this dichotomy was a pragmatic one. 'Not being able to enlarge the one,' he suggested, 'let us contract the other; for it is from their difference that all the evils arise which render us unhappy.' This advice may be sensible. The distance between our expectations and reality forms the basis for some modern theories of happiness. But by the same token it seems to throw us back onto the fear of limits with which this chapter started.[25]

The finite dimensions of our planetary home are incontrovertible. But in the hands of power, the injunction to limit our expectations is deeply problematic. If we teach our kids there are no limits at all, they will become disillusioned and dysfunctional adults. If we teach them the world is a dark and foreboding prison, they will never achieve their full potential. If we ignore the limits to economic growth, we risk irreversible damage to our lives and livelihoods. If we appear to turn back the tide of progress, we risk a return to the barbarism of the cave.

But retrenchment and denial are not the only response to the challenge of limits. Adaptation offers a more creative alternative. Applying our limitless ingenuity and boundless imagination in adapting to the real world is the foundation for an endlessly creative endeavour. 'Human and earthly limits, properly understood,' wrote the conservationist Wendell Berry, 'are not confinements, but rather inducements . . . to fullness of relationship and meaning.'[26]

Beyond our material limits, he was suggesting, lies another world. A place worth visiting. An investment worth making. A destination worth reaching. Tomorrow is another country. They do things differently there. Beyond the limits to affluence lies an affluence that only limits can reveal to us. Limits are the gateway to the limitless.

4

The Nature of Prosperity

'Those only are happy (I thought) who have their minds fixed on
some other object than their own happiness.'
John Stuart Mill, 1873[1]

'Hence in a season of calm weather
Though inland far we be,
Our Souls have sight of that immortal sea
Which brought us hither.'
William Wordsworth, 1804[2]

In the autumn of 1826, John Stuart Mill suffered what might nowadays
be called a mental health crisis. The man sometimes credited with
being the founder of classical economics had a complex and troubled
personality. Former British Prime Minister William Gladstone once
called him the 'saint of rationalism'. That rationalism yielded the
'happiness calculus' on which today's economics is built. And yet
he was driven by strong moral sentiments. He fiercely championed
progressive social policies, favoured the redistribution of wealth and
was a staunch advocate of the rights of women and the abolition of
slavery.[3]

At the age of 20, he fell into a deep depression that lasted right
through the 'melancholy winter' of 1826 and into the rest of that
decade. He almost didn't survive it. 'I frequently asked myself, if I
could, or if I was bound to go on living, when life must be passed
in this manner,' he confessed, recalling the episode more than four
decades later in his *Autobiography*. 'I generally answered to myself
that I did not think I could possibly bear it beyond a year.'[4]

To anyone with direct or indirect experience of mental illness,
Mill's account of this dark period is deeply moving. It's one of the

calamities of modern capitalism that mental ill-health now accounts for one of the largest and fastest-growing categories of disease world-wide. Depression costs the global economy more than $1 trillion each year. The human cost is even higher. In the US, the suicide rate has risen by almost a third since the beginning of the century. Trends in mental illness amongst young people are particularly distressing, with suicide now the second most common cause of death for those aged between 15 and 29.[5]

How this can be happening in a world that is unimaginably richer than it was in the early nineteenth century is both tragic and puzzling. It clearly points us towards an essential truth: that living well is not just about having more. And this truth is a liberating one. It offers the tantalizing possibility that we could live better with less.

Such an outcome is by no means a guaranteed outcome, of course. But one thing is clear. If we are to live well, within the limits of a finite planet, we need a better conception of social progress than the one encoded in the myth of growth. Understanding the nature of prosperity – what it means to live well – is an essential stepping-stone towards a postgrowth narrative. In this chapter, I want to propose a very specific answer to that question. It's an answer beautifully illustrated by Mill's own life.

The 'calculus' of happiness

The saint of rationalism was widely recognized as a child prodigy. He learnt Greek at the age of 3. He was reading classical philosophers in their original language before he was 12. Under the tutelage of an attentive but authoritarian father, he began to study political econ-omy when he was just 15 years old. For five years before his crisis, he had been immersed in the work of the philosopher Jeremy Bentham, who happened to be a close family friend.[6]

Perhaps ironically, given the impact it had on Mill, the work itself concerned the pursuit of happiness and its relationship to right and wrong. Bentham taught that something is right in so far as it leads to an increase in happiness and wrong in so far as it doesn't. Social progress happens, he said, when the general happiness increases. If it were only possible to develop a framework for adding up happiness, then perhaps we would have a reliable guide not just to our everyday decisions, but to the prosperity of the nation as a whole. Consequently, argued Bentham, the role of the state should be to pursue the 'greatest happiness for the greatest number' of people. This was the theory that Mill was later to popularize, some forty years after he first started to study it, under the name 'utilitarianism'.[7]

Economics today has a bad rap. But it's useful to understand that our modern theory has its roots in social activism. Utilitarianism was a bold, almost heroic move on the part of a generation of increasingly secular thinkers, disaffected with religion and distrustful of the power of the priests. One of their aims was to challenge what was seen as the unjustified moral authority of the church. In a sense, it was a deliberate attempt to do away with concepts like 'natural law' and the 'natural order': the same concepts that were embedded in the cosmology of *The Knight's Tale*. The utilitarians believed these ideas to be a surreptitious form of tyranny used by a religious elite intent on laying claim to secular power.

At the age of 16, Mill understood this bold ambition instinctively. Reading Bentham, he realized immediately the magnitude of the shift in moral authority that was implied. 'The feeling rushed upon me,' he wrote later in his *Autobiography*, 'that all previous moralists were superseded, and that here indeed was the commencement of a new era in thought.' In retrospect, the accuracy of this assessment is remarkable. Economics began to dominate our world. Its equations coded our sense of right and wrong. Its prescriptions coloured our vision of social progress.

The early economists were trying to 'democratize' moral right and wrong; and in the process to wrest power away from the church. They were stupendously successful in at least a part of that task. The extent to which economics itself not only usurped but eventually abused that power is a salutary lesson from history. Power tends to corrupt, as the British parliamentarian Lord Acton once remarked. Absolute power corrupts absolutely. It's a theme we'll return to in Chapter 9.

Since that time, the meaning of the word 'utility' has changed. In Mill's day, it was a kind of direct proxy for happiness. Bentham starts from the premise that we all desire happiness. That's what makes its pursuit an appropriate role for government. Economists today use 'utility' to refer to the worth or value of something. They tend to measure utility in monetary terms. The argument that we are driven to maximize our expected utility then assumes a very different meaning. But perhaps it's easier to see now why the pursuit of GDP growth is seen as an irreducible good by economists and policymakers alike. It's a direct descendant of Bentham's proposal that the aim of policy should be to achieve the greatest happiness.

However reasonable the underlying idea, its translation into the myth of growth relies on one particular, somewhat suspicious assumption: namely, that money is a good proxy for happiness. If income is the same thing as (or closely related to) utility and utility is the same thing as (or closely related to) happiness, then surely higher income should lead inescapably to happiness – if not at the individual level, then certainly at the aggregate level? The trouble is, it doesn't. Or at least, not entirely.

Who's happy now?

In 1974, the economist Richard Easterlin asked a seemingly innocent question: does economic growth improve the human lot or does it not? Clearly, it ought to if the economic equation of income with happiness is to hold. But the answer he uncovered was both surprising and confusing: sometimes it does; sometimes it doesn't. In some circumstances, having more money makes us happier; in others it doesn't. There's now a mass of statistical evidence that unpacks this ambivalent relationship.[8]

One clear finding is that more income does a lot to increase happiness when incomes are very low to start with. Looking across countries, for instance, there's a rapid increase in measured happiness as the average income of the nation rises from next-to-nothing to around $20,000 per person. Lifting the poorest out of poverty matters. Proper nutrition, safe water, basic services: all these things make a material difference to people's lives. And the result is clearly reflected in their reported happiness.[9]

Beyond that point, though, the additional benefits of having more money seem to diminish quite rapidly. Eventually, they peter out altogether and sometimes they even go into reverse. Some very high-income countries (like the US) have happiness scores which are below those of much poorer countries (like Chile and Costa Rica). Quite astonishingly, they also have lower life expectancy. It's a very perverse finding. If the aim of economic growth is to improve life and to increase happiness, then why don't richer countries always look happier than poorer ones? How can happiness sometimes be lower in rich countries than it is in poorer ones?[10]

Looking at happiness inside the richer nations reveals some even more curious findings. Over time, the average level of reported happiness within a country really doesn't tend to change that much. In the US, for example, the General Social Survey reports the average happiness scores haven't changed by more than 5% between the highest and the lowest values since the mid-1970s. There was a very slight (2%) rise in happiness between 1976 and the early 1990s. Since that time, though, the average happiness score has fallen by around 3%. And this has happened even as the economy has more than tripled in size. In other words, getting richer on average hasn't helped Americans get happier at all over the last four decades.[11]

On the other hand, richer people within America (and within other countries too) tend to be happier than the poorer people around them. Differences in income measured within each country lead to marked differences in reported happiness. Relative deprivation definitely matters. So does social exclusion. In Germany, there's still a happiness divide between the former East Germany (where average incomes are lower) and the West (where they're higher). Being richer than those around you really does seem to make people happier. And vice versa: being poorer sucks.[12]

Curiously, it isn't just the poorest who suffer in countries where there are big differences between the rich and the poor. Inequality affects everyone. Society as a whole is less happy when things are unequal, as the sociologists Kate Pickett and Richard Wilkinson have shown so clearly. Could this be one explanation for the counter-intuitive finding that happiness hasn't changed much in the richer countries over time? Perhaps the happiness gains from higher GDP are getting cancelled out by rising inequality? It's still something of a puzzle that the increased happiness of the rich doesn't outweigh the decreased happiness of the poor. Particularly as the average income triples over time. But the evidence that more equal societies are happier than less equal ones leads to a pretty straightforward conclusion. Levelling up our societies could have massive benefits in terms of people's happiness.[13]

Taking these findings together, it becomes obvious that – from a utilitarian perspective – we should be aiming to close the inequality gap, not widen it. This in itself would tend to improve the 'greatest happiness of the greatest number'. But to be doubly sure, we should also be aiming constantly to focus on the wellbeing of the poorest in society. The pursuit of GDP growth guarantees neither of these things. And in some cases, as we've seen from recent history, it can actually undermine both of them.

In short, there are important, even essential, aspects of happiness that money just can't buy. An account of the size of the economy tells us nothing about our wider human aspirations and our societal needs. Cashing out happiness (quite literally) in monetary terms makes a fatal category error. It isn't so surprising to ordinary people – although it sometimes does seem to surprise economists – that the pursuit of money will at some point begin to depart from the pursuit of happiness.

One obvious way out of this bind might be to use happiness rather than the GDP as our indicator of the nation's prosperity. The British economist Richard Layard has been particularly eloquent in arguing that this would be more in keeping with the original ideas of Jeremy Bentham and more informative as a measure of social progress. But even that idea, true as it may be to utilitarianism, runs into some problems.[14]

The limits of rationalism

Mill's analysis of his own mental health crisis is a strangely intellectual one. Depression was an unexpected and slightly annoying failing of his own internal logic. The timing was arbitrary and inconvenient. But his analysis of it is fascinating, nonetheless. Particularly for what it reveals about the nature of prosperity.

Five years studying utilitarianism gave Mill what he believed would be his mission in life: 'to be a reformer of the world'. His conception of his own happiness was 'entirely identified with this object'. It seemed to work well for him at first. Looking around at the social and political changes that were happening early in the nineteenth century, he could well imagine that the world was getting better. He felt himself to be a part of that improvement. He had a sense of solidarity with those engaged in the same work of social reform.

And then one day, in a moment of melancholy, he posed what he thought was an innocent question: what if these reforms were somehow magically realized? 'Would this be a great joy and happiness to you?' he asked himself. Maybe it's never a good idea to engage in existential reflection when you're already feeling low. It's likely to reveal some uncomfortable truths. And that's exactly what happened to Mill. 'An irrepressible self-consciousness distinctly answered "No!"'

'At this my heart sank within me: the whole foundation on which my life was constructed fell down,' he confessed. The next few paragraphs in his *Autobiography* seek to analyse the trap he had caught himself in. He had fully hoped and expected to find his own happiness by chasing a project to pursue the happiness in society. He still believed intellectually that the project was worth pursuing, but in relation to his own happiness, '[t]he end had ceased to charm,' he explained. 'I seemed to have nothing left to live for.'

His rational 'resolution' of this paradox is a strange one. He continues to maintain that happiness is 'the test of all rules of conduct, and the end of life'. But from this point on he claims that it can only ever be attained by not making happiness an end in itself. 'Those only are happy,' he writes in the famous passage cited at the top of the chapter, 'who have their minds fixed on some other object than their own happiness; on the happiness of others, on the improvement of mankind, even on some art or pursuit, followed not as a means, but as itself an ideal end. Aiming thus at something else, they find happiness by the way.'

There's something vaguely unconvincing in this explanation. It slides away from reason somehow, into a kind of contorted apologia. For if happiness at the personal level cannot be attained except in passing, by not looking at it, so to speak, then how effective is a 'calculus of happiness' going to be as the guide to public affairs? It's weirdly reminiscent of the 'measurement' problem in quantum mechanics. The observer irreducibly interferes with the observable world. The harder we look, the less we see what's there. Until we're forced into the uncomfortable position of accepting that there is no 'there'. Happiness is just a mirage, then. Is that the conclusion?

Intellectually, the resolution appears to satisfy Mill of the validity of the utilitarian project. It must have done. He spent another three or four decades refining his vision of it. He published the defining treatise on it. But he admits years later that it failed to alleviate his unhappy mood. From the depths of despair, he looks around for someone to talk to about the way he's feeling. After briefly considering his father in this role, he dismisses the idea immediately. 'Everything convinced me that he had no knowledge of any such mental state as I was suffering from, and that even if he could be made to understand it, he was not the physician to heal it.'

There's a hugely revealing section of his account that was deleted from the final published version. Without blaming either of his parents, he reflects ruefully on their ill-suitedness to each other and its impact on his life. 'In an atmosphere of tenderness and affection, [my father] would have been tender and affectionate,' he writes, 'but his ill-assorted marriage and asperities of temper disabled him.' He paints a picture of a household divided at its core and with no emotional stability. 'I thus grew up in the absence of love and in the presence of fear,' he concludes.[15]

Happiness may be hard to find. But the roots of misery can sometimes be excruciatingly clear. Mill's crisis reveals a deeply unhappy childhood. This arid land was obviously an immensely productive place to pursue the life of the mind. But its compensations are too dry to nourish the roots of a desiccated soul. And any narrow configuration of happiness that misses this multi-dimensional truth is blown out of the water completely.

To some extent, Mill seems to have understood this point. From that moment on, his own version of utilitarianism begins to separate out different kinds of pleasure on the basis of their qualities – as though he has come to an understanding that happiness can never be a single one-dimensional thing. All pleasures are equal, but some are more equal than others. A child prodigy can want for a love that no amount of intellectual adventure can satisfy.

At another point in the early draft of his *Autobiography*, Mill admits something fundamental. It's a failing that has so often been thrown at modern economics. 'In our schemes for improving human affairs,' he writes, 'we overlooked human beings.' What he doesn't quite acknowledge, here or anywhere, is that this failing in particular undermines the reliability of a simple 'happiness calculus' and leaves the entire edifice of a utilitarian economics standing on foundations of sand.[16]

The good life

This is an uncomfortable but not entirely unpredictable place to find ourselves. Happiness is not a simple one-dimensional thing. Nor can we approach it by rushing headlong towards it. We cannot accurately monitor its presence or calculate the sum of its parts. It doesn't fully reflect the complexity of the human heart. It doesn't reliably capture the many, different dimensions of human wellbeing. We can certainly offer it as an alternative to the pursuit of money. But happiness, just like the GDP, may end up measuring, in RFK's words: 'everything, in short, except that which makes life worthwhile'. Neither the pursuit of happiness nor the pursuit of money offers us a reliable guide to what we might call the 'good life'.

What we've stumbled on here is a problem as old as the hills. In his famous essay 'The Living Standard', the Nobel Prize-winning economist Amartya Sen argued that neither money nor utility can bring us a very reliable guide to the quality of life in a given society. Prosperity depends rather on the 'capabilities' that people in society have to flourish or to function well. Social progress, he argues in *Development as Freedom*, should be thought of as a continual increase in those capabilities. Sen's arguments owe something to the work of the ancient Greek philosopher Aristotle, who grappled with very similar issues almost two millennia ago. In a book called the *Nicomachean Ethics*, he deals very precisely with the problem confronting Mill – and facing us here in this chapter. What does it mean for human beings to live well?[17]

Aristotle's starting point looks disarmingly familiar. The greatest good for human beings is something he calls *eudaimonia*, a word derived from the Greek word for good (*eu*) and the word for spirit (*daimon*). It's often translated into English as wellbeing. But in Aristotle's view this sense of wellbeing isn't just about the presence of pleasure or the absence of pain. Instead he defines it in terms of virtues. *Eudaimonia* is 'activity of the soul in accordance with virtue' (*aretē* in Greek). This sounds a bit moralistic, as though human beings are somehow saints, constantly craving moral goodness. If it were true, of course, it might well lead to a better society than one fixated on self-interest. And a better economics as well. But it would also be a misunderstanding of Aristotle's ideas.[18]

At the time he was writing, the word *aretē* had a much broader meaning than the English word 'virtue' has today. For someone – or something – to be virtuous meant simply that they were capable of functioning well: to the very best of their potential. A virtuous cook is one who cooks pretty good meals. A virtuous knife is one that cuts extremely well. A virtuous poet would compose astonishing poetry. A virtuous person is someone who functions excellently (or flourishes) in all possible capacities as a human being. Moral virtues, as we would understand the word 'virtue', are simply a subset of the broader ways in which human beings are capable of flourishing or functioning well. A morally virtuous person is someone really good at being 'good'.

The sense of virtue implicit in Aristotle's description of the good life has more in keeping with the English word 'virtuosity' (the quality of being 'good at' something) rather than the word 'virtuousness', which simply implies being good – as judged against a particular moral code. Virtuosity brings with it a sense of the context of an act or a performance. A knife isn't virtuous just because it's very big, or even because it's very sharp. A Samurai sword wouldn't be much good as a kitchen knife, for instance, though it's clearly bigger and a whole lot sharper than an ordinary kitchen knife. Virtuosity depends not just on the particular qualities of a thing or a person, but also on the context of an action or a situation. The context of cutting up carrots is massively different to the context of engaging in mortal combat. In most people's kitchens.

Aristotle went so far as to articulate this understanding in a far-reaching principle. Each virtue, he said, is flanked by two vices. One of these relates to a deficiency in the functioning embodied in a particular virtue. The other relates to an excess of it. Sometimes, the knife just needs to be sharper, if it is to do the job assigned to it. Other times it needs to be blunter. Sometimes, incomes do need to be higher, if people are to have any chance of a decent life. Other times, higher incomes bring the diseases of affluence that troubled the American liberals.

This principle begins to make sense of the confusing data about the relationship between happiness and the GDP. Sometimes people really do need more income to have any chance of a decent life. Sometimes the 'mere accumulation of material things' that so alarmed RFK leads only to an erosion of happiness, purpose and dignity. The simple single equation of growth in the GDP with social progress – if it ever was remotely fit for purpose – now very clearly falls apart.

Stay healthy

As the global pandemic began to exact its torments on our lives, our responses to it betrayed fascinating clues about our own priorities. Almost overnight, though with no explicit instruction, we began to greet each other differently. Especially in our virtual correspondence. I must have received a thousand emails which all began with some version of this slightly awkward, deeply human opening line: 'I trust that you are well in these strange and difficult times.' I probably wrote as many myself. Each one signed off with a precautionary 'stay healthy'. 'Kind regards' and 'best wishes' were forsaken for the much more personal 'take care'.

We were beginning to learn how much health matters to us. It was always there in the sociological evidence. Physical health is a deeply important component of prosperity. Whenever you ask people what matters in their lives, health comes at or close to the top of the list. Health for us; health for our families and friends. A genuinely prosperous society must have health at its heart. Neglecting that priority, as we learned from the coronavirus, is devastating in all sorts of ways. Prosperity of any kind begins to look pretty elusive when you or those you love are suffering or dying unnecessarily.[19]

Casting prosperity as health has another foundation. Aristotle's *Ethics* was dedicated to Nicomachus, which happened to be the name of both his father and his son. Nobody seems entirely sure which one was the intended recipient. Maybe it was both. As it happens, though, we do know that Nicomachus senior was a physician. And the conceptual model underlying the *Ethics* seems to owe a lot to the notion of health. Balance is absolutely key to healthy physiological functioning. Both deficiency and excess are signifiers of imbalance and poor health.

Physical health must surely be fundamental to the nature of prosperity. We are at the beginning and the end of the day biological animals. We are living in a material world. Our most solid foundations are based on continuous material exchange. We breathe in. We breathe out. We feed. We shit. We fuck. What seems so mundane is literally vital. Life depends on it. Vitality resides in it. How we carry out these physiological functions matters enormously, as I am going to argue later on. But the first key lesson from all this is that a genuine prosperity depends on the intrinsically material process of our physical lives.

The philosopher Hannah Arendt has even suggested that this visceral materiality is the only chance for contentment human beings have. 'There is no lasting happiness outside the prescribed cycle of painful exhaustion and pleasurable regeneration,' she writes in *The Human Condition*. And 'whatever throws this cycle out of balance', whether it's misery and wretchedness or riches and great fortune, 'ruins the elemental happiness that comes from being alive'.[20]

I want to come back to this argument in Chapter 7. It has massive repercussions for our understanding of the role of work in a post-growth society. And it receives some interesting confirmation from modern theories of neurobiology. But for now, of course, we have to admit that physiological functioning doesn't exhaust what people have in mind when they're asked about the good life. More than the material is involved in living well, as Robert Kennedy pointed out in Kansas. My proposal is that here too we can cast prosperity in terms of health.

Prosperity as health

Again, the sociological evidence is useful to us here. Beyond the pre-occupation with physical health, people speak of their love of family, the importance of friendship, the attachment to community. We long for security and safety and a sense of home. We want to belong; but we also yearn for individuality. We crave significance; but we are also looking for meaningful ways to participate in society.[21]

The psychologist Abraham Maslow once proposed a 'hierarchy' of human needs with subsistence as the foundation for every-thing. People only turn their attention to 'higher' social and psy-chological needs once material needs are satisfied, he suggested. Later in life, he changed his mind, proposing instead a 'duality' of human needs, some physical and some psychological or social. Social and psychological health are not add-ons, it seems: 'nice-to-haves' once our material needs are met. We now know that mental health is absolutely critical to our survival as social beings. Without it we become isolated and disoriented. We seek solace in addic-tions of one kind or another. Drink or drugs entice us. Shopping becomes our defence against despair. Addiction offers the prom-ise of salvation. But it leads us towards stress and sickness and suicide.[22]

In some fascinating experimental work carried out in the 1970s, the psychologist Bruce Alexander overturned our understanding of how addiction operates. The dominant view at the time was that substances like heroin were simply too powerful for people to resist without engaging in a 'war on drugs' that involved severe social and legal punishment. To prove this power, psychologists kept rats in cages with the option to drink from pure water or water laced with morphine. Inevitably (it would seem), the rats chose the morphine over the water and eventually their addiction killed them.

Alexander looked at the experiment and realized there was something wrong with it. The rats were invariably kept in solitary confinement in empty cages with little or nothing in the way of interaction or entertainment. He took some of these morphine-addicted rats and introduced them to what he called Rat Park: a huge plywood box fitted out 'as a happy home and a playground' on the floor of his addiction lab in Simon Fraser University. Almost immediately their addictions began to disappear. 'The opposite to addiction is not sobriety,' argues the best-selling author Johann Hari. 'The opposite to addiction is connection.' Social health is not inferior to physiological health. Both of them are essential to survival.[23]

Tangled up in all of this is the role of desire. We long to love and be loved. We search for a sexual partner, a companion, a mate. We are looking for someone to share our joys and commiserate in our pains. Someone to raise a family with. Once again I suggest we can employ the metaphor of health. We can cast desire in terms of sexual or reproductive health, if you will: a part of 'life's longing for itself', as the poet Kahlil Gibran once described it.[24]

And finally there's also a capacity in human beings for transcendence. Sometimes, the need to lose oneself in life's intensity and its mystery. Sometimes, a yearning for meaning and purpose. Occasionally, a desire for desire itself. None of this necessarily presupposes any particular kind of cosmological reality beyond the material world. But its existence as a phenomenon in human life suggests a fifth domain of spiritual health (Figure 1) without which it's hard to make sense of people's aspirations for the good life.

Within each domain, we may expect to find both virtue and vice – in the sense that Aristotle talked about it. Excellent health is a balance between deficiency and excess. This doesn't necessarily mean that we can cure deficiencies by simply adding more of something. Nor that we can put a halt to excess by taking something away again. The domains of health are deeply entwined with each other. Sometimes an excess in one place is an indicator of a deficiency in another. Sometimes the way to curb excess is to create abundance elsewhere.

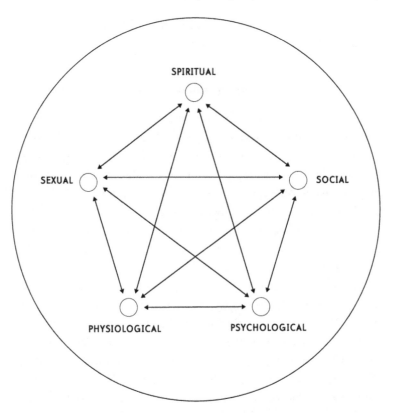

Figure 1 Prosperity as health: human functioning in five domains

These possibilities are all obscured by the flawed idea that more is always better. Once uncovered, they reveal new pathways towards prosperity.

What's most fascinating about this framework – and in particular the idea that virtue lies in achieving an appropriate balance within and between each of these dimensions – is that it effectively rules out the possibility that the good life can be reflected in any meaningful way through a continual accumulation of material or financial wealth. It makes clear that society has taken a profoundly wrong turn in its pursuit of prosperity. A wrong turn that started way back when Mill was building the foundations for a utilitarian economics. A trajectory that simply went on meandering into the wilderness from that point on. Tantalizingly, there were times when Mill almost recognized this uncomfortable truth.

Trailing clouds of glory

The most moving part of Mill's mental crisis is the account of his slow recovery from it. The first glimpse of light came when he found himself in tears, reading a passage from a book called *Memories of a Father* by the French historian Jean-François Marmontel. The passage in question describes the death of Marmontel's father, vividly eliciting the distress of the family. It dwells in detail on the determination of the young Marmontel to comfort his family and make them feel 'that he would be everything to them – would supply the place of all that they had lost'.

'A vivid conception of the scene and its feelings came over me,' wrote Mill in his *Autobiography*. 'From this moment my burden grew lighter. The oppression of the thought that all feeling was dead within me was gone. I was no longer hopeless: I was not a stock or a stone. I had still, it seemed, some of the material out of which all worth of character, and all capacity for happiness, are made.' The capacity to empathize, perhaps even identify, with the young Marmontel rescued Mill from the prison of his own intellect and allowed him to begin a slow, hesitant journey back into the world.

It wasn't a particularly easy one. He would relapse sometimes for months at a time, slipping headlong into episodes of darkness. One day in the autumn of 1828, he started to read the work of the English poet William Wordsworth. In poetry, Mill found a balm that lay beyond the intellect. 'What made [his] poems a medicine for my state of mind,' he explained, 'was that they expressed, not mere outward beauty, but states of feeling, and of thought coloured by feeling, under the excitement, of beauty.'

He was particularly taken by a poem called *Intimations of Immortality*, in which Wordsworth struggled with the loss of youth and the impermanence of life. 'I found that he too had had similar experience to mine,' wrote Mill. 'He also had felt that the first freshness of youthful enjoyment of life was not lasting.'

But he had 'sought for compensation and found it, in the way in which he was now teaching me to find it'.

Wordsworth's famous ode is renowned not just for the beauty of its language, but also for its appeal to an almost transcendental dimension to human experience. Something far from the rationalism that haunted Mill, but close to the idea that spiritual health constitutes an essential element in human prosperity. We're most connected to this domain when we're young, claims Wordsworth, because our memory of its glory is still strong. 'Our birth is but a sleep and a forgetting,' he muses:

> The Soul that rises with us, our life's Star,
> Hath had elsewhere its setting,
> And cometh from afar:
> Not in entire forgetfulness,
> And not in utter nakedness,
> But trailing clouds of glory do we come.

As we grow up, the brilliance of this transcendental beauty slowly fades. But it never entirely disappears, says the poet. And sometimes, 'in a season of calm weather', he suggests in my opening epigraph, our souls may still catch a glimpse of 'that immortal sea'.

The final stage in Mill's recovery began when he met the woman who would eventually become his wife. Harriet Taylor was married, with two sons already, when they were introduced at the dinner party of a mutual friend in 1830. Their subsequent close friendship was the subject of some lively speculation. Harriet herself described her early relationship to Mill as that of a soul mate. She didn't leave her husband. In fact, they had a third child in 1831 and remained married until his death in 1849. Nor is there any evidence of a physical intimacy between Mill and Taylor during those early years. But it's clear that within a very short space of time they developed an unusual intellectual and emotional intimacy. It was a relationship that was to sustain Mill – and contribute to his intellectual work – for the rest of his life.[25]

What remains behind

Empathy, transcendence, poetry, love. This short episode in Mill's life is fascinating for all sorts of reasons. Through it, the 'saint of rationalism' stumbles on, but never quite assimilates, an utterly subversive vision of what a genuine prosperity might mean. Beyond the greatest happiness of the greatest number, his own experience seems to suggest, lies a much more sophisticated, a much more radiant, a much more human terrain.

By the time they were free to marry in 1851, both John Stuart Mill and Harriet Taylor Mill suffered from chronically poor health. Seeking physical relief, they would travel south from time to time in search of a warmer climate. It was on one of these trips, just seven years after their wedding, that Harriet was taken ill with a severe lung infection. She died in Avignon on 3 November 1858. And it was there in Avignon that Mill decided to buy a small cottage so that he could be 'as close as possible to the place where she is buried'. He lived there for much of the rest of his life.[26]

It was in Avignon that he wrote the first draft of *The Subjection of Women*. 'All that is most striking and profound belongs to my wife,' he wrote of it. There too he finally completed *Utilitarianism*, his exposition of the 'happiness calculus' that had absorbed so much of his life. Perhaps in the end, it was this rationalism which offered him a stoic refuge in tragic circumstances. His favourite poet, William Wordsworth, had suggested as much in *Intimations*:

> Though nothing can bring back the hour
> Of splendour in the grass, of glory in the flower;
> We will grieve not, rather find
> Strength in what remains behind.

Our love of nature; our innermost emotions; our empathy for others; our sorrow at the transience of life; our unfathomable connection to the earth itself; our capacity for contemplation; our inherent desire to strive for a better society. These are the psychological – and perhaps spiritual – dimensions of the human condition.

It's compelling to wonder what kind of economics we might have inherited from a narrative capable of holding such richness in its grasp. It's intriguing to ponder on what might yet emerge from a postgrowth vision informed by this abundance.

5

Of Love and Entropy

'We are such stuff
As dreams are made on; and our little life
Is rounded with a sleep.'
William Shakespeare, 1611[1]

'S = k log W'
Ludwig Boltzmann, 1877[2]

On 28 October 1905, the Austrian physicist Ludwig Boltzmann gave what was to be his last lecture for a public audience. It took place on a Saturday evening at the Vienna Philosophical Society. Its title was strange. 'An Explanation of Love and of Entropy Using the Principles of Probability'. Entropy is a measure of the disorder of a physical system. An ultimate expression of natural limits. Love offers perhaps the highest example of human flourishing. An ultimate expression of human prosperity. How these two things relate to each other is the subject of this chapter.[3]

Boltzmann's career was unusually stormy. He spent much of his professional life mired in controversy, and this lecture was no exception. By mixing up physics and philosophy with the most exalted of human emotions, he managed simultaneously to delight the open-minded and upset his strait-laced colleagues. The die-hard physicists found his excursions into philosophy unfathomable. The dyed-in-the-wool philosophers disliked a physicist wandering around in their patch. Neither of them could figure out what love had to do it.

It's extraordinary to think that one of the greatest physicists of the nineteenth century should have spent so much of his life fighting battles which, in hindsight, put him so far ahead of his time. They would eventually take a toll on both his physical health and his peace of mind. But his students adored him. And his public lectures were always filled to capacity with a lively audience, drawn to his wide-ranging arguments and his dry sense of humour.

Sadly, there's no surviving transcript of the love and entropy lecture. But a few people have taken a creative guess at its content. Boltzmann was fascinated by Darwin's theory of evolution, which the Austrian physicist would often frame as the struggle for available energy. Everything we are and everything we do requires access to free energy. It's likely Boltzmann used this occasion to explore the way in which this universal struggle could have led to the emergence of a complex species with an extraordinary array of aspirations and emotions – including, of course, love.[4]

In doing so, he would have addressed two of the most fundamental objects of inquiry in this book: the question of limits on the one hand; and the nature of our aspirations for the good life on the other. So, with only a passing apology for putting words into Boltzmann's mouth, I want to offer an interpretation of that last lecture as a kind of rough guide for a lonely planet. An instruction manual in how we might flourish as human beings in a finite world.[5]

Counting calories

Let's start with physical health. What does it mean for human beings to achieve excellent functioning in physiological terms? Broadly speaking, this question is equivalent to asking what it means for people to be really, truly healthy. That's a huge question, of course. Our bodies evolved over millions of years under very specific conditions and developed a rather complex set of system requirements to achieve optimal health. But some of these requirements are relatively easy to understand and deeply revealing about the relationship between health and society.

The most straightforward of them is the body's energy balance. Human beings need a certain number of calories each day to maintain a healthy body weight. The precise number varies according to age, height, gender and the amount of exercise we take. But it's generally between about 1,500 and 3,000 calories a day. Fewer calories than needed and your body will wither and weaken. More than required on a regular basis and you will gain weight. The idea of counting calories has emerged for a reason. The energy balance is critical in the struggle to maintain a healthy life.[6]

Calorie counting, believe it or not, works through one of the most fundamental laws in physics: the first law of thermodynamics. Calories are a measure of energy. Thermodynamics is the study of energy transformations. The first law tells us that energy is always conserved through physical transformations. The calories we consume are transformed in physical processes within our body. But the energy is always conserved along the way.

Our bodies use energy to maintain basic functions: breathing, circulation, digestion, cell reproduction and growth. They also need energy for physical exercise, walking, running, lifting things. Whatever's left over from the calories we consume will be stored in the body as fat (a form of chemical energy). This is where the first law comes in. If your calorie intake exceeds the basic maintenance energy needed to keep you alive plus the energy you exert through physical activity, the excess energy is stored in the body, usually as fat. Likewise, of course, if your calorie intake is insufficient to cover these two things, you will lose weight, because your body will start burning fat (and eventually muscle) in order to source its energy needs. The human body is a thermodynamic organism. It obeys the laws of thermodynamics.

Good physiological health is in part a balance between having too many and having too few calories. If you consistently have too few calories, you will eventually die of starvation or malnutrition. But if you persistently take in more calories than your body needs, you will over time become overweight and eventually obese. Being overweight massively increases your chances of developing conditions like hypertension (raised blood pressure) and hyperglycaemia (high blood glucose levels). And these in their turn increase your risk of suffering from non-communicable – or 'lifestyle' – diseases such as heart attacks, strokes and diabetes. Lifestyle diseases shorten your life-expectancy, reduce your life quality and lower your resistance to infectious diseases.[7]

Counting calories isn't all there is to health, of course. Calories come in different kinds. Proteins, carbohydrates, fibre, minerals, vitamins: each of these is essential for proper health. The balance between them matters. So too does their quality. 'Good' calories, for example, with a slow release of sugar into the bloodstream, are better than 'bad' calories, which release their energy all in a rush. The body's metabolism struggles to stabilize blood sugar levels when constantly exposed to high 'glycaemic index' (GI) foods. Over time, this chronic instability leads to severe health problems.[8]

In short, once fully grown, the healthy organism maintains itself and defends itself from attack, not through a continual, relentless increase in consumption, but through healthy balance. In Aristotle's terms, the 'virtue' of excellent physiological functioning is flanked by two distinct and very different 'vices': undernutrition on one side and overconsumption on the other. Virtuous physiological functioning (excellent health) lies somewhere between them.

Out of balance

What happens when this careful balance meets an economic system designed for growth? It depends critically on the context. Where deficiency is in play – where there's too little food – then growth works in favour of health. But when excess is in play – where there's too much food already – continually indulging in more is a recipe for disaster. It's a particular example of the more general case we explored in the previous chapter. More is only better when there is not enough. When there is already an excess, it simply serves to make things worse.

One of the tragedies of capitalism is the way in which it has presided over both deficiency and excess – even in something as basic as nutrition. One in five children worldwide suffers from physical stunting caused by undernutrition. And yet almost two-fifths of adults over 18 are overweight. Worldwide obesity has tripled since 1975. Childhood obesity has increased a startling ten-fold. Not surprisingly, the incidence of lifestyle diseases has also accelerated. More people now die of obesity than they do of undernutrition.[9]

Quite often you'll hear how complicated it is to tackle the obesity epidemic. Experts will talk of the complex interplay of nutritional, psychological and physical factors. A few years ago, a government study attempted to map these relationships. The visual 'obesity system map' that came out of the exercise was so complicated it resembled nothing much more informative than a plate of densely woven spaghetti. It was virtually useless in terms of either understanding or communicating anything other than the supposed complexity of the problem. And although this was never the intention, it effectively put a stop to any concerted attempt to tackle the root causes of the problem.[10]

Actually, the core dynamic underlying the problem is blindingly simple. Healthy body weight is determined by the balance between calorific input and physical exercise. The economic model of the food sector depends on selling more and more food. If we were all getting more and more active, then – up to a point – we might be able to offset the increase in consumption. But we're not. In fact, the opposite is true. On the whole, people have been getting less physically active – particularly in richer countries – for some time.

Across the world, almost 30% of adults (rising to 37% in high-income countries) now engage in insufficient physical activity to maintain proper health. Meanwhile, global revenues from fast food (which typically has high calorific content) have increased dramatically. The combination of low physical activity and ready availability of fast calories has tipped the calorific balance irresistibly in the direction of excess. The profit motive built into the food production system continually drives this imbalance forwards.[11]

It's entirely possible in principle to resist these perverse incentives. A good starting point would be to provide our kids with the foundations for more active lives. It's definitely much easier for younger people to exercise. Their muscles are stronger; their metabolisms are faster; their joints are more flexible. The young are designed for robust physical activity. Which is why it is shocking that worldwide more than 80% of school-age adolescents are now deemed to have insufficient physical activity. This is nothing short of a tragedy waiting to happen in a world of calorific excess.[12]

Another reason to start young, of course, is the desperately short-lived nature of youth. As the body matures, the metabolism changes. We are assaulted by illness and damaged by accidents. The ease with which we once maintained our fitness diminishes. At the time we need it most, our own ability to help ourselves seems to decline. Any number of physiological feedback mechanisms further deter us from success. As our weight increases, it gets harder to exercise properly, reinforcing the spiral.

Obesity has impacts on our mobility. Immobility has an impact on mental as well as physical health. As our morale declines, we turn to food for comfort. We find it easy to confuse what we desire with what our body really needs. A simple deficiency in relation to water or sleep or fresh air can seem like a desperate need for sugar or saturated fats or carbs. But giving into a sugar craving messes up our insulin balance, overworks our kidneys and our adrenal glands and sends our bodies into a constant sugar addiction. Good news for the food industry. Disaster for us.[13]

The outcome is entirely predictable. Diabetes, high blood pressure, respiratory problems, back and joint pain and increased risk of dementia. Early estimates suggested that almost three-quarters of coronavirus deaths were associated with at least one underlying health condition. The 'comorbidities' of Covid-19 were all alarmingly familiar. Many of them were associated in some way with obesity.[14]

The more we suffer these imbalances, the worse things get. As mobility declines, the muscles get weaker, the joints get stiffer. One day, we're just bending down to pick something up from the floor – a task that seems progressively harder as the years unwind – and something gives. The easy mobility of youth is gone, apparently for good, and we are at risk of spending the rest of our lives immobile. At the very least, we begin to resign ourselves to a severely diminished quality of life. We become less active, less healthy, less fulfilled, more unhappy. We begin to believe that this is the best that we can expect from our physical health for the rest of our lives.[15]

Take back control

None of this is necessary. At any stage of our lives it's possible, in principle, for each of us to take back control of our physical health. To eat better, exercise more (or differently), change our lifestyle, pick up the pieces and return to the balance that the body itself craves. At the individual level it's demonstrable. But rolling back the statistical tide of societal ill-health requires us to confront its underlying dynamic. That dynamic has two key components: human nature on the one hand and the structure of the economy on the other.

It's clear to anyone who's tried how hard it is to go against our nature. We evolved in a very particular world, at a very particular time. The environment of evolutionary adaptation, as biologists call it – the place we 'grew up' as a species – was a place where high-energy foods such as refined sugars and saturated fats were in desperately short supply. Better access to them conferred an advantage over others. Our brains began to reward us by delivering the 'feel-good' chemical dopamine whenever we received an unexpectedly intense burst of calories. Hundreds of thousands of years later, they're still doing it.[16]

We're trapped in a paradox of fitness. The human organism was adapted to an environment of calorific scarcity. The capitalist economy has evolved to deliver calorific overload. In an environment of scarcity, craving these foods was 'adaptive'. It improved our fitness for survival. In an environment in which they are plentiful, the same craving can be damaging and dysfunctional. By making these once-limited resources available in places where there were huge deficiencies, capitalism has done us a service. By creating a model in which economic profitability depends on continuing to sell more and more, it has placed us in a profound danger.

Human health can't be achieved through continually increasing calorie intake; it isn't consistent with ever-rising food consumption. Health and exponential growth are mutually inconsistent models of prosperity. Left to our own devices, with no more than simplistic advice for guidance and surrounded by temptation, we need wills of iron to resist the lure of our own dopamine response to sugar and fat – particularly when we are surrounded by messages that deliberately seek to undermine that resistance. Maintaining virtue (in Aristotle's sense) is proving statistically impossible in an economic model predicated on growth.

Health is a balancing act. It's a dance played out between our diet, our physiology and our choices in life. It's an art we must learn.

Sometimes the hard way. And yet we do not teach it to our kids. We give them nothing of the skills or the resilience that they will need to maintain their health once the early years of easy vitality are gone. Worse than that. We are treating our kids as an opportunity sample for an aggressive marketing strategy. We do our very best to hasten disease by exposing them to impossible temptations to engage in diets that are self-evidently catastrophic for their long-term health. Nor do we teach people to prepare for the time when youth is over. Inevitably, as you age, things change. You will not break the world record for 100 metres. You will not thrive in violent contact sports. You will have to accept that your body has certain limitations.

None of this prevents us from living long, healthy and active lives. We ourselves are ruling that out by failing to understand and to communicate the nature of physical health. That we've done it at all is unfortunate. But that we've done it in the name of profit. That we've condoned it in the name of growth. That we've wilfully confused excess for progress. That is almost inexcusable.

Even now, we're inclined to downplay capitalism's role in the health crisis playing out across the world. This is a tragic mistake. The trends that led to this point will only worsen as time goes on. By embracing and understanding the underlying failure, we have a chance to reverse it. Capitalism has failed to respect the most basic of limits: those that regulate and maintain our health and vitality. Beyond growth lies a model of prosperity as health that is not just achievable, but desirable. Better by far than the one we have too easily resigned ourselves to.

Order out of chaos

We could say, very loosely, that health depends on the body's ability to create and maintain order: to replenish cells, to prevent decay, to achieve optimal balance and excellent functioning. When we die, that ability disappears and the carefully maintained structure of the physical body begins to deteriorate rapidly: to lose its internal order. Very soon even the material constituents of the body break down and dissipate into a more chaotic disorderly state.

This movement from order to chaos is a particular expression of what the physicist Arthur Eddington once called the 'supreme' law of nature: the second law of thermodynamics. In his 1927 Gifford Lectures, Eddington remarked:

> If someone points out to you that your pet theory of the universe is in disagreement with Maxwell's equations – then so much the worse for Maxwell's equations. If it is found to be contradicted by observation – well, these experimentalists do bungle things some-times. But if your theory is found to be against the second law of thermodynamics I can give you no hope; there is nothing for it but to collapse in deepest humiliation.[17]

The second law of thermodynamics is the one that tells us that entropy (disorder) always tends to increase. It was Boltzmann whose interpre-tation of the second law transformed entropy from an abstract con-cept into something instantly recognizable from our everyday lives. Things tend to move from a more orderly state to a more chaotic one – rather than the other way around, he said.[18]

You can probably think of a thousand examples. The continuing battle to keep a teenage bedroom tidy. The gradual running down of essential appliances. The increasing need for maintenance of an old family car. The unholy tangle of your earphone cables, when you definitely put them away tidy. These phenomena are so familiar they seem natural to us. They reflect a profound truth.

Left to their own devices, the general tendency of physical systems is to move from order to chaos. A world in which the opposite hap-pens is an improbable one. Garden sheds, kitchen drawers and kids' bedrooms don't spontaneously tidy themselves up over time. Cables, threads and ropes don't spontaneously untangle. Counteracting the tendency of the world towards chaos requires a continuous effort. In thermodynamic terms, this 'effort' means applying available energy to the situation. That's the job of our lungs and our beating heart in the human body. The function of housework and repair workshops and maintenance contracts in the economy. The work of the carbon cycle in the stability of the earth's atmosphere.

Order is clearly possible in the universe. Life itself is evidence of that. But the entropy law tells us something profound about achieving it. The energy you used to create order becomes less and less available in the process. Energy itself moves from low entropy to high entropy as it carries out work. Even as you create your own small haven of order, by applying energy to the situation, the entropy in the overall system increases. The tidiness of the drawer, the fitness of the human body, the progress of the economy, is always only achieved at a cost.[19]

Each reversal of entropy is carried out at a price. That price is an increase in entropy overall. The available energy becomes unavailable. Its low entropy has turned to high entropy. The universe is a little less orderly than it was before.

Perhaps you tidied that bedroom using only your own muscle power. The chemical energy in your body was used by the muscles to pick things up, put them away: lift, carry, move. The energy in your muscles is transformed into movement and heat. Dissipated into the environment. No longer available to perform more work. The cruel logic of the entropy law is that the order you created by tidying the room is always less than the entropy you created in the process.

'A microscopic mist'

There's a popular formulation which expresses the laws of thermodynamics in terms of the rules of a game in which:

1 You can never win.
2 You can't even break even.
3 You can never leave the game.

Anything we do on planet earth – and, as far as we know, this is true of every other place in the universe – is subject to the second law: you can't ever break even.[20]

What's true of tidying a room is also true of whole economies. Creating civilization is an enormous effort. You need huge volumes of available energy to do it. Our modern society was built on fossil fuels. The chemical energy in coal, oil and gas has delivered us all kinds of miracles. These fuels gave us an unbelievable chance to play the thermodynamic game. But not to win it. As they get burned, their energy is dissipated as heat. The carbon that was once locked up in these fuels is dissipated into the atmosphere, causing climate change, just as the second law predicts. Entropy inevitably increases.

Our best chance for a sustainable world is to use the stream of renewable energy that arrives each day on the earth in the form of solar energy. That energy is captured through the process of photosynthesis. It supports our food chain. It delivers our own ability to do useful work. It also creates the wind and the waves. It drives the cycle of water and nutrients in the biosphere. Using it to generate heat and electricity and work is like surfing a tide of available (low entropy) energy. 'In a different way from the past,' said Herman Daly's PhD supervisor, Nicholas Georgescu-Roegen, '[we] will have to return to the idea that [our] existence is a free gift from the sun.'[21]

The trouble is that even that gift is not entirely free. The solar tide is massive. Just a few days of sunlight is worth more in energetic terms than the entire stock of natural resources. But it falls on the earth with an extremely low intensity, 'like a fine rain, almost a microscopic mist'. To be useful this energy must be concentrated and captured. To capture it we must use materials. That depends in its turn on using up available energy and creating more entropy. The solar flux is free. But capturing it still has a cost, in terms of materials, in terms of energy and in terms of disorder. Wherever we look, the process of creating order carries a price.[22]

This price must be paid not just to create order but also to maintain it. There's a reason why financial depreciation is hardwired into standard accounting practices at both corporate and national levels. It's there to account for the 'running down' of capital equipment. Left to their own devices in a sun-drenched world, physical assets tend to fall apart. Using them tends to accelerate that process. Iron turns to rust. Concrete turns to dust. Even silicon chips degrade over time. Depreciation is the economic manifestation of the inevitable march of entropy.

The bigger the economy, the higher this cost. An infinite economy (the ultimate end of eternal growth) means infinite depreciation.

Infinite maintenance costs. An infinite need for available energy to turn back the tide of entropy. At the end of the day, the myth of growth is a thermodynamic impossibility.

Staying in the game

A kind of hubris haunts our culture. It's the hubris of Reagan's refusal to countenance limits in 1983. The hubris of green growth today. The hubris of the addicted gambler and the delusional narcissist. I can challenge nature and win. I can beat the odds and get away with it. I can be the one to break the rules. The one to outgame the game.

We see this hubris at play in our belief that good health is simply a matter of will power. It's not the fault of capitalism that obesity is accelerating and lifestyle diseases are increasing. It's human nature that's at fault. All we have to do is reverse a million years of evolution and rewire our brains. Let's fix that up before we mess with capitalism. How hard can that be? We see it too in our defiance of the thermodynamic limits to endless economic growth. Who cares about the entropic price we pay for relentless expansion? We can still maintain order in our own tidy corner of the world for as long as it's possible to export the chaos somewhere else. And hope it never comes back to haunt us.

More than a century after Boltzmann's lecture in Vienna, chaos has come knocking. The entropic price of ignoring the rules of the game is evident all around us. In the climate emergency. In the biodiversity crisis. In the curious attack that the coronavirus launched on our most fundamental beliefs and assumptions. Its demands are more and more pressing. Its price is higher than ever. Its message is that we chose the wrong way to play the game. Ignoring and rewriting the rules won't work.

What if there is another way to stay in the game? A way that respects the rules. A way that learns to live well – within the rules. A way to live better than we could ever have imagined. This is the vision of prosperity, the vision of the good life, that I'm searching for here. In imagining a postgrowth world, we're encouraged to believe that we are somehow adopting either a ridiculously naïve or else an irredeemably defeatist attitude to the challenge of living well on a finite planet. Yet any serious exploration of thermodynamic limits and the nature of human prosperity says otherwise. Our challenge is to find the ways and means through which materiality guides our human aspirations towards greater prosperity.

To be able to follow this path we must leave behind the mantra of more. Balance, not growth, is the essence of prosperity. When it comes to physiological functioning, this is abundantly clear. Growth is a very particular phase in the development of the organism. Beyond that phase, excess is as dangerous to our physical health as deficiency. Growth becomes a damaging metaphor for social progress at exactly the point where deficiency turns to excess. Optimal health automatically embodies a dynamic of balance. A dynamic that's fundamentally different from the one embodied in relentless growth.

Can't Buy Me Love

Beyond the realm of physical health lies an even more surprising terrain. Physiological functioning is inherently material. Achieving physiological health requires certain minimal material conditions. Good nutrition, sufficient water, proper exercise, protection from the elements. All of these imply an irreducible materiality. The other forms of health in the previous chapter (Figure 1) are fundamentally different from this. They are essentially relational. They impose no *a priori* materiality beyond the inherent physicality of the subjects and objects of these relationships.

Identity, affiliation, role, purpose, belonging, friendship, self-actualization, love: these are the attributes of excellent psychological health. Often, admittedly, we seek material satisfactions of these non-material needs. The symbolic role of consumer goods in our emotional lives is well documented. Fashion, gift-giving, display, all depend on the pliable currency of material stuff.[23]

Exchange is fundamental to many of these. But to materialize that exchange – as we consistently do in consumer capitalism – is dangerous. By obscuring the nature of relational health, we're in danger of undermining it, as the Beatles pointed out in their 1964 hit song *Can't Buy Me Love*. Substituting material exchange for emotional expression is a sure-fire way of damaging love.[24]

This doesn't mean that love entirely escapes the thermodynamic game. Love and entropy are intimately linked. Love is an emergent property of a thermodynamic universe. It's a relationship between physical beings. It expresses itself within a material world. Love appears as the most unlikely pinnacle in an entire universe of improbability. It's the most spectacular victory in our ongoing struggle to bring order out of chaos.

But at no point is love inherently bound by that struggle. At no point is love brought down by entropy. Never does love demand entropic transformation. Our passage through the high ground of emotional wellbeing is not impeded by the logic of entropy. And the extraordinary implication of this freedom is that it places our highest aspirations – momentarily at least – beyond the realm of scarcity and struggle. It liberates human prosperity from the endless march towards chaos, even as our material existence remains firmly in the game.

This isn't necessarily what Boltzmann was talking about that evening in Vienna. But he almost certainly referred to the undeniable thermodynamic basis for our material being. He probably highlighted the sheer improbability of human existence. He might have underlined that even our complex emotions represent unlikely accumulations of order in a mainly entropic universe. That human progress itself is at best an island of order in an ocean of chaos.

He may well have pointed out that even these unlikely and hard-fought achievements must be temporary at best. None of it lasts forever, as Shakespeare has Prospero point out in *The Tempest*:

The cloud-capp'd towers, the gorgeous palaces,
The solemn temples, the great globe itself,
Yea, all which it inherit, shall dissolve,
And, like this insubstantial pageant faded,
Leave not a rack behind: We are such stuff
As dreams are made on; and our little life
Is rounded with a sleep.[25]

Leaving the game

Boltzmann was born on 20 February 1844, during the night between Shrove Tuesday and Ash Wednesday, as the dying strains of the Mardi Gras ball gave way to repentance and the glamour of the feast turned to sackcloth and ashes. It was to this fact that he would sometimes attribute the volatility of his own personality, alternating between joy and despair. It's likely that a modern diagnosis would suggest a bipolar disorder. Intensely social at times, he would host lively soirées in the family home, where he'd play the piano for students and colleagues. But his wife, Henriette, would often find him still hunched over his writing at 5 a.m., struggling to lay out the arguments in one of his numerous intellectual battles.

By mid-1906, just nine months after the love and entropy lecture, those battles were taking their toll on him. He was plagued with asthma and angina. His eyesight was beginning to fail. It was obvious to his family that he was exhausted. For the first time, that summer, he was forced to cancel his lectures in the University of Vienna, unable to hold the fragments of his life together. Seeking respite, Boltzmann and his wife travelled to the Italian village of Duino, near Trieste, with their 15-year-old daughter, Elsa. The trip was the fulfilment of a promise to Henriette, who had long wanted to visit the castle there, perched high on a rocky promontory above the Adriatic Sea. Its dramatic outlook was a frequent attraction for visitors and visionaries. It was during a stay at the castle in 1912 that the German poet Rainer Maria Rilke would find inspiration for his most famous work: the *Duino Elegies*. The poem speaks of the transience of human life and of an infinite transcendental beauty that lies beyond it.

On Wednesday, 5 September 1906, a couple of days before their return to Vienna, Henrietta and Elsa left Ludwig alone in the house to get one of his suits cleaned in preparation for the new term. A short while later, Elsa returned to the house to find her father hanging by a short cord from a window casement. His body was still warm. But his struggle was already over. He was 62 years old.

He would not survive to see the victory of his ideas. He would not live to understand the importance of his work. He would not witness his daughter Elsa find love with one of his own doctoral students, Ludwig Flamm. He would not attend their wedding. He would never meet the four grandchildren they bore him.

On his tombstone in the Vienna Central Cemetery was engraved a mathematical equation:

$$S = k \log W.^{26}$$

It represents what Albert Einstein would later call Boltzmann's Principle: the law that entropy tends always to increase. The most likely state of the world is chaos. But out of this chaos can emerge the most unlikely, the most extraordinary and the most profoundly beautiful kinds of order. The complexity of the human species. The subtle balance on which our health depends. Our enormous potential for creativity. And our propensity to encounter the most intense and the most beautiful of human emotions.

6

Economics as Storytelling

*'Many circumstances conspire to extinguish scientific discoveries,
especially those that cause discomfort about our culture's
sacred norms.'*
Lynn Margulis, 1999[1]

*'[E]very now and then a new idea turns out to be on the mark, valid
and wonderful.'*
Carl Sagan, 1996[2]

The biologist Lynn Alexander (later Lynn Margulis) joined the University of Chicago's early entrants programme in 1954 when she was just 15 years old. Soon after she arrived there she bumped (quite literally) into the astronomer Carl Sagan as she was bounding up the stairs of Eckhart Hall and he was making his way down. He was a 19-year-old grad student in physics, 'poised to launch his astronomical career'. She was a 'fast-moving, enthusiastic, ignorant girl'. There's a photo of the two of them from around that time, taken on campus. He is holding court at the centre of a group of students sitting on the lawn. She is gazing on in admiration. Three years later they were married.[3]

As power couples go, Lynn and Carl Sagan were something else. He was already on his way to becoming the most celebrated astronomer in the US when they met. Within a few years, he would be a prolific science writer and renowned science commentator. His gaze was invariably turned outwards: towards the cosmos. From a very early age, he had been intrigued by the possibility of discovering life elsewhere in the universe. Lynn's work led her in a completely different direction: towards the microcosm. She became fascinated by a different kind of alien life: the bacteria that inhabited planet earth for three billion years before humans even arrived on the scene.

Shortly after their wedding, Lynn enrolled in a Master's course at the University of Wisconsin. Already pregnant with their first child, she was often sleepy in class. But years later she could still remember clearly the day her professor read out a short passage about the work of early biologists on the neglected concept of symbiosis: the living together of organisms from different species in the same place over a protracted period of time. It was in that moment, she recalled, that 'the course of my professional life was set forever!'[4]

That early fascination eventually led her to a theory which revolutionized our understanding of life on earth – and our conception of nature. Its birth was not an easy one, precisely because of the 'discomfort about our culture's sacred norms' to which Margulis alludes in the opening epigraph. But its relevance to our inquiry here is profound. Not least because it overturns one of capitalism's most cherished beliefs: that competition is the most fundamental driving force in nature – and that it is therefore the most effective basis for an economy.

Yes, competition exists. Yes, as we saw in the previous chapter, the second law of thermodynamics is everywhere in operation. But competition is not the only response to the ubiquitous struggle for survival, claimed Margulis. Animal and plant life evolved from bacteria through symbiosis. Evolution happens as much through cooperation as it does through competition, she insisted.

The power of metaphor

In his book *Narrative Economics*, the Nobel Prize-winning economist Robert Shiller highlights the power of cultural memes to influence economics. There is an uneasy osmosis between the domain of reason and the world of sentiment, he suggests. It's a point no better illustrated than by Mario Draghi's famous remark in 2012 that the European Central Bank would do 'whatever it takes' to stabilize the euro in the aftermath of the financial crisis. Those three words – plus a massive €2.6 trillion programme of asset purchases – conjured up a spirit of heroism, sacrifice and indomitable power. They are credited with rescuing the ailing European currency and preventing financial disaster in Europe. Very similar language was used to 'calm markets' during the early months of the coronavirus crisis.[5]

If this gives the impression that economic performance is just a confidence trick, there may be some truth to the idea. The annual Davos ritual certainly owes more to narrative control than it does to reason. But there is a deeper, more challenging point here. The authority of economics – indeed of any science – depends on our ability to understand and to communicate it. Conceptual models and metaphors are essential for that task. Cast-iron facts and impeccable logic are useless to us without a frame of reference – a conceptual language through which to convey meaning to ourselves and coherence to others.

Narrative plays this role in science. The economist Deirdre McCloskey once declared that economists are 'tellers of stories and makers of poems'. The philosopher Richard Rorty claimed that it is 'pictures rather than propositions, metaphors rather than statements, which determine most of our philosophical convictions'. The theologian Sarah McFague argued that our models of the world are all just 'metaphors with staying power' and that these metaphors are 'ways of knowing', not simply ways of communicating. To achieve staying power, the metaphors themselves must *resonate*. They must reinforce or be reinforced by our experience of the social world. But here's the tricky part. Social resonance works as a filter. It selects *in* those ideas that chime with our social world and selects *out* those that don't. Separating scientific truth from the social context becomes near impossible. Science's hard-nosed objectivity vanishes.[6]

Darwin's theory of evolution offers a prime example of all this. Its central metaphor asserts that life is always and everywhere a relentless 'struggle for existence'. The thermodynamic aspect of this struggle – the one that concerned Boltzmann – is a more or less quantifiable feature of material processes. But the 'struggle' itself is not an objective reality. It's a metaphor. A powerful one for sure. It evokes seemingly trustworthy visions of life as the domain of scarcity, irreconcilable conflict, endless competition and the inevitable dichotomy of victory or defeat. But it is still a metaphor.[7]

In the hands of the Social Darwinists, the narrative turned dangerous. It was the political theorist Herbert Spencer who coined another metaphor: the 'survival of the fittest'. By casting life as a struggle and bestowing a 'natural' supremacy on the survivors, Spencer's metaphor promotes the dubious doctrine that 'might is right'. It sowed the seeds for eugenics: a doctrine of pursuing racial purity which had profound and tragic consequences well into the twentieth century – most notably of course during the Holocaust – and is visible in the xenophobia and racism still haunting society today.[8]

Darwin himself was deeply taken with the metaphor of struggle. He attributes this to his reading of Thomas Malthus's famous *Essay on Population,* which argued that population will always outstrip the means to nourish it, leading to an inevitable and irreducible suffering. The essay was enormously influential across intellectual society in the early nineteenth century. In his *Autobiography,* Darwin writes explicitly:

> In October 1838, that is, fifteen months after I had begun my systematic enquiry, I happened to read for amusement 'Malthus on Population', and being well prepared to appreciate the struggle for existence which everywhere goes on from long-continued observation of the habits of animals and plants, it at once struck me that under these circumstances favourable variations would tend to be preserved, and unfavourable ones to be destroyed. The result of this would be the formation of new species. Here then I had at last got a theory by which to work.[9]

The central metaphor at the heart of evolutionary theory came from an economist. Not just any economist, as it happens, but one with a very specific set of political views which involved (for example) withdrawing support from the poorest in society because it was a lost cause. Suffering could never be eliminated, so why bother trying, Malthus concluded. No wonder economics was dubbed 'the dismal science'. Just how wrong Malthus was in all sorts of ways has been widely pointed out. But his alignment of economics with the inevitability of struggle developed into a very common Victorian meme.[10]

Writers fell over themselves to depict the carnage playing itself out in nature. In a work once described as 'the defining poem of the Victorian age', Alfred Lord Tennyson bewailed the cruel savagery of 'Nature, red in tooth and claw'. A long 'scientific poem' which was originally called *The Origin of Society* and published posthumously as *The Temple of Nature* proclaimed:

> Air, earth, and ocean, to astonished day
> One scene of blood, one mighty tomb display!
> From Hunger's arm the shafts of death are hurl'd
> And one great Slaughter-house the warring world![11]

The author was Charles Darwin's own grandfather Erasmus Darwin.

The idea that life itself is 'nasty, brutish and short' was nothing new. A hundred and fifty years earlier, the philosopher Thomas Hobbes had argued that, when left alone in 'a state of nature', society is nothing more than a 'war of all against all'. Hobbes's *Leviathan* was massively influential in the development of political thought. And I want to come back to it again in Chapter 9. But the reality is that, at the time it was written in the mid-1600s, one half of the country was literally at war with the other, through absolutely no fault of their own. The English Civil War was an unseemly power struggle between monarchy and Parliament. Hobbes's metaphor was drawn from his own social world. It was repeated word for word by the Swedish botanist Linnaeus in a pamphlet written in 1790 to which Malthus and Darwin must both have had access.[12]

Metaphor is complicit in science. As the philosopher Thomas Kuhn once pointed out, there is no 'naked eye'. We see the world through our own distinct cultural lens. The lens through which scientists saw nature in the nineteenth century was tinted irredeemably by a fast-growing, brutally disruptive form of capitalism which was leading to huge social inequalities, horrendous working conditions and the disenfranchisement of vast swathes of the population from the land, from political power and from economic self-sufficiency.[13]

'Far from reading the ethos of the jungle into civilized society,' wrote the historian Theodore Roszak, 'Darwin read the ethos of industrial capitalism into the jungle, concluding that all life had to be what it had become in the early milltowns: a vicious "struggle for existence".[14]

Capitalism has coloured our view of nature. But once appropriated by Darwin, the metaphor of struggle bequeathed a mantle of renewed authority on capitalism. Look! This is how it works in nature! Scarcity leads to struggle. It must be right! Struggle justifies competition. Competition eliminates the weak and allows the fittest to survive. It isn't just inevitable, it's profitable. Selfish behaviour is adaptive. Let's encourage it further. The endless and unseemly scramble to reach the top of the pile is legitimized by the desire for growth. Nature – once again – becomes capitalism's apologist.

Growth matters when there is a material insufficiency. That much we've firmly established. So up to a point, some of this might just work. The trouble is knowing where that point is. And knowing how to stop when we get there. Capitalism has failed on both these counts. It established rules it borrowed from a prejudiced view of nature and imposed them tyrannically on the operation of the market.

At the same time, it failed to protect the environment. It failed to protect society. It left gaping holes in its own financial system. And it stumbled, at least twice in the last hundred years, into massive and damaging economic crises. We still haven't recovered from the second and we're already facing a third. But the truth is that the lessons from the first haven't yet been learned either. They too point to our over-reliance on Darwinian metaphor.

The glittering prize

The Great Depression precipitated by the stockmarket crash of 1929 has been called with some accuracy a 'crisis of over-production'. Technological innovation driven by oil and coal had generated massive increases in productivity, to the point where our ability to produce had outstripped desire for the product. Supply was plentiful but demand was insufficient. Prices fell, confidence plummeted, investment slowed, unemployment soared, and it took a decade and a half (and the military expenditure of the Second World War) to get the global economy back on track.[15]

We might at that point have reflected more deeply on what it is that humans really need. And how best to organize production. We might have looked more critically at our obsession with productivity narrowly defined. But instead capitalism responded by stimulating desire. Never again should we suffer from insufficient demand. So along came a whole new industry designed to manufacture not products but desire. To stimulate the demand that capitalism needed to maintain the engine of growth. To further its cause, it drew on another metaphor, borrowed from an emerging 'evolutionary psychology': the insatiability of human desire.[16]

What's most striking about this turn of events is how it turned Mill's utilitarianism completely on its head. Post-war consumer capitalism trades not on happiness but on discontent. Post-purchase dissonance is an expression that psychologists use to describe the disappointment we sometimes feel on realizing that our latest purchase doesn't fulfil what it promised. At first sight, it's just a curious anomaly. On deeper reflection, it turns out to be the structural basis for the success of consumerism. The engine of consumer society is discontent.[17]

This is more than a rhetorical claim. Let's take consumerism's more ostentatious charms: the glitter and bling, the endless parade of new and exciting products that keeps us shopping. Novelty lies at the beating heart of capitalism. Innovation is vital to enterprise. Joseph Schumpeter called it *creative destruction*: the continual throwing over of the old in favour of the new; the relentless search of the entrepreneur for new markets and new products to fill them with. These are the rewards that innovation and productivity can bring.

For this to work, novelty must occupy a pivotal place in the human heart. The marketers had to persuade us just how much we love new stuff. Admittedly, they were pushing on an open door. There is of course a genuine desire for novelty in the human psyche. Conspicuous consumption signifies status and power. But novelty also signals hope. It holds out the promise of a brighter and shinier world for ourselves and for our children. Consumerism thrives on this promise. The job of advertisers is to ensure that we never forget it.[18]

Consumerism's most glittering prize is the promise of immortality itself: an earthly paradise of never wanting, never needing, never lacking for anything imagination can dream of. 'The human animal is a beast that dies. And if he's got money, he buys and buys and buys,' says Big Daddy in Tennessee William's play *Cat on a Hot Tin Roof*. 'And I think the reason he buys everything he can is that in the back of his mind is the crazy hope that one of his purchases will be life everlasting.' Suddenly, we find ourselves in the grip of a powerful social logic. Economic structure on the one hand and human psyche on the other bind us into an 'iron cage' of consumerism.[19]

The first crack in the shiny surface appears with the realization that the system itself is rooted in anxiety. Adam Smith called it the desire for 'a life without shame'. Shame magnifies consumer needs. Advertisers know this only too well. They play on the power of misplaced shame. 'What does your car (house, holiday, laptop, toilet roll . . .) say about you?' they ask, in ever more seductive ways. In Smith's day, a much less expansive set of goods could stave off shame. He illustrates his argument by reference to a simple linen shirt, 'the want of which would be supposed to denote that disgraceful degree of poverty, which, it is presumed, nobody can well fall into without extreme bad conduct'. Nowadays the basket has expanded massively, as indeed it must for the system to work: fast cars, fast food, fast sex, fast fashion. If we ever stop coveting the fruits of innovation, the economy starts to fail. Unemployment rises. Instability beckons.[20]

This is precisely why anxiety must tip over into outright dissatisfaction if capitalism is to survive. Discontentment is the motivation for our restless desire to spend. Consumer products must promise paradise. But they must systematically fail to deliver it. They must fail us, not occasionally, as psychologists have observed, but repeatedly. The success of consumer society lies not in meeting our needs but in its spectacular ability consistently to disappoint us.[21]

This might seem at first like a dark and hopeless conclusion. I don't believe it is. It's an essential recognition that consumerism is, and always was, a construct. A necessary element in a story that is no more real than the tooth fairy. A fanciful but unfulfilling dream sold to us by the architects of growth in order to perpetuate a socially constructed myth. 'Our enormously productive economy demands that we make consumption our way of life,' wrote the marketeer Victor

Lebow in the 1950s, because 'we need things consumed, burned up, worn out, replaced, and discarded at an ever-increasing pace.'[22]

Nature as struggle; profit as a competition; consumption as insatiability: this is the unholy trinity of a Darwinian capitalism. Is this real life? Or just a mirage in the desert of economic dogma? At best it is a historical contingency, only as real as the social context that shaped our conceptions and informed our metaphors for nature. To recognize this relativity is to loosen the chains that bind us to a dysfunctional prison of our own making. From here we can begin to understand both why consumerism must eventually fall. And how to replace it. That process too starts with metaphor.

The limits of competition

Competitive struggle isn't the only possible response to scarcity. It just happens to be the one embedded in capitalism. It's legitimized by a metaphor for nature which was itself derived through a capitalistic lens. But this is all just narrative framing. There is another, much richer story to be told. Lynn Margulis dedicated her life to telling it.

When she was a young research student, evolutionary theory was dominated by neo-Darwinism: an uneasy synthesis of Darwin's work and the Moravian scientist Gregor Mendel's novel ideas about genetics. Darwin saw evolution as a process of gradual change. Mendel saw genetic inheritance as the transfer of fixed characteristics. How could an ongoing transfer of fixed characteristics lead to the massive evolutionary change that we now know took place? This was the question the young Margulis asked herself. The neo-Darwinian synthesis held that it was chance mutations in the genetic code which led to the emergence of new species through the process of natural selection – the struggle for existence of the 'selfish' genes themselves. Blind chance and relentless competition were the dominant metaphors for progress.[23]

To Margulis this was all unsatisfactory. She would ask over and again where the empirical evidence for it could be found. It was possible in laboratory conditions to induce mutations in the genetic code of fruit flies, for instance. The trouble was that these mutations led only to sick or dead flies, rather than to evolutionary improvements on the species, even less to whole new species. Margulis's early exposure in Wisconsin to the marginalized idea of symbiosis led her in a completely different direction.

She was still in her twenties when she published her ground-breaking paper on endosymbiosis: the biological process by which one kind of bacteria takes up residence inside another kind of bacteria to form a third, more complex nucleated cell. As Margulis went on to show, this symbiotic collaboration was the starting point for the evolution of all other life on the planet. Plants, animals, human beings: we are all the improbable result of an evolutionary pact between bacteria. This inheritance is coded into every cell of our body. We use it to metabolize, to grow, to reproduce. 'We are walking communities,' said Margulis. 'Ten percent or more of our body weight is bacterial, and it's just foolish to ignore that.'[24]

Evolution is not the relentless struggle for existence that neo-Darwinians say it is, she claimed. When single-celled bacteria got together to create nucleated cells, they not only found a way to survive together, they provided the foundations for all life on earth. We would not be here without symbiosis. New species are a collaborative effort. Evolution emerges out of a cooperative response to the changing conditions of life. Collaboration played an absolutely essential part in our existence.

There is struggle in nature. There is death and predation and scarcity. Sometimes the struggle for existence is a desperate fight for survival. The race between predator and prey is real. But competition is not the only response. And believing it is has led us disastrously astray.

Embedding competition so thoroughly into our economic and social institutions is to mistake metaphor for reality. It's a dangerous mistake. It's a 'critical blind spot that lies unexamined within capitalist doctrine', writes the competition lawyer Michele Meagher in her wonderful debunking of free market myths, *Competition Is Killing Us*. 'We need to act on the knowledge that we are being governed by a defunct system of beliefs that is driving us off a cliff,' she insists.[25]

Once you've nailed down a set of rules and institutions that systematically prioritizes competition over cooperation, profit over wages, quantity over quality and today's consumption over tomorrow's security, then it is too late to know when to stop and too difficult to stop. You're locked into an economic system that permits no fine distinction between greed and need and offers only the crudest of levers when the economy is careering out of control.[26]

Gaia is a tough bitch

Would we do any better by eliminating competition altogether? Or is there still some role for the frontier spirit? Surely, competition can sometimes bring out the best in us. It can teach us respect for others. It can offer a sense of achievement. Sporting prowess, artistic endeavour, the rigour of the martial arts: all of these bear witness to the benefits of competition. So too does the ability occasionally to pit ourselves against unlikely odds, as Ellen MacArthur did in the Southern Ocean. Or as Lynn Margulis did in overturning our understanding of evolution.

Early in her career, Margulis had teamed up with the British scientist James Lovelock to help expand and expound his theory of Gaia: the proposal that the dynamic conditions of life on earth are regulated by the sum of all its living inhabitants. The name Gaia (an ancient Greek name for mother Earth) was suggested to Lovelock by the novelist William Golding, author of *Lord of the Flies*. It was intended as a metaphor to communicate a complex theory to a wide audience. It was certainly successful in that aim.

Lovelock conceived of Gaia as a single planetary organism. This encouraged a popular conception that the planet was regulated by some kind of benevolent goddess who would make everything alright. Margulis believed this vision was wrong. Gaia is not an organism, she said. An organism doesn't eat its own waste, she pointed out. And Gaia is not benevolent. 'Those who want Gaia to be an Earth goddess for a cuddly, furry human environment [should] find no solace in it,' she insisted. 'Gaia is a tough bitch – a system that has worked for over three billion years without people.'[27]

Margulis was no fluffy, rose-tinted optimist. Cooperation was essential to evolution, she discovered. But that doesn't mean the world is a warm, fuzzy, infinitely collaborative place. Margulis herself was adamant about that. Gaia's concern for planetary balance has little or nothing to do with her benevolent oversight of human affairs. Making one metaphorical mistake is not going to be corrected by making another.

We're in a familiar place. The good life is not about extremes. It is about virtue. Virtue is not about excess. It is about balance. Our most adaptive strategy is one that holds a place for competition without sacrificing the value of cooperation. One that recognizes the struggle without defaulting to fight or flight in every response to danger. One that honours the frontier spirit without losing sight of the essential intimacy of caring for each other. In our confrontation with limits, the possibility is always open to us to adapt to them with courage and ingenuity and skill rather than seek to power through them with brute force and ignorance.

We are back at the bridge in Potter Heigham. We are confronted with a choice. To adapt and thrive or to struggle and fail. The post-growth option is clear. If we recruit limits as our mentor, we have the chance to follow their wisdom towards our fullest potential as human beings.

Virtuous metaphor

How we approach this choice depends on the values that motivate us as human beings. Are we open to change? Do we care about tradition? Are we driven by achievement? Are we motivated by a concern for others? All of these qualities inform the human spirit. And they bear a fascinating relationship to each other, as the work of the psychologist Shalom Schwartz reveals. In a body of research spanning several decades, he has shown that it is possible to organize human values around two distinct tensions in the human psyche (Figure 2).

The first is the tension between self and other. We are continually torn between selfish and altruistic behaviours. Both evolved in human beings over time. Self-preservation served us well under conditions of fight or flight. But concern for the other was fundamental to our

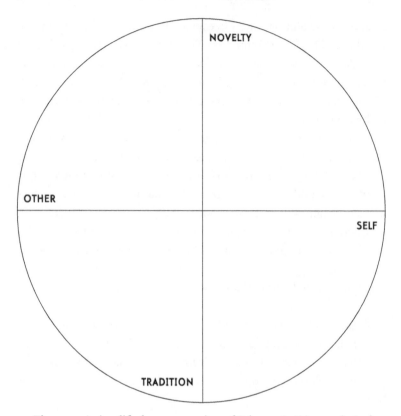

Figure 2 A simplified representation of Schwartz's 'Circumplex' of
Human Values

evolution as social beings. It remains vital to our concepts of parenting and care. It's the foundation for community and solidarity. The
same tension is familiar in developmental psychology. Differentiation
and affiliation shape our earliest experiences. As kids we start out
utterly dependent on other people. Pretty soon we begin to want to
separate ourselves from our parents and distinguish ourselves from
our siblings. But even as adults we continue to experience the need
to belong, the desire for safety, the longing for a respectable place in
society.[28]

The second tension is between novelty and tradition. We've already
seen how the desire for novelty plays a crucial role in consumer capitalism. Marketers exploit this aspect of human behaviour constantly

in the drive to maintain and stimulate consumer demand. So long as entrepreneurs innovate and consumers crave novelty, a 'virtuous circle' creates an expansionary momentum that drives growth forward. Novelty-seeking behaviour is continually incentivized for exactly that reason.

The pursuit of novelty is not in itself dysfunctional. In evolutionary terms, it was clearly adaptive. It allowed us to solve problems of scarcity, to create conditions amenable to life and to develop social systems that could respond quickly to fast-changing conditions. But relentless novelty-seeking isn't always adaptive. Aside from its role in speeding up the consumption of energy and materials, novelty involves risk. Innovations don't always succeed and are often disruptive. Continuous disruption undermines the stability needed to raise families and form cohesive social groups. The counter-balancing values of conservation and tradition are essential to the success of human society.

In other words, there are profound, biological reasons for the evolution of these two distinct tensions in the human psyche. It makes sense, then, to suppose that human flourishing involves a healthy balance between opposing values. It is meaningful to speak, in Aristotelean terms, of a 'virtuous' value orientation: one that is finely balanced between the poles of each psychological tension. Or perhaps one that moves seamlessly and responsively around the value 'circumplex' shown in Figure 2 as conditions demand.

In an ideal world, this is the kind of flexibility that would create a truly resilient society, adaptive to changing conditions. But it's specifically not how our economies work. In fact, Schwartz's 'map of the human psyche' is enormously revealing in allowing us to understand capitalism's core dysfunction. In single-mindedly following the Darwinian metaphor, we've created an economic model which systematically privileges one particular quadrant of the human heart. The selfish, novelty-seeking hedonist (the upper right quadrant in Figure 2) is the perfect companion to the restless, competitive entrepreneur. It's a great system for accelerating material growth But it's poorly aligned with a genuine and lasting prosperity.

By the same token, the way forward now seems much clearer. It's not a heroic demand to change human nature. It's not even about curtailing human possibilities. It's about realizing that there is a different story to be told. A story that recognizes the breadth and depth of the human soul. A story that accounts for affinity with tradition as well as our desire for novelty. A story that acknowledges our roots as evolutionary creatures in an inherently collaborative response to the struggle for existence. A story that offers us the tantalizing freedom to become not less, but more fully, human.

Bear necessities

The competitive response is, of course, deeply engrained in us. Not just by genetics. Two people are walking in the mountains when they find themselves confronted by a bear. One of them immediately takes off his backpack, digs out his trainers and puts them on. 'What's the point of that?' says the other. 'You're never gonna outrun a bear.' 'I don't need to outrun the bear,' comes the reply. 'I just need to outrun you.' The joke illustrates some of the worst possible ways to react – should you ever find yourself in their place. There's some much better advice out there. Top of the list is: don't run away; you're acting like prey. Somewhere near that comes: stay calm; don't panic.[29]

Much easier said than done, of course. Fight or flight is coded into our neurochemistry. In response to a perceived threat, our 'sympathetic nervous system' creates a rapid, involuntary response which prepares our bodies for fast, aggressive action. A flood of hormones is released, sending signals to all the organs that regulate our energy levels. Insulin is suppressed and glycogen is increased, discharging a burst of glucose into the blood stream. The heart rate rises, sending extra blood to the muscles. We begin to breathe faster, sending more oxygen to the brain. Non-urgent body functions are put on hold so that all our resources can be dedicated to countering the immediate threat.[30]

Arousal happens so fast that often we barely register it. We find we've automatically ducked to avoid something, reached out to grab something, yelled a warning to a child in danger, without consciously formulating any of these intentions. This 'sympathetic' response evolved just like our values did. Just like our appetites did. The human nervous system was laid down during a time when physical dangers had quite precise characteristics: they were urgent and they were deadly.

Once the danger is past, the 'parasympathetic' nervous system kicks in, reducing the heart rate, calming the breathing and releasing insulin into the blood stream. This cooling-off mechanism is as important as the revving-up one. Maintaining a state of heightened arousal for long periods of time places enormous physical strain on the human body. It creates huge stress on the vital organs, reduces our ability to relax and in the long term creates the conditions for chronic stress, morbidity and depression. Could this tendency provide some explanation for the crises of physical and mental health confronting us?

Modern society is founded on stress. Insecurity at work. Competition between firms. Social comparison at every turn. Let's go shopping for a moment. You start out with the best of intentions. Your sister is getting married next week. You want to look your best. Through the doors of the department store you're met with bright lights and upbeat music. Soon after that you encounter the first mirror. Standing nearby is a full-size image of an impossibly perfect model who has done insane things to themselves to look like that. But you're not to know. You're not being asked to know. You're being asked to compare yourself – as unfavourably as possible.

You won't even know it, but your stress levels are already rising. Cortisol is being pumped through your nervous system. Your rational decision-making faculties are diminishing. Your sense of urgency is accelerating. Very soon, if a sale is on, you'll find yourself scrapping for bargains with the best of them. And even in a more sedate environment, judicious product placement and subliminal messaging will guide you relentlessly towards purchase. Online shopping is no less geared towards hyperarousal.

Anxious, hyperactive consumers are the inevitable consequence of our obsession with growth. Shopping will keep people in jobs, we're told. It will also line the pockets of shareholders. It will put tax in the hands of government, of course. It keeps the economy growing.

But don't let's pretend. The stress you are feeling in the simple act of looking your best for a family wedding has little to do with the happy-ever-after. It's a definitive strategy to manipulate our nervous system to maximize profit. It's not even designed to lead to long-term fulfilment. As we saw already, it's much better for the economy if it doesn't.

This competition has even more pernicious outcomes. It drives a social inequality that is not confined to income or even to happiness. The damage happens at a neurochemical level. 'The less [well off], less educated and more stressed segments of the population rely on the same neural reward system as those who are better off,' writes the neuroscientist Peter Sterling in his fascinating book *What Is Health?* But they have far fewer opportunities to experience these rewards. And the more space that is taken away from community and given over to consumerism, the fewer these opportunities become. The poorest in society are 'at greater risk for all sorts of addiction', argues Sterling, precisely because they must look elsewhere for satisfaction. Inequality plays a critical role in the sharp rise in obesity that we explored in Chapter 4, he claims.[31]

Addiction, despair, suicide and violence: these are the fruits of our insistence that selfish competition is the only feasible response to struggle. Even in the most extreme circumstances, the fight or flight instinct is not as useful as we believe it to be. Quite close to the 'don't panic' motif on the 'how-to' lists from helpful bear confrontation websites is useful advice about staying together. Stand tall if it's a black bear; stay as still as you can if it's a grizzly. Your heart is pounding. Your blood is pumping. Your neurochemistry is in overdrive. And yet even there, in acute danger of a life or death struggle for existence, your best chances of survival are in keeping a cool head and acting collaboratively.

Many of the challenges we face in modern society are not in fact of this kind at all. The prospect of scarcity doesn't usually represent an imminent threat to life. It is rather a set of conditions that we must continually navigate in pursuit of prosperity. Material limits are real. But characterizing each and every limit as a violent struggle for existence is counterproductive. In fact, it may seem paradoxical. But even under extreme duress, anxious and aggressive action rarely works in our favour.

The inner game

This paradox is well known in sports psychology. Competitive sport is a form of ritualized conflict. Playing tennis, for instance, we confront an opponent who is projecting missiles at us across a net constantly for a couple of hours. Successful blows are tallied up to rank our progress from moment to moment in a contest where the final score is victory or defeat. The game is meant to simulate a violent conflict with a definitive outcome. Yet it's common knowledge that to treat each moment as an imminent threat to survival is a recipe for failure. The fight or flight response reduces the body's ability to play the kind of elegant passing shots or stunning volleys that characterize tennis at its best.

Good tennis players know this. The 'inner game' of tennis is all about techniques for achieving a specific mindset which is conducive to optimal performance. Players will resort to all sorts of routines and rituals to create and protect it: breathing, visualization, relaxation; the bouncing of the ball a set number of times before the serve. The aim is to allow hard-earned skill and the body's instinctive coordination to work seamlessly together to create perfect tennis. Even winning or losing must temporarily be taken out of the picture to allow peak performance to emerge.[32]

The Hungarian-born psychologist Mihalyi Csikszentmihalyi called this optimal state of mind 'flow'. People 'in flow' report an unusual clarity of mind and precision of movement. They experience a sense of confidence and control over the task. But there is also a sense of being lost in the moment, sometimes even being carried along by a momentum that is entirely outside of oneself. People describe a sense of wonder, a connectedness to the world, a feeling of satisfaction that goes beyond happiness or the gratification of pleasure. Even asking the question of whether you are happy during this experience makes little sense. As a musician in one of Csikszentmihalyi's studies described it:

You are in an ecstatic state to such a point that you feel as though you almost don't exist. I have experienced this time and again. My hand seems devoid of myself and I have nothing to do with what is happening. I just sit there watching it in a state of awe and wonderment. And the music just flows out of itself.[33]

Flow is most likely to happen, it's been found, when there's a good balance between your level of skill and the degree of challenge you face. When your skill is not up to the challenge, you are likely to panic or take fright. When your skill is higher than the challenge, there's a tendency to lose concentration or even get bored. When skill and challenge are high, the conditions are perfect. Two well-matched opponents produce the best tennis you can possibly watch. At the height of the match, the players are not so much competitors as collaborators in a state of flow.

Skill and training improve our capacity to find flow. But the experience is not restricted to sport or art. Even the simplest everyday activity can generate flow. With training it's possible to develop a state of mind where you remain in flow through all kinds of different situations. Achieving flow becomes an aim in itself. It's a very different aim than pleasure or contentment. But it brings with it one of the highest levels of fulfilment it is possible for human beings to experience.

More fun, less stuff

A warning is probably called for here. There's a rather simplistic popularization of language which speaks of 'going with the flow'. Stay calm, take it easy, chill out, relax: the thrust of all these injunctions is to counter the automatic activation of the sympathetic nervous system. Useful in bear territory. And in today's over-stimulated society, it warrants some repetition. But too much relaxation can also reduce our motivation to act, where action is in fact what's needed. It becomes a denial that there is any struggle at all. And that's clearly misleading.

Margulis's life, for example, was not one devoid of struggle. She personified the ideal of a dedicated scientist in a terrier-like pursuit of the truth. No tennis player ever won Wimbledon by chillaxing on court. An entirely laid-back tennis player will miss the stretch volley, underpower the serve and never bother to run back to retrieve an overhead lob. Flow definitely carries some sense of laidback ease. But it's a very dynamic sense of relaxation and can embrace quite strenuous, concentrated activity. The ideal of flow, then, is a perfect balance between being highly focussed and being totally relaxed in the moment.[34]

Virtuous psychological functioning, just like physical health, is all about achieving balance. This is particularly true of flow. Its highest pinnacle is a state of extraordinary fulfilment. Flow exemplifies with extraordinary clarity the kinds of dividends that remain available to us in a postgrowth world. Dividends which are often obscured by capitalism. A continual emphasis on accumulation and the relentless pursuit of more renders balance almost impossible to achieve. Flow offers us better and more durable satisfactions than consumerism ever does.

Even more striking is the possibility that these satisfactions could be more sustainable in ecological terms. That flow activities could offer us the potential to live better with less. To have more fun with less stuff. Clearly, this isn't always so. There are some high-challenge, high-skill activities that are probably a real blast – and also have a massive environmental footprint. Heli-skiing in Davos comes to mind, for instance. But it's fascinating to wonder if there is a set of activities which have minimal environmental impact and yet have the potential to lead to intrinsically satisfying 'peak' experiences.[35]

Czikszentmihalyi has proposed exactly this. His argument starts from the idea that human beings have two different kinds of goals. Material goals are those that 'aim at the preservation of the organism in its present state'. Transcendent goals are those that reach beyond our material needs 'to create ideas, feelings, relationships, objects that did not exist before'. Devoting our attention to one of these goals diminishes our potential to devote it to the other. By focussing our attention on flow, we can tread more lightly on the planet, he suggests.[36]

My colleagues Amy Isham, Birgitta Gatersleben and I wanted to test this hypothesis. We examined the link between flow experiences and environmental impact from people's leisure experiences in the US. We found a very distinct set of high-flow, low-impact activities across the sample. The activities themselves were familiar from the literature on flow. They centred on five key themes: physical sports, craft and creative activities, social interactions, romantic relationships and contemplative practices like meditation. All of these activities have low environmental impacts. But people engaged in them report high levels of flow and high levels of wellbeing.[37]

Clearly, these things aren't always easily attainable – particularly in today's overly materialistic society. In a separate study, we found that simply favouring materialistic values is enough to undermine people's potential to experience flow. The damage created by consumer capitalism is not restricted to its impact on the planet, it seems. We like to believe that material affluence represents progress. But in some very specific ways, the focus on material things actively impedes our ability to reach our potential.

Flow is not a supermarket commodity. None of the practices identified in our study are easily marketable products, in spite of the best efforts of advertisers to persuade us that they are. Each of them requires an investment in time and skill – a theme I will come back to later. But the return to that investment is enormous. It offers us a route towards the highest peak of human fulfilment at a fraction of the environmental cost of consumerism. And it seems to be something that is available to anyone who pursues it. The inner game has no gatekeepers. Flow offers us the foundation for a postgrowth world that is not just as good as but significantly better than the broken promise of capitalism.

Makers of poems

Lynn Margulis's seminal paper 'On the Origins of Mitosing Cells' was published in 1967. It revealed that our dominant metaphor for nature, one drawn from the social environment of early capitalism and assimilated thoughtlessly into economics, was fundamentally mistaken. Struggle may be inevitable. But our response to it is not. We are not confined to the naïve and painful prison of relentless competition for life. Evolution itself is the result of a historical collaboration of epic proportions.

It's difficult to conceive just how radical this idea was at the time. Her paper was turned down fifteen times before it was finally published in the *Journal of Theoretical Biology*. For more than a decade, the work was more or less ignored by mainstream biology. Her first draft of a book expanding the theory was rejected by the same publisher who commissioned it. And yet *Symbiosis in Cell Evolution* is now considered one of the classics of twentieth-century biology. It heralded a 'quiet revolution' in evolutionary thinking.[38]

That 1967 paper was published under her married name, Sagan, even though Lynn and Carl were divorced. Perhaps it was a fitting tribute to her time together with the man who had inspired her love of science. Perhaps it was partly her work he had in mind when he made the remark cited at the top of this chapter: '[E]very now and then a new idea turns out to be on the mark, valid and wonderful.' Margulis herself was sanguine about the marriage. Their 'passionate foray into loveland' had 'a rocky start and equally abrasive end', she wrote. At one point, before the wedding, she had made a tape recording to remind herself of all the reasons why marrying him would be a 'stupid, self-destructive move'.[39]

Some of those reasons were clear. They were both fiery, inquisitive, passionate human beings. They both had high ambitions for their own professional life. This was still an age, in spite of an emerging feminism, when women were expected to stay home and look after the kids. 'It's not humanly possible to be a good wife, a good mother and a first-class scientist,' wrote Margulis after the failure of her second marriage. 'No one can do it – something has to go.' There is a sense too that, right from the start, Carl Sagan and Lynn Margulis were gazing in different directions.[40]

We are all symbionts. The first multicellular organisms were the product of symbiosis. The lichens under the bridge at Potter Heigham are symbionts. Human existence too is a living embodiment of collaboration. We are born of the ability to meet and stay together long enough to create things that are new and wonderful and different. The day after the birth of their first child in 1959, Carl Sagan wrote in his diary: 'It feels strange adding our fiber to the red thread. I've never before had so strong a feeling of being a transitional creature, at some vague intermediary position between the primeval mud and the stars.'[41]

A decade or so later, Sagan was to assemble the first 'time capsule' sent into space from earth, a 'message in a bottle' for any intelligent life that might stumble on it. The Voyager Golden Record was a 12-inch gold-plated copper disc containing images and sounds that had been carefully selected to represent life on earth. Two such discs were launched on the two Voyager spacecraft that left the earth's orbit in 1977. Both discs are out there still, wandering their lonely trajectories through the Milky Way.[42]

Margulis meanwhile was passionately earthbound. As late as the 1990s, she was still being portrayed in the media as 'science's unruly earth mother'. It's not unlikely she delighted in that reputation. She would often accuse her critics of mistaking Darwin's intentions and 'wallow[ing] in their zoological, capitalistic, competitive, cost–benefit interpretation' of evolution. Towards the very end of her life, Margulis was asked in an interview whether she ever tired of being called controversial. 'I don't consider my ideas controversial,' she replied. 'I consider them right!'[43]

We are all 'tellers of stories and makers of poems'. Economics is a form of storytelling. The myth of growth has dominated our cultural story for a century or more. Science proceeds through metaphor. That much is inevitable. In defence of this inevitability, Margulis would often cite her favourite poet, Emily Dickinson, whom she affectionately referred to as her next-door neighbour. (The two women both lived in Amherst, Massachusetts.) 'Tell all the truth but tell it slant – ,' wrote Dickinson:

> Success in Circuit lies
> Too bright for our infirm Delight
> The Truth's superb surprise
> As Lightning to the Children eased
> With explanation kind
> The Truth must dazzle gradually
> Or every man be blind –[44]

But Margulis knew too that we should never allow ourselves to be seduced by the power of narrative. To do so is to end up believing in fairytales. This too was a lesson that a 'fast-moving, enthusiastic, ignorant girl' managed to teach the world.

7

The Return to Work

'Work and its product, the human artefact, bestow a measure of permanence and durability upon the futility of mortal life and the fleeting character of human time.'
Hannah Arendt, 1958[1]

'The reward of labour is life. Is that not enough?'
William Morris, 1890[2]

In October 1957, just a few months after Lynn Margulis and Carl Sagan were married, the Soviet Union sent the first orbital satellite into space. It was one of those odd moments in history that dramatically reshapes the social world. The launch of Sputnik kicked off the space race, intensified the arms race and heightened the Cold War. It was also a huge blow to US self-esteem – not to be the first nation to reach space. But it provided the stimulus for John F. Kennedy's 1961 announcement of the Apollo 'moon shot' programme: to put a man on the moon before the end of the decade. The goal was achieved. Though he never lived to see it.[3]

Sputnik also heralded a new relationship between humanity and planet earth. As the political philosopher Hannah Arendt remarked in the Prologue of her 1958 masterpiece *The Human Condition*, going into space would allow us to see and appreciate our earthly home for the first time in history. It was a reminder that 'the Earth is the very quintessence of the human condition'. And nature itself, 'for all we know, may be unique in the universe in providing human beings with a habitat in which they can move and breathe without effort and without artifice'.

Others saw in Sputnik a gateway to the beyond. For Carl Sagan, it was the beginning of that quest for life elsewhere. A US newspaper headline from the day celebrated the launch as 'one step toward escape from [our] imprisonment to the earth'. Arendt was intrigued by that sentiment. It didn't surprise her. In contemporaneous science fiction, she had already seen a deep-seated 'rebellion against human existence'. And she recognized there a common dream that technology would liberate us from the struggle for existence. But for her that dream was self-defeating. Modern society was in no position to appreciate it. [4]

We no longer recognize those 'higher and more meaningful activities for the sake of which this freedom would deserve to be won', she believed. The outstanding characteristic of the age is one of thoughtlessness, she said. We have become mired in 'heedless recklessness or hopeless confusion or complacent repetition of "truths" which have become trivial and empty'. It might almost have been written for the post-truth world in which we have increasingly found ourselves. Her response was an appeal for reflection. 'What I propose, therefore, is very simple,' she wrote in *The Human Condition*. 'It is nothing more than to *think what we are doing*.'[5]

Arendt's work resonates with the ideas in this book for all sorts of reasons. The human condition both prescribes and circumscribes the possibilities for happiness. It connects the irredeemably material nature of our existence with the irrepressible creativity of our aspirations and our dreams. Arendt's forensic examination of the 'active life' (*vita activa*) offers an incisive analysis of the world of human work. The aim of this chapter is to explore that world in more detail.

Work is essential to the human condition. It is a vital component of our prosperity. It provides, as we shall see, the conditions for hope. Yet under the yoke of capitalism it has been caught in a paralysing trap. I want to explore the nature of that trap. But I also want to sketch the outlines of an escape plan. A postgrowth economy, I shall argue, allows us to return work to its rightful place at the heart of society.

Life on the frontline

Something extraordinary happened when Covid-19 forced almost every country in the world into an extended period of lockdown and brought much of the economy to a juddering halt. Suddenly, over-night, we began to understand which tasks in society really matter. Healthcare, food provision and basic utilities were the jobs we could not do away with. Care workers turned out to be vital. They were the absolute frontline in a battle to contain the virus. Workers on farms and in food supply chains mattered. Shop assistants and delivery workers mattered. Waste collection and cleaning mattered. Cleaners mattered more than we ever imagined they could.

There was something massively ironic about this revelation. It would have been farcical if it hadn't been so tragic. These were, in many cases and for slightly different reasons, the jobs that had been systematically undervalued for decades. These were the people who had been used and abused, overworked and underpaid long before the crisis struck. In the long years of austerity, in particular, resources in the care sector had been systematically decimated, leaving vital workers facing unrealistic 'productivity targets' and living stressed, overburdened lives. Frontline health workers were facing burnout long before the coronavirus pandemic.[6]

A study of food and farming, conducted the year before the out-break of the virus, made an astonishing and shameful finding. Even in a rich country like the UK, there were workers in the food produc-tion sector who could not afford to feed themselves properly. Those responsible for providing the most basic services to society had to visit the rapidly rising number of 'food banks' to stay alive. To have to accept donations from strangers for essential goods that you yourself have laboured to produce is such an extraordinary perversion of eco-nomic value that it had to be witnessed to be believed.[7]

The entire concept of a market economy – and its advantage over a subsistence economy – is that labour can generate what is called a surplus. Each worker can produce more than is required for their own survival. These surplus goods can be exchanged for income. This income can be spent elsewhere on things that other workers have produced. Yet here were workers in the most vital sector in the economy apparently generating a *negative* surplus: unable to feed themselves and their families without resorting to charity.

It was no better in the low-paid, 'unskilled' sectors such as delivery and distribution warehouses and cleaning. Often working on zero-hours contracts without holiday pay or sickness benefits, people in these sectors quite literally worked themselves to death because they could not afford to do otherwise. These were the people the economist Guy Standing calls the 'precariat'. Whole communities who depended on precarious, poorly paid jobs for their livelihoods. People who increasingly found themselves at the bottom of the pile: disadvantaged, disenfranchised and disillusioned.[8]

It would be a mistake to suggest that here alone lay the roots of the populism that began to grip politics in the years before the pandemic. More accurately, that populism was a symptom of the same distorted economic system that systematically captured the gains of capitalism for a few and excluded too many from access to basic rights and dignities. But these were incontestably the sectors where increasing precarity of pay and declining conditions of work were pushing people inexorably towards a rising sense of isolation and alienation: it's your bloody GDP; not ours.

Labour's love lost

Arendt makes a critical distinction between labour and work. It's not an instinctively obvious one. But as she pointed out in *The Human Condition*, the two words continue to persist in almost every language across the world. So perhaps it's modern society's elision of them that is odd and maybe the distinction is still useful to us. What's clear is that her characterization of labour (as opposed to work) captures very precisely the activities left behind by capitalism: the jobs the pandemic revealed as being so essential to human flourishing.

Labour maintains the conditions for life. It delivers the baseline for health. It creates the foundations for society to flourish. Those who 'labour' sometimes fall outside the market economy altogether. Housework, parenting, caring for the elderly, are often unpaid altogether. Yet their value to society – and to life itself – is absolutely vital. 'Labour assures not only individual survival but the life of the species,' said Arendt. It is this kind of activity which corresponds most closely to the biological process of human existence: growth, metabolism and eventual decay. 'The human condition of labour is life itself,' she wrote.[9]

It's an interesting echo of William Morris's wonderful exchange in the novel *News from Nowhere*, written in the late nineteenth century. The novel's narrator, referred to as Guest, is travelling through a utopian land called Nowhere where work is undertaken willingly, for no apparent payment. At one point, Guest asks his guide (a man named Old Hammond), 'How do you get people to work when there is no reward of labour?' '"No reward of labour?" said Hammond, gravely. "The reward of labour is *life*. Is that not enough?"'[10]

It sounds bizarre to us today. It's also potentially dangerous in a society where those who labour suffer the indignity of poor conditions and inadequate rewards. But that is part of the point that Morris was making. *News from Nowhere* is a critique of a system where labour is seen solely as a resource for the extraction of a surplus that labour itself never receives. In Nowhere, goods are shared equitably and on the basis of need. And under these conditions the labour required to produce them might very easily be its own reward.

A part of that reward flows from our nature as physical animals. Morris and Arendt, in different ways, both make this point. Our animal nature equips us to labour. This isn't surprising. Labour is essential to life. We evolved in ways that endowed us with the means to fulfil the conditions of life. This is true, of course, in the biological sense of being animals who labour to give birth as well as in the everyday sense of biological animals who must engage in physical labour to survive. Labour is a design characteristic of the human species.

The development of tools made labour more effective. Much later, industrialization brought a huge surge in available energy (fossil fuels) which allowed us to substitute hard graft with machines. In the process, it 'freed' us from many (although not all) of the tasks that constitute labour in Arendt's sense of the word. As we became less active, less conditioned to labour, we became increasingly distanced from any sense of reward and now quite often 'suffer' these activities rather than 'enjoy' them. In Chapter 4, I touched on Arendt's view that happiness is only to be found in the 'painful exhaustion and pleasurable regeneration' of physical labour. It's a view that's almost totally alien to us.

Sometimes, belatedly noting our own need for physical activity, we will drive to the gym, sign up to exercise classes, train for marathons, just to retrieve that sense of physical wellbeing that comes from an active physical life. And we will do all this while barely noticing that we live in a society where physical labour is denigrated as unpleasant, unnecessary and unrewarding. Our default program is to delegate as much of this work as we can to people who are demoted to the lowest ranks in society. We are even supposed to think of this freedom from labour as a benefit. Arendt and Morris both identified it as a profound loss.

Love and Saint Augustine

Hannah Arendt was born in 1906 in Hanover, Germany just a few weeks after Boltzmann's tragic death in Duino. She was brought up in the Prussian city of Königsberg (now Kaliningrad), the only child of middle-class Jewish parents of Russian descent. Her father died when she was 7 years old and Hannah was raised by her mother in a house with a library full of philosophy and poetry. This early immersion in literature formed her education. 'You see, all the books were in the library at home; one simply took them from the shelves,' she explained in an interview later in life. 'For me, the question was somehow: I can either study philosophy or drown myself, so to speak.' She decided to study philosophy.[11]

Like Mill, she was reading the classics from an early age. Like him, she was instinctively drawn to the intellectual life (what she would later call the *vita contemplativa*). Intellectual inquiry would remain a life-long passion and provide the inspiration for her final (unfinished) book. But for Arendt, unlike Mill, the life of the mind was always to be balanced by a recognition of our embodied nature as animals living in a material world. This recognition lies at the core of *The Human*

Condition. It flowed in part from her experience growing up in the Germany of the 1920s.

It wasn't a good time to be Jewish. She noticed as a schoolgirl that she was treated differently. But in the care of a mother who instilled in her a sense of her own worth, this treatment simply reinforced her strength of mind and fiery character. At 15, she was expelled from high school for leading a student rebellion against a teacher who insulted her. As a young university student in Marburg, she fell in love with her teacher, the philosopher Martin Heidegger, with whom she had a brief and passionate affair. His attention to the processes of human thought was to have a profound influence on Arendt. 'Passionate thinking' became the foundation for much of her life's work.

But the affair didn't end well. Heidegger was seventeen years her senior and married with kids. His ambitions for her were not her ambitions for herself. At one point, he tried to persuade her to abandon philosophy altogether, on the grounds that it was no profession for a woman. Politically, they were a million miles apart. Heidegger responded to the rise of Nazism by acceding to the politics of the day and eventually joined the Nazi party. Arendt resisted its advance with every fibre of her being and ended up getting arrested in Berlin for collecting evidence of anti-Semitic sentiment. She escaped prison by sweet-talking the arresting officer but then had to flee for her life, travelling through the mountains by night to reach what was at the time Czechoslovakia. From there she made her way to Paris, where she worked for several years rescuing young European Jews and relocating them to *kibbutzim* in Palestine.[12]

Asked later why she chose this very grounded, pragmatic work at that point in her life, she acknowledged that a part of the reason had been her disillusionment with the intellectuals (Heidegger included, of course) who had capitulated to the Nazis. 'I didn't believe that Jews and German Jewish intellectuals would have acted any differently, had their own circumstances been different,' she explained. 'I thought that it had to do with this profession, with being an intellectual.' Amazingly, she remained lifelong friends with Heidegger. But the marriage of visceral experience with her instinct for the life of the mind was to push her work in very specific direction: towards the same tension between material limits and human aspirations that lies at the heart of this book.[13]

Shortly after the end of her affair with Heidegger, she wrote her doctoral dissertation on the concept of love in the writings of Saint Augustine. She opens her exploration with an account of the idea that love is a form of craving. 'The good [that] love craves is life,' she wrote. 'And the evil [that] fear shuns is death.' What follows is an extraordinary examination of the same fierce dilemmas she was later to explore in *The Human Condition*. 'All "having" is governed by fear, all "not having" by desire,' she wrote. 'Only a present without a future is immutable and utterly unthreatened.'

This early writing contains the roots of her argument that the only true happiness lies in labour – because it is first and foremost an inevitable part of being alive. In its purest form, it is a state where the future is diminished to nothing, the past is irrelevant and only the present remains. 'The happy life is the life we cannot lose,' she wrote in *Love and Saint Augustine*. The only life we cannot lose is our inevitable participation in the struggle for existence. Or, as she was to express it later, the reward of labour 'is the human way to experience the sheer bliss of being alive which we share with all living creatures'.[14]

Arendt also realized that this existential happiness does not end our craving. As mortal beings, we are continually and painfully aware that we will eventually die. The more we lift ourselves out of the physical conditions of labour, the more time we have to understand the ephemeral nature of our existence. The more successful we are in maintaining our physiological functioning and the less immersed we are in the process of labour, the more clearly we see that our lives are lived in a condition of unending insecurity. Solving the struggle for subsistence enters us into another kind of struggle.

Our craving for life becomes a desire for immortality. For permanence. For something solid beyond the unending cycle of exhaustion and rejuvenation to cling onto. This is where Arendt's distinction between labour and work comes in. Beyond the continual struggle of labour lies the painstaking work of world-building. The uniquely human response to a world of impermanence is to try and construct a world of permanence: a world that is not entirely and incessantly subject to the unforgiving cycle of regeneration and decay. This other world is what Arendt calls the world of human artifice. It's the sum total of our creation over and above the task of physical maintenance and sheer survival. It is the objective of what Csikszentmihalyi might call our transcendent goals.

The rewards of flow

Work, in Arendt's view, is the activity which allows us to build and maintain the durability of the human world. Whereas labour involves care and sustenance, work is the domain of creation and creativity. It calls on craft and skill and vision. It is about the dreaming of dreams and the making of things. Our world-building activities, according to Arendt, are not so much about staying alive as staving off our fears of death. As she wrote in the opening epigraph: 'Work and its product, the human artefact, bestow a measure of permanence and durability upon the futility of mortal life and the fleeting character of human time.'

The doing of work may not offer the same elemental happiness that comes from the visceral labour of care. But craft and creativity still offer enormous potential for fulfilment. Work offers us the chance, in the words of the anthropologist Mary Douglas, 'to help create the social world and find a creditable place in it'. The ability to participate in the life of society is vital to our psychological and social health. For the individual, it provides the means to belong. For society, it provides the mechanism for cohesion.[15]

The task of world-building calls on us to invest our skills as makers, as crafters, as architects, as designers, as engineers, as musicians, as teachers, as dancers. And because this investment absorbs our attention – our 'psychic energy' – it can lead directly to the experience of flow introduced in the previous chapter. Csikszentmihalyi notes that people often experience flow at work more easily than they do in their leisure time, particularly in a world overloaded with vicarious, passive pleasures. Work is the place where skills develop and challenges are met. The conditions of flow are already present. To find these things outside of work requires a particular kind of effort and attention that often goes missing in our hurried and harried lives.[16]

Flow is not always immediately pleasurable. It doesn't necessarily offer the instantaneous rewards associated with eating or drinking or making love. It often proceeds through arduous, exhausting and even risky endeavour. Sport, craft, music, art: classic flow-inducing activities are notoriously difficult to perform well. That's the point: to raise both challenge and skill to achieve excellent human performance. But flow can nonetheless be enjoyable, says Csikszentmihalyi, because it offers us the exhilaration of 'going beyond the requirements of survival'.[17]

His distinction between pleasure and enjoyment (or fulfilment) is a fascinating one. Pleasure is a powerful source of motivation for human beings. But it is a conservative force that tempts us continually into comfort and relaxation. Enjoyment, on the other hand, 'nourishes the spirit' because 'it involves a triumph over the forces of entropy and decay'. Enjoyment requires more effort than pleasure. Its rewards are often delayed. But that doesn't mean that flow is all delayed gratification.[18]

Work itself, the allocation of attention, the application of skill, the dedication of effort, can bring its own intrinsic rewards. Our immersion in the task can lead, under the right circumstances, to the highest and most intense forms of fulfilment it is possible for humans to experience, as we saw in the previous chapter. Both work itself and the world it creates are vital to healthy psychological and social functioning. One of the most interesting dimensions of this experience is that people temporarily lose their sense of individuality. Flow erodes the boundary between self and the world.

This isn't to suggest that work is an entirely selfless endeavour. On the contrary. The outcome of work, the artefact, plays into a powerful economy of regard. A beautiful design, an exceptional performance, a magnificent building: all of these things receive social acclaim. The achievement of excellence is inevitably mired in extrinsic reward. Often allocated in arbitrary ways, good work reaps social rewards that can be incomprehensibly fickle. The desire to do well and to be seen to do well is an immensely powerful motivation for human beings. It is exactly what the 'hidden persuaders' played on, in the aftermath of the Second World War, to create a culture of consumerism.[19]

Its application to the extrinsic rewards of good work is no less powerful. The culture of celebrity is concerned almost entirely with the appropriation of the rewards of work. In its worst forms, even the underlying skill is irrelevant. Craft, skill, effort and creativity often bear no relation to the rewards themselves, which are claimed instead, sometimes even plagiarized, through the pliable currencies of style and popularity. Just as pleasure can stand in the way of enjoyment, so extrinsic regard can usurp the intrinsic value of creation. But for the duration of the task at least, the experience of flow allows us to dispense with the necessities of the ego and to merge individual action into the building of a common endeavour.

When the task itself is a shared or collective one, this loss of individuality can be enhanced considerably. There is a wonderful scene in the Australian director Peter Weir's 1985 film *Witness* which depicts the raising of a barn in an Amish community in the US. Federal agent John Book (played by Harrison Ford) has taken refuge there after he's been shot trying to protect an Amish mother, Rachel Lapp (played by Kelly McGillis), and her young son, the eponymous 'witness' to a violent crime. Ford's presence is a clear threat to the integrity of the community. He has already managed to stir up all kinds of tensions and rivalries – not least over McGillis's affections. But during the barn-raising scene all of this is forgotten.

Weir dispenses with dialogue entirely for this sequence and points his camera lovingly at the spectacle of a community working together. His cinematography celebrates the harmony of shared participation in a common project. The reward of labour is profoundly physiological. The rewards of work are deeply psychological and intrinsically social. The reward of labour is life. The reward of work is flow; and a share in the 'intimations of immortality'.

Bullshit jobs

It's blindingly obvious that paid employment today looks nothing like this utopian dream of restorative labour and fulfilling work. Early capitalism wasn't much like that either, as Mill and his contemporaries could so easily see. And already in the 1950s, when Arendt was writing, the conditions of both labour and work under capitalism were a cause for alarm. Today things look even worse. They may become worse still if trends towards automation in pursuit of productivity continue to disenfranchise and immiserate work.

Capitalism systematically denigrates labour. That much we have already seen. The essential tasks of care and maintenance are consistently (and dangerously) undervalued. But capitalism has also undermined the work of craft and creativity. And the reason for this is pretty basic. The aim of world-building is to offer us security. To be successful in that task, human artefacts must endure over time. They must abide. They must offer the permanence that is missing from the natural world. Without this quality of durability, the human world fails in its most essential task: to offset the anxiety of our own impermanence, to diminish the fear that continually undermines our happiness.

But the quality of durability is inimical to capitalism. Obsolescence and innovation are its continual watchwords. Permanence and longevity are a direct threat to its structural integrity. Capitalism necessitates consumerism. Its voracious appetite provokes, in Arendt's words, a 'grave danger that eventually no object of the world will be safe from consumption and annihilation through consumption', a fear given credence by Victor Lebow's demand that consumerism becomes a way of life, 'that we seek our spiritual satisfactions, our ego satisfactions in consumption', because nothing less than this will do if we are to keep the system going.[20]

Of course, in the long run, durability itself is little more than a convenient short-term fiction. Human artefacts are as bound by the second law of thermodynamics as nature is. Even the most durable structures, 'the cloud-capp'd towers, the solemn temples', will crumble and eventually fall. Arendt is perfectly aware of this. What concerns her is the dysfunctional acceleration of this process. Durability is the first casualty of the restless innovation that keeps capitalism going. Craft and creativity are subjugated to mass production in pursuit of increased efficiency and the expansion of profit.

Neither the visceral rewards of care nor the psychological returns on craft and creativity are remotely of interest to capitalism. The modern economist, said the author of *Small Is Beautiful*, Fritz Schumacher, is brought up to believe that work is 'little more than a necessary evil'. Employment is seen as a cost to producers, to be reduced or eliminated if at all possible (by replacing people with machines), and a sacrifice to workers, to be endured at best and only in exchange for wages.[21]

Under this dystopian configuration, Schumacher concludes, 'the ideal from the point of view of the employer is to have output without employees, and the ideal from the point of view of the employee is to have income without employment'. The world-building function of work collapses entirely. Decent work gives way to precarious, under-paid labour on the one hand and what the late anthropologist David Graeber called bullshit jobs on the other: jobs which are neither satisfying nor valuable to society.[22]

This is a part of the point that Arendt was making. Capitalism's need to generate more and more consumption has eroded the distinction between biological maintenance (labour) and the creation of a durable human artifice (work). Clothing and fashion offer a powerful example of this. Clothes protect us. They're part of the care and maintenance economy. But as we saw in Chapter 5, fashion is deeply implicated in our psychological, social and reproductive needs: identity, distinction, professionalism, coolness, affiliation, attractiveness, desire. All of this is mediated by how we look and what we wear.[23]

The elision between material and non-material needs is probably inevitable. Every society we have any evidence for attributes symbolic meanings to material goods. It might just be an indelible human trait. Goods are not just goods, as the economist Kelvin Lancaster once remarked. They become a symbolic language, a social conversation, through which we tell each other stories – about how important or how clever or how desirable we are. The idea that we could stop people engaging in this symbolic world is ludicrous. There is too much at stake. As a respondent in a study of the role of desire in consumer behaviour once remarked: 'Noone is going to spot you across a crowded room and say "Wow! Nice personality!"'[24]

But in the hands of consumer capitalism, the elision between the material and symbolic role of goods has been massively accelerated. It's driven the productive economy towards a persistent decline in durability dressed up as relentless novelty. The enormous success of the advertising industry has been to persuade us that physiological needs are the very least of the functions delivered by clothing.

The purpose of this elision has been exactly the one foreseen by Arendt: to speed up the consumption of clothing and stimulate the rising demand the fashion industry requires to maintain its growth targets. The paradoxical outcome of this process is that the industry can only really survive by undermining its own purpose. Far from assuaging our anxiety about the impermanence of the world, fashion must continually provoke it. Only so are we persuaded to indulge endlessly in its fickle attractions.

The robots are coming

You would think that when it comes to labour, socialism would have something better to offer than capitalism. Perhaps there is a socialism for the twenty-first century which does. But Arendt was as critical of mid-twentieth-century socialism as she was of capitalism. She praised Marx's good intentions in drawing attention to the plight of workers. But socialism's strategy to emancipate labour from drudgery was as flawed as capitalism's, she argued. Both of them relied on replacing workers with machines and assumed that the gains would flow to society.[25]

Keynes had a similar belief. In an essay written in 1930, he dared to look beyond the immediacy of the Great Depression towards a time when the 'economic problem' would be solved. 'For the moment, the very rapidity of these changes is hurting us and bringing difficult problems to solve,' he wrote. 'But this is only a temporary phase of maladjustment.' Within a couple of generations, he insisted, there would come a time when, liberated by technology, the 'struggle for subsistence' would be over and we would 'devote our further energies to non-economic purposes'. Like Mill, Keynes saw this postgrowth world as an improvement on the continuous competitive struggle to produce and consume. It would be a place where we 'would once more value ends above means and prefer the good to the useful'.[26]

What capitalism and socialism both failed to see was how the endless replacing of people with machines undermines the social function of work. In capitalism, in particular, that function is coded into the structure of the economy through the systematic pursuit of labour productivity. We saw in Chapter 2 how that pursuit has both served and undermined society. When labour productivity was growing at 4 or 5% each year, and markets for consumer goods were expanding fast, the rewards were shared around more equitably: even if the impact on the planet was untenable. The subsequent stagnation in labour productivity growth has driven inequality and precipitated capitalism's decline.

The strangest part about this historical decline is that it has coincided with massive increases in automation. It was accompanied by the emergence of the internet and the rapid globalization of the economy. It accelerated even with the birth of the smartphone, unprecedented leaps in social connectivity and the 'deepening' of artificial intelligence. All of these things were supposed to boost our productivity enormously. But their gains have been elusive at the national level for some time now – particularly in the advanced economies.[27]

What makes this elusiveness particularly odd is the persistent recurring cultural meme which would have us believe that 'the robots are coming'. And that they will lead to a massive surge in productivity. They will be cheaper than us. They will be better than us at making things. They will be more persuasive at selling, cleverer at advising, better at teaching our kids and more sympathetic than we are in caring for the elderly. And before very long they will outclass human beings at writing books and making music too. They will take our jobs, our livelihoods and possibly even usurp our place on the planet.[28]

In some versions of this story, human beings will be unimaginably richer as a result of all this and live the life of Riley. In others, we will be newly enslaved by an emerging master race: the robots themselves. Humans will just be a footnote in the history of evolution. In others again, we will live in a divided world, where those who own the hyper-automated means of production will grow unimaginably rich;

while those who don't will live lives of penury. In yet another version of this dystopian tale, the process itself will grind to a halt because there won't be enough income for ordinary people to purchase the extraordinary output from all this robot productivity.

But where is this massive boost of hyper-productivity today? At the level of the economy as a whole, it's virtually invisible. For sure, some sectors are charting massive gains. At the margin (as economists like to say), labour productivity is still rising. In the high-tech sectors, in mass manufacturing, in niche applications, we are still capable of making enormous strides in the demise of human usefulness.

In March 2016, Google Deepmind's *AlphaGo* successfully demolished the supremacy (and the peace of mind) of the world's undisputed Go champion, Lee Sedol. Autonomous (self-driving) vehicles are the inevitable future of personal transport, we're told. Pepper, the humanoid robot designed to read human emotion, has been touted as a revolution in hospitality, education and possibly even (for those who can afford the price tag) personal care. But far from distributing wealth across society, the gains from this colourful margin remain firmly with the owners of capital in a few now almost monolithic corporations. Average labour productivity growth has been falling since the 1960s and is now going into reverse. And meanwhile the ticket machines at your local railway station are as likely as not 'out of service' waiting on an underpaid engineer.[29]

Maybe the robots really are out there waiting. Maybe they will turn everything around – and either save or destroy us. Quite likely, their presence is already in action. It's entirely credible that the ambivalent role of technology has been part and parcel of capitalism's demise. Perhaps we are already living in a kind of two-tier economy. In one sector, let's call it the 'fast' sector, accelerating technology drives rapid productivity growth and reaps enormous dividends for the owners of capital. In another sector, let's call it the 'slow' sector, labour productivity growth is increasingly elusive, margins are squeezed, wages are depressed and investment becomes difficult or impossible.[30]

It might seem at first like an abstract problem in economics. One that could be fixed by a bit of redistribution between the rich and the poor. But on a closer inspection there's something more worrying going on here. The fast sector is, for the most part, engaged in replacing manual labour with machines for the purpose of mass production of material goods. The slow sector depends intrinsically on human skills and tasks. It's more about the services we provide for each other than it is about material goods. It's more about the time we spend than it is about the stuff we sell. It's intrinsically less damaging to the planet.

The slow sector, it turns out, is a highly desirable place to be. It's exactly the labour of care and the work of craft and creativity that we have been exploring in this chapter. But its fate hangs in the balance. Not delivering the rapid gains and easy profits of labour productivity growth, it's often left to rack and ruin at the margins of capitalist society. This is the Cinderella economy, the economy left behind by austerity, the economy that went missing in action, dismissed from the minds of politicians and economists until we discovered how desperately we needed it.[31]

This is the economy that matters. It's the economy whose services matter. Whose jobs matter. Whose work matters. This is the economy that delivers prosperity: health, employment, longevity, creativity, durability, fulfilment. It is on the resilience of this economy that our future wellbeing – perhaps even our survival – depends. This is the economy we must rescue as the foundation for a postgrowth society.

The work of art

For Arendt, the purest expression of work lies in the creativity of art. Dismissed by capitalism as unproductive or merely decorative, art plays a vital cultural role in building and maintaining the human world. 'Nowhere else does the sheer durability of the world of things appear in such purity and clarity,' she wrote. 'It is as though worldly stability becomes transparent in the permanence of art, so that a premonition of immortality, not the immortality of the soul or of life but of something immortal achieved by mortal hands, has become tangibly present, to shine and to be seen, to sound and to be heard, to speak and to be read.'[32]

The work of art is in part to hold up a mirror to the world. To extol its virtues and to expose its vices. To allow us to see ourselves as we really are. And to dream of who we might become. Rembrandt's etching of *The Good Samaritan* asks us to question the morality of good intentions. Caryl Churchill's *Serious Money* is a savage indictment of human greed. Margaret Atwood's *MaddAddam* trilogy explores the power of community and the endurance of love.

Writer Ben Ketai's iconic study of money and violence in the web TV series *StartUp* exposes late capitalism's dark underbelly. One of his protagonists, Ronnie Dacey (played by Edi Gathegi), is the lieutenant in a street gang called LH7 from the Little Haiti district of Miami. He bursts into the lives of cryptocurrency whizz kid Izzy Morales and her 'South Beach' financier Nick Talman, threatening vengeance over an unpaid loan. But very soon Ronnie begins to see Araknet (the eponymous startup) as a passport out of the toxic cycle of poverty, drugs and violence in which he's trapped.

It's only later, with his family safely settled in an uptown neighbourhood, that a deeper truth begins to dawn on him. Escaping Little Haiti was the easy part. Evading the violence that injustice brings is much more difficult. Part-way through the third season, with Araknet still on a knife edge between success and failure, his allegiance to LH7 catches up with him. Ronnie begins to understand that he still has responsibilities to those he left behind in the 'hood. But when he tries to explain this to his wife, Tam, she's not impressed. 'We are good here. I like it here. You said you like it here,' she pleads. 'Why you wanna go and blow all that up?' Ronnie's response is damning. He's come to the realization that their new life is no better than their old. His new line of work is 'no different than thugging'. 'Araknet is a gang,' he tells Tam. 'It ain't no different than LH7. We just do this shit from behind a desk.'

The writer's message is clear. In the hands of a raw and unbridled capitalism, even what seems like decent work is already corrupted. Its only counterpoint, as Gathegi's character slowly discovers, is a morality anchored in dignity and respect for life. But in a broken society disfigured by power and privilege, even this unassailable virtue must fight relentlessly for purchase. The violence of the streets will always lie on the tainted conscience of capitalism. Shamed. Dishonoured. Wading in blood. Luxemburg was right.

The work of art is sometimes to reveal these darker truths. To connect us viscerally to the suffering in the world. To uncover the demons that lurk in the human soul. But its task too is to shine a light on the 'angels of our better nature'. Maya Angelou's *On the Pulse of Morning* revels in the ties that connect us to each other. David Mitchell's *Cloud Atlas* offers a tantalizing counterpoint to humanity's will to power. Iris Murdoch's *The Sea, the Sea* hides a mystical jewel within a tale of vanity and betrayal.

The work of art helps us transcend what Arendt once called the 'banality of evil'. It lifts our eyes from the horizon of the everyday and reveals the patterns that connect us to each other and to the world. And beyond all this, the transformative power of art breaks down the barriers of the past and acquaints us with new possibilities for the future. It may just be the most important work of all.

The life of the mind

Capitalism's distortion of work is nothing short of tragic. In giving everything over to an accelerated process of wasteful consumption, we are returned inevitably to impermanence. We undermine the very purpose of meaningful work. We destroy the fabric of the human world. Capitalism arouses our cravings for immortality, whilst continually reminding us that nothing is secure. It drags us insistently into the harsh light of hyperarousal, while refusing to satisfy us. And all of this is done in the name of sustaining its own momentum. The visceral contentment of labour is lost. The value of work is destroyed. The opportunities for flow, for peak experience and for the solidarity of a durable human world evaporate.

We are left with a society where labour is denigrated, work is unfulfilling and the human artifice is as durable as a gossamer mist. We are thrown back into a neo-Darwinian nightmare, driven by the law of the jungle. We are mired in gangland, hounded by the relentless pursuit of money and power. Ruled by Fargonomics. The poor and the dispossessed suffer first. But the tragedy belongs to everyone.

It's a tragedy that's entirely avoidable. There is a vision of labour that is consistent with our nature as physical beings in a material world. There is a vision of work that offers us the opportunity to learn, to develop, to create, to participate, to help build the social world and find our place in it. There is vision of human flourishing which teaches us to develop and prize the skills we need to face the challenge of living well. Arendt saw that vision more than six decades ago and wrote about it with extraordinary clarity.

When Germany invaded France in 1940, she had fled with her second husband, Heinrich Blücher, to the US, where they settled together in New York City. It was there that she wrote *The Human Condition*. It was there, in the 1960s, that she witnessed the new spirit of a nonviolent protest that was beginning to transform America. She became an enthusiastic supporter of the peace movement and developed close alliances with the students bringing riots to campuses across America. The same riots that brought hope to RFK as he set out on the Presidential campaign trail in 1968. When the peace activists boycotted classes at the University of Chicago in protest at the Vietnam War, Arendt's was the only course they continued to attend.[33]

It was in New York too that Hannah nursed Heinrich through a prolonged period of ill-health that worsened progressively through the late 1960s. Despite the labour of caring for him, she took it on willingly. She once confided to a friend that 'life without him would be unthinkable'. When he died in October 1970, she was devastated. Looking around for a project to absorb her attention once again in the dignity of work, she returned to her early engagement with the theme of 'passionate thinking'.[34]

The Life of the Mind was her final, unfinished work. *The Human Condition* was always intended as a precursor to this deeper, more fascinating project: an exploration of our capacity for contemplation (*vita contemplativa*). She had planned the book as three distinct volumes on three distinct topics. She completed the second volume on Saturday, 29 November 1975. On Thursday, 4 December, she invited some friends to dinner in her New York apartment, perhaps to celebrate the achievement. The first page of the third and final volume was already sitting in her typewriter on the writing table. She would never return to it. That evening she suffered a massive heart attack and by the time the doctor arrived she was pronounced dead at the scene. She was 69 years old.

The page in her typewriter was blank except for two epigraphs with which she wanted to open the final volume. One was an epigraph she had used to conclude the previous volume. A quote from the Roman senator Cato, renowned for his moral integrity. The other was a verse from the German writer Johann Wolfgang von Goethe's tragic play *Faust*:

> If I could banish magic from my way;
> Unlearn the incantations one by one;
> And stand before you, Nature, all alone:
> Then would the toil of being human pay.[35]

Neither epigraph is enough to know exactly what her intentions were for that final, unwritten volume. Both point to a restless desire for an unvarnished truth which grounds the potential for human fulfilment in the reality of a finite material world. Both highlight the rewards that belong to this quest. Amongst those rewards is the ability to 'think what we are doing'. And by doing so, to reap the benefits that come from understanding the human condition and finding our place in the world.

8

A Canopy of Hope

*'The roots of our future will bury themselves in the ground and a
canopy of hope will reach into the sky.'*
Wangari Maathai, 2006[1]

*'Having deep roots and a strong trunk
Is the Way of long life and clear vision.'*
Lao Tzu, ~500 BC[2]

Wangari Muta Maathai grew up in the district of Nyeri on the slopes
of Mount Kenya. In those days, in the 1940s, the foothills of the
Central Highlands of Kenya were scattered with hundreds of wild fig
trees called *mugumos* in the local Kikuyu tongue. Their tough bark
was the colour of elephant skin. Their gnarled roots drilled deep
channels through the rocky earth to the groundwater below. They
bore a small round fruit which ripened to a warm orange colour, and
their branches were alive with the song of the tinkerbirds and turacos
which feasted on them.[3]

The *mugumo* near her childhood home threw a 60-foot canopy
across lush, fertile undergrowth. Close by was the source of a clear,
babbling stream that provided the family's drinking water. When
Wangari was sent to collect water and firewood, her mother would
always remind her not to take wood from the tree itself or even from
the undergrowth around it. 'Why not?' the young girl would ask.
'Because that's a tree of *Ngai* [the Kikuyu name for God],' she was
told. 'We don't use it. We don't cut it. We don't burn it.'[4]

In 1960, Wangari left Kenya for the US. She was one of three
hundred bright, young African students studying in North America as
part of what became known as the 'Kennedy airlift'. The scheme was
the brainchild of Tom Mboya, a rising star of the Kenyan liberation

movement. In 1959, he had raised enough funding to bring the first cohort of students over. But as the date approached for the second-year intake, he was running out of cash. Appeals to the US State Department were rebuffed. So Mboya approached John F. Kennedy for help.

JFK was about to launch his 1960 Presidential campaign and was immediately supportive. He managed to secure funding from the Joseph P. Kennedy Jr Foundation – set up in memory of his elder brother, who was killed in action in the Second World War. When the news came out that the (Democrat) Kennedys were funding the scheme, the (Republican) State Department miraculously managed to reverse the previous decision. But Kennedy's support for the scheme had been crucial. He was to go on and win the 1960 election by a narrow margin – with the undisputed help of 68% of the African American vote.[5]

Oblivious to any of this, the 20-year-old Wangari took up her place at Mount St Scholastica college in Kansas, to study biology. From there she gained a Master's degree from Pittsburgh, before returning to Kenya to take a Ph.D. and then a teaching post at the University of Nairobi. It was to be almost a decade before she revisited the land of her birth on the slopes of Mount Kenya. What she found there shocked and saddened her. The new owner of the land had cut the tree down to grow tea. The lush undergrowth had disappeared. The soil was arid. The stream that bubbled up from the earth where the roots had broken through the rock was gone.[6]

Over and again, across Kenya, Wangari found the same story repeated. With the memory of childhood, she mourned its loss. With the eyes of a scientist, she grasped its devastating logic. Without the fig tree, there was no easy access to the groundwater. Without its shade, the undergrowth was lost. Without its roots, the soil became unstable. Landslides devastated the mountainous slopes. The drinking water dried up. The birds fell silent. The land and its people suffered the consequences.

Wangari realized that her mother's simple folklore had coded for a lasting protection of the natural resources on which the lives and livelihoods of rural Africans depended. 'Before the Europeans arrived,' she wrote, 'the peoples of Kenya did not look at trees and see timber, or at elephants and see commercial ivory stock, or at cheetahs and see beautiful skins for sale.' But as capitalism – and debt – encroached further and further into African ways of life, simplistic fables offered scant protection against the harsh new reality. Swept away by the requirements of the money economy, the integrity of the natural world was gone in the space of little more than a generation.[7]

The mother of all virtues

The story of the *mugumo* is symptomatic of capitalism's failure to protect nature right across the world. It's the same as the story of the decline of the redwoods, bemoaned by RFK in 1968. It's the story of palm oil in South East Asia and cattle ranching in the Amazon today. The deforestation of planet earth has contributed to the climate emergency, accelerated the loss of biodiversity, depleted scarce resources, overturned the culture of indigenous peoples and deprived humanity of the widespread and enormous benefits of trees. It's been driven by a system of incentives that has prioritized short-term profit over long-term wellbeing. And it's been encouraged by the conviction that the only value in nature is that which can be reaped from it in market exchange.[8]

The short-sightedness inherent in all of these examples is an extraordinary indictment of the economic system that has presided over them. This has all been documented extensively by many other people elsewhere. And it's not my intention to rehearse the detail of those failings here. In Africa, in Asia, in Latin America, the truth of Rosa Luxemburg's insistence that capitalism can only really proceed by plundering cheap resources from beyond its own dominion has been played out ever since she pointed it out more than a century ago.[9]

Developing the foundations for a postgrowth economy demands more of us than bemoaning the massive damage inflicted on society and the planet through the power of accumulation. Just as we need to unravel the dynamic through which human work is degraded and distorted under capitalism's yoke, so we need to delve more deeply

into the machinery of capital itself before we can arrive at the transformation of values on which a different kind of economy might be
built.

My starting point for that exercise is the concept of prudence: the
ability to act wisely in the face of an uncertain future. For Aristotle,
prudence (*phronesis* in the Greek) was a kind of practical wisdom: the
ability to act in a way that is consistent with living well. St Augustine
saw prudence as knowing what to strive for and what to avoid. In
moral and religious thought, prudence is regarded as one of the four
'cardinal virtues' and by some as 'the mother of all virtues' because it
involves a recognition of one's moral duty to the future. In economics,
prudence is used in a very specific way to refer to people's saving and
investment behaviour.[10]

There's a link, of course, between economic prudence and our lay
interpretations of the word. Putting aside some of our income now
in expectation of future rewards holds some of the common meaning
of prudence as concern for the future. But in capitalism, as we shall
see, prudence evolves into a restless motivation to accumulate – a
powerful driver of economic activity.

The English word 'prudence' comes from the Latin *prudentia*.
And this word was a contraction of *providentia*, which literally means
seeing ahead: that is, looking into the future. In classical philosophy,
foresight was a component of wisdom. Someone who could see ahead
was wise enough to make good decisions about how to act now. Lao
Tzu's 'clear vision', cited at the top of the chapter, expresses some of
this sense.

The Italian artist Titian manages to catch the concept well. His
Allegory of Prudence shows the faces of three men. An older man,
whose features are only seen in profile, looks to the left (the past) of
the picture. A young man, also seen in profile, is looking to the right
(the future). A middle-aged man, who is seen face on, is looking out
of the painting at the viewer (the present). Above the three men is a
Latin inscription which translates as something like this: 'By learning
from the past, the present acts with foresight so that the future is not
spoiled by today's actions.'[11]

The painting makes clear that prudence calls for an awareness of extension over time. It entails learning from the past and preparing for the future, as well as acting in the moment. There's an interesting paradox here. The visceral happiness of labour to which Arendt alludes is available only when our awareness stays in the present. When exhaustion or regeneration are salient, they anchor us in that moment. But when the conditions of labour are eased or the joy of satiety is past, our awareness is more easily drawn away from the present. We remember that our lives extend beyond the day-to-day, minute-by-minute struggle for existence. Our memories and our regrets, our concerns and our anxieties, inevitably distract us. We are drawn inexorably towards the uncertain (and ultimately certain) future. This is the mental space where prudence must operate.

The worm at the core

This conceptualization of prudence is a profoundly useful one. Particularly, when it is taken in conjunction with Arendt's analysis of the human condition. It reminds us that we are not just physical beings immersed in a material world. We are also temporal beings living out our existence across a finite period of time. Awareness of our own impermanence plays a critical role in motivating our attempts to build a more durable world.

There's no evidence that prudential behaviour is exclusively a human phenomenon. All kinds of species appear to act in prudential ways. Squirrels hoard nuts in expectation of future hunger. Birds build nests in expectation of the need to lay eggs and protect their young. Beavers build dams in order to slow down fast-running water and fashion a secure home. Ants build colonies to create thriving, industrious, 'prudential' societies.

Does this mean that other creatures have an awareness of what is to come? Do they learn from the past in order to make good decisions about the future? In some cases, yes, as Pavlov famously showed by training dogs to behave in certain ways in expectation of reward. In other cases, 'prudential' behaviour may simply be instinctive behaviours that have evolved over millennia. When getting it wrong carries the penalty of extinction, then getting it right ends up being coded in the genes. At a signal from a lookout, an entire herd of gazelles will instinctively know when to run under threat from an approaching cheetah.[12]

Whether or not awareness of death exists in other species, we know for sure that it does in humans. According to the psychologist Sheldon Solomon, our own mortality is the 'worm at the core' of human existence. It creates an anxiety that can 'eat up the soul'. And it can exacerbate the discord that leads to conflict. But it can also motivate the highest and noblest of our ambitions. Recognizing the brevity of life we are drawn endlessly into the work of world-building in all its myriad forms.[13]

The aim of work, says Arendt, is nothing less than the desire to approach immortality. To achieve this aim, we continually sacrifice time, material resources and money now in order to deliver benefits at some later date. Prudential behaviour in humans, in other words, involves a substantial diversion of material resources away from the present in favour of the future. We sacrifice consumption today in favour of returns tomorrow.

In economics, this process is called investment. Investment is our commitment to the future. Sometimes to our own future. Sometimes to the future of our children, our family or our community. Sometimes to the future of humanity itself. 'A society grows great,' according to a well-known proverb, 'when old men plant trees under whose shade they know they will never sit.' Or indeed when poor, disenfranchised women in rural Africa do the same.[14]

Foresters with no diploma

By the mid-1970s, Wangari was married to the Nairobi politician Mwangi Mathai and the couple had three young children. In his 1974 election campaign, Mwangi had vowed to create full employment for his entire constituency in the outskirts of Nairobi. Once elected to Parliament, he was tempted to forget the bargain he'd struck with voters. But the rising unemployment in Kenya was impossible to ignore. Wangari was determined to try and fulfil his ambitious election promise.

The lessons from the lost *mugumo* in her childhood home still haunted her. Deforestation was destabilizing the land and devastating the lives of the poor. So she launched a business whose sole aim was to nurture seedlings and plant trees. The plan was to employ poor people to plant trees in the gardens of the rich. Sadly, the business model fell foul of a broken economy in a highly divided society. The poor couldn't wait until the end of the month for their income. And the rich refused to advance the funds that Wangari needed to make the enterprise work. The seedlings she had managed to nurture sat idle in the family compound.

Wangari refused to give up. She talked through the idea with colleagues in the United Nations Environment Programme, headquartered in Nairobi, and with the support of the National Council of Women of Kenya she came up with a plan that would support rural women's ability to improve their land and their livelihood. A name was needed for this new endeavour. So she chose one that reflected the social vision she had for the project in which communities themselves would invest time and resources in planting trees. She borrowed the Swahili word *harambee*, which means 'pulling together'.

On World Environment Day, 5 June 1977, Save the Land Harambee was launched. Wangari led a procession to plant seven seedlings in Kamukunji Park in downtown Nairobi, one for each of seven fallen community heroes from Kenyan history. The declared aim of the programme was to plant one tree for every person in Kenya. Within months, they were overwhelmed with demand for seedlings, so Wangari began to teach women how to run their own community nurseries. When she asked for help from professional foresters, she was met with complicated advice and frosty disapproval. 'You need people with diplomas to plant trees,' she was told.[15]

Undeterred, Wangari and her community of 'foresters without diplomas' set about learning for themselves. 'Anybody can dig a hole, put a tree in it, and nurture it,' she would say to them. 'Use your woman sense.' She developed a simple plan with ten steps to enable communities to form groups, plant trees and report back on progress. Soon, women in communities all over Kenya were growing seedlings and planting trees. Eventually, they would plant in rows of a thousand or more, to create 'green belts' that would restore the earth and the Kenyan landscape to its 'cloth of green'.

Success came at a price. Barely a month after the World Environment Day procession, Mwangi left her. In a striking echo of Lynn Margulis's own reflections on marriage, Wangari would later write of that time: 'I had tried to be a good politician's wife, a good African woman, and a successful university teacher. Is it that those were too many roles for one person to excel in?' Or was it simply that Kenya was not yet ready to accept an educated independent woman intent on changing the dysfunctional society she saw around her? In the divorce petition filed by her husband, Mwangi was quoted as saying that she was 'too educated, too strong, too successful, too stubborn and too hard to control'.[16]

At one point during the divorce proceedings, Wangari queried something her husband's lawyer had asked her. The lawyer turned to the judge and said: 'Your honor, did you hear what she asked me? If she dares ask me a question in court what do you think she does to my client at home?' She realized then she would lose the case. But worse was to follow. When she criticized the decision in a magazine interview a few days later, she was asked by the court to retract the remarks. When she refused, she was sentenced to six months in jail for contempt.[17]

In prison, she experienced only kindness and generosity of spirit from her fellow inmates. When she explained why she was there, one woman said: 'We have to pray for the judges so they will judge fairly and justly tomorrow.' Her lawyers came to a compromise that freed her after only a few days. But the experience made her painfully aware of the political realities in Kenya. She became convinced that she had to tackle the deep roots of the disempowerment of the Kenyan people – and in particular of Kenyan women.[18]

Investment as commitment

The Green Belt Movement Wangari helped to found became a powerful force for political and social change. It slowly expanded 'from a tree planting movement into one that planted ideas as well'. Not surprisingly, those ideas were even less welcome than the trees. As long as the women weren't politically engaged, the authorities could turn a blind eye to them. Once people began to ask *why* trees disappear and to campaign for political freedom to change things, the movement was far less tolerated.[19]

Wangari and her fellow activists endured two decades of opposition and repression. Over the course of that time, she was to lose her job, her home and, for a while, access to her children. In 1992, she discovered that her name was on a list of people targeted for assassination. She barricaded herself in her house and started contacting as many international journalists as she could to make them aware of what was happening and to bear witness to what she knew would be her imminent arrest. Three days later, the inevitable happened. Losing patience with standoff, the police broke through the barricade, marched her out of the house and pushed her into a waiting car, leaving the door to her home wide open behind them. It was Mwangi, her ex-husband, who came by to secure the property while she was in jail.

Released on bail, the first thing Wangari did was to join a hunger strike to protest against the detention of political prisoners. She ended up in hospital after being knocked unconscious. During a demonstration in 1999 to protect the Karura Forest, outside Nairobi, she and several others were attacked by armed security guards and she was struck viciously over the head. Bleeding profusely, she reported the attack to the local police. They refused to act. But the protest had been witnessed by foreign journalists and provoked international outrage.

Before long, the political momentum was slowly swinging in the Movement's favour. Their long investment in the future of the land and the livelihoods of its people was beginning to pay off. The days of routinely selling off public forests to private developers or giving them away to members of the government were numbered. In 2002, when she stood as a candidate for the successful National Rainbow Coalition, Wangari Maathai was elected to Parliament with 98% of the vote.

The simple act of planting a tree entails a kind of sacrifice. Not always one as huge as those made by the heroes of the Green Belt

Movement. But always one that demands some kind of investment: time, energy, resources. The return to that investment is the creation of what Wangari called in the epigraph to this chapter a 'canopy of hope'. Literally, in the case of trees, the deep roots and protective foliage that stabilize the climate, improve the soil and protect the livelihoods of those who depend on them. Metaphorically, a symbol of the strength of our commitment to the future.

Sometimes, working with women frustrated by the slow pace at which trees grow, Wangari would remind them that 'the trees they are cutting today were not planted by them, but by those who came before'. Investment in the land and in forestry and in the stabilization of soils and the protection of the climate connects the past to the present and the present to the future. Sometimes to a future we will not even see.[20]

What's true of forestry is true of the investments we make in ourselves and in each other. Investment in health is a commitment to our future quality of our life and our longevity. Investing in skills is a commitment to our capacity for rewarding work and for flow. The time spent with our kids, our families, our friends, creates the social bonds that ground our prosperity in shared experience. Investment in the work of craft or in the creative arts is a commitment to the durability of the human world. Investment is our commitment to the future.

The casino economy

It's clear that capitalism has strayed a million miles from this fine ideal. Investments are judged on the basis of the short-term financial returns they yield for investors. Investment itself is seen as the process of making money from money. Prudence still matters. It has a formal definition in economics as the rate at which consumers sacrifice present consumption in order to save for an uncertain future. But this kind of prudence says little about the destination for savings, the wisdom of investments or their role in creating a more sustainable world.

Productive investment requires us to build and maintain the physical assets needed to provide for economic goods and services. But alongside this 'real' economy there has been an exponential rise in the size and complexity of the 'financial' economy. This trend was in evidence long before the global financial crisis. Banks were increasingly lending to each other rather than to non-financial firms. Financial derivatives of all kinds, hedge funds, collateralized debt obligations, credit default swaps, sub-prime mortgages, insurances, futures markets: these were the arcane components of a financial architecture that few understood and which led more or less inexorably to the collapse of Lehmann Brothers in 2008.

Even to a lay viewer, the evidence is damning. Instead of financing the real economy, finance was busy financing finance. Ratings agencies colluded in the game. Regulators turned a blind eye to malpractice. Sometimes they even changed the rules to facilitate the process. Speculation was driving a kind of casino economy. The most powerful financial institutions in the world were almost literally betting that the future doesn't really matter. The 'age of irresponsibility' is what the former UK Prime Minister Gordon Brown once called it.

Sooner or later, the bubble had to burst. And when that happened, in September 2008, it was only the public purse – taxpayers' money – that saved the global economy from collapse. It did so, as we saw in Chapter 2, by bailing out the rich and imposing austerity on the poor. The privatization of profit and the socialization of costs have been the hallmarks of capitalistic investment from the beginning. Without some shift in this dysfunctional logic, investment's commitment to the future is irredeemably broken.

Shortly before the 50th World Economic Forum convened in Davos, Larry Fink, the head of BlackRock, the world's largest asset management company, published his customary 'annual letter' to CEOs. Climate change is rapidly changing people's perspective on investment risk. 'I believe that we are on the verge of a fundamental reshaping of finance,' he wrote. 'In the near future – and sooner than most anticipate – there will be a significant reallocation of capital.'[21]

A recent assessment of global sustainable investment found that 'climate finance' – investment in technologies such as renewable energy which reduce climate emissions – has indeed been growing and now exceeds half a trillion US dollars a year. But this number falls far short of the $1.6–3.8 trillion in clean energy investment needed to achieve the Intergovernmental Panel on Climate Change's 1.5° target. Outside of climate finance, there is even less prudence. The protection of natural 'biodiversity' accounts for a minute 0.002% of the global GDP.[22]

Meanwhile, governments around the world are still subsidizing fossil fuel investments with taxpayers' money to the tune of more than $5 trillion per year. More than 6% of the world's GDP is being spent on short-sighted investments that could make our world unliveable in the space of decades. Redirected towards investments in renewable energy and low-carbon infrastructure, these perverse subsidies could more than fill the climate investment gap.[23]

Fink's protestations are an interesting signal of changing times. But marginal shifts in investor preference will not be sufficient to rescue us from the age of irresponsibility. There is a fundamental need to prune the corrupt and decaying branches of capitalism and return investment to its proper role in society. The handwringing in Davos in the innocent early days of 2020 may have been mostly theatrical. But with the hindsight of a global pandemic, the irony of the situation is painfully evident. The proper role for investment is to deliver a sense of durability against the impermanence of the natural world. In the hands of capitalism, that role has been perverted. In seeking to enrich the few, it has served to undermine security for everyone.

The return to prudence?

The last few years have witnessed a rising pressure to 'divest' (or disinvest) funds from unsustainable or unethical industries, and to invest in assets that protect our future prosperity. The rise in climate finance is one of the manifestations of this 'divest-invest' movement. Pension funds (and some sovereign wealth funds) have begun to divest from fossil fuel investment. Central banks are aiming to support this trend by requiring all financial institutions to assess climate-related risk. Governments have been painfully slow in imposing the prudential regulation that is needed to accelerate these changes. But shareholders (and fund managers) are already beginning to exercise their power to reject companies which damage the environment, exploit supply chain labour or short-cut good governance. Ethical and sustainable investors are beginning to demand that their money should work for the common good.[24]

The fact that some of these ethical funds perform better than their rivals comes as a surprising challenge to conventional wisdom. But it's no real mystery. The value of investment today lies in the performance of the economy of tomorrow. And it's becoming increasingly clear that the future will look rather different from the bankrupt financial architecture of the past.[25]

Tomorrow's economy will be built around renewable and 'regenerative' technologies; around fair wage deals and transparent governance; around the protection and restoration of social and environmental assets rather than their systematic destruction; around enterprise in the service of community and in harmony with nature. The first movers in this new investment landscape will (rightly) benefit from its many dividends. So too will the rest of society.

To date, the divest-invest movement has confined itself mainly to the domain of climate finance. But it seems to me that we must understand the task ahead in a much deeper sense than this. Seeing investment as a commitment to the future calls on us to build and maintain the physical infrastructure for a very different kind of life. One in which it is possible for people to live in ways that are not just more sustainable and more resilient, but also healthier and more fulfilling than life under capitalism.

The obvious foundation for this new portfolio must be what we might call *ecological investment* – the allocation of resources to the protection of the climate, the land, the oceans, the rivers, the forests, the habitats of living creatures: our earthly home. This part of the portfolio – which is mostly neglected under capitalism and only partly emerges within sustainable investment – is an absolute prerequisite for a lasting prosperity.

Next I think we can take our cue from Arendt's distinction between labour and work to define two categories of productive assets: those that facilitate the maintenance of life (let's call these *care investments*) and those that contribute to the creation of a fulfilling durable human world (let's call these *creative investments*). Care investments are those that allow us to maintain the everyday fabric of society: homes, hospitals, schools, shops, systems of provision for food and the biological necessities of life. Creative investments are those that provide for the durability of the human world – what Arendt calls the human artifice: communal spaces, meeting places, artistic venues, works of art.

Just as the material and symbolic value of goods cannot be entirely distinguished from each other, so the two kinds of investment must inevitably overlap. But the distinction is nonetheless a useful one because it begins to specify the sectoral focus of our investment intentions. On the one hand, we must prioritize and support those frontline services that have proved themselves most vital during the coronavirus crisis. On the other hand, we must begin to take seriously the task of investing in the infrastructure of a resilient, low-carbon world.

When nation after nation imposed varieties of lockdown to curb the spread of the virus, towns and cities were suddenly empty of cars. In their place came people on foot and on bikes, reclaiming streets that had become more and more inaccessible to them. This long-forgotten public space became the site for a new sense of shared prosperity: a world in which our own nature as active, physical and social beings was allowed to thrive. The benefits of investing in 'liveability', building the infrastructure of a resilient, fulfilling, active zero-carbon world, have never been more obvious.

At the end of the day, the role of investment in economics is the same as it is in forestry. The same as it is in our individual lives. The same as it is in our social world. To create a canopy of hope. To protect and maintain the conditions on which our prosperity depends. To leave the world a stronger, more resilient place for our children. As Titian's *Allegory* suggests, the exercise of prudence stretches backwards and forwards through time. But it bestows at least some of its virtue on the continuous present. Investing in the future is the best – perhaps the only – way to render our own lives meaningful today.

Jubilee

Wangari's life was itself a kind of investment. In her final book, *Replenishing the Earth*, she writes movingly of the values that motivated her work. She describes in particular how a commitment to service lay at the core of the Green Belt Movement. 'Selfless service is the basis for much of what we admire in those we see as exemplars of what is best in humanity,' she said. 'People who represent a model not only of self-empowerment but also of how to motivate others to act for the common good.'[26]

Her life was a continual search for solutions to the problems facing Kenya and many other poor developing countries: the disempowerment of women; the decline in rural livelihoods; the destruction of the soil; the loss of the *mugumo* from the land near her childhood home. In her search for the origins of these problems, it isn't surprising that she was led at one point to the crushing debt burden that is carried by the poorest countries in the world. It was – and continues to be – one of the most pernicious outcomes of a dysfunctional capitalism.

In the name of development, the richest economies have benefitted disproportionately from the financial flows into and out of Africa. Between 1970 and 2002, African economies borrowed $540 billion and paid back $550 billion, but still owed the lending agencies almost $300 billion. Not content with identifying these injustices, Wangari took up arms against them. In 1998, she assumed the role of co-chair of the Jubilee 2000 Africa campaign, with an aim to enact a Jubilee – a cancellation of the worst of the debt in the poorest countries in the world – in the year of the millennium.[27]

The campaign had enormous traction with celebrities and politicians around the world. And it did eventually lead to the cancellation of some $100 billion in debt. But the battle was by no means won. Today the financial flows out of Africa – including debt service payments, repatriated profits and capital flight – are two and a half times larger than the financial flows into the continent. As the anthropologist Jason Hickel has argued, 'rich countries aren't developing poor countries; poor countries are effectively developing rich countries – and they have been since the late 15th century.' This injustice persists in the twenty-first century. The worsening debt crisis massively hampered Africa's ability to deal with the coronavirus.[28]

Wangari Maathai is no longer there to fight that cause. She died of complications from ovarian cancer in 2011. But the spirit of her work continues to inspire communities far beyond her native land. Her investment in trees, in people and in justice had a stunning simplicity to it and revealed a singular courage. Her persistence and her personal sacrifice enabled communities, empowered women, supported livelihoods, stabilized soil, absorbed carbon from the atmosphere and rejuvenated rural landscapes across Kenya and around the world.

She would have been the first to recognize that the journey towards sustainable livelihoods, healthy soils and vibrant communities in Africa is far from over. And that the setbacks associated with a broken financial system remain a significant impediment to prosperity. But she would not have stopped fighting them. 'A stumble is only one step in the long path we walk,' she once said, 'Dwelling on it only postpones the completion of our journey.'[29]

It was this extraordinary spirit that led to her being awarded the Nobel Peace Prize in 2004 and a place in the hearts of people all over the world. The Green Belt Movement she founded has planted more than 50 million trees in Kenya alone and inspired the planting of hundreds of millions more across the planet. Her commitment exemplifies what investment can and should be in a postgrowth world. Her canopy of hope stretches out of Africa and shines a powerful light into the uncertain future.[30]

9

The Art of Power

'We've come here to let you know that change is coming whether you like it or not. The real power belongs to the people.'
Greta Thunberg, 2018[1]

'If you have a path to go on, you have power.'
Thich Nhat Hanh, 2007[2]

Bobby Kennedy's opposition to the Vietnam War in the 1968 Presidential campaign was inspired, in part at least, by a Vietnamese monk named Thich Nhat Hanh, who travelled to the US to canvass for peace in his native land.

Born in 1926 in the city of Hué in central Vietnam, Thich Nhat Hanh was just 7 years old when he came across a drawing of the Buddha, sitting cross-legged on the grass, radiating serenity and peace. The image was in such stark contrast to the conflict and suffering the boy saw around him, it was to set the course of his entire life. At 16 years old, he enrolled at the Tu Hieu monastery in Hué as a novice monk in the Vietnamese Zen tradition of Buddhism.[3]

By the time he'd completed his studies, Vietnam was on the brink of all-out war. The former French colony was slipping away from western influence, to the dismay of the US and its allies. When the French finally withdrew from the region in 1954, the country was split in two along the 17th parallel, just north of Hué city, setting the scene for twenty years of tragic American involvement in an ultimately disastrous military engagement. Officially, it was a civil war between the newly formed countries of North and South Vietnam. But everyone understood it for what it was: a brutal tussle for power in the Cold War being played out between the US and the Soviet Union.[4]

As the conflict escalated in the 1960s, first John F. Kennedy and then Lyndon B. Johnson committed ever-greater resources to the battlefield, to the rising dismay of many Americans. Thich Nhat Hanh saw the consequences first-hand. He made up his mind to travel to 'the source of the war' and campaign for peace. Accepting an invitation to give a seminar at Cornell University in Ithaca, New York, he left his native land for the first time in May 1966.[5]

Neither side had been keen to hear Thich Nhat Hanh's anti-war message in Vietnam. But it received a warm reception from those in America uncomfortable with their country's involvement in the conflict. In January 1967, the civil rights activist Martin Luther King Jr nominated him for the Nobel Peace Prize. 'Here is an apostle of peace and nonviolence,' he wrote in his nomination letter, 'separated from his own people while they are oppressed by a vicious war which has grown to threaten the sanity and security of the entire world.' The two men campaigned for peace together at a conference in Geneva in June of the same year.[6]

Less than a year later, King was dead: another victim of another assassin's bullet. During a peace demonstration in Philadelphia, Thich Nhat Hanh was asked by a US reporter whether he was from the north or south of Vietnam. 'If I said I was from the north, he would think I was anti-American,' wrote Thich Nhat Hanh years later. 'If I said I am from the south, he would think I was . . . pro-American. So I smiled and said: "I am from the center."' It was true, as it happened, in a literal sense. But it was also a rejection of the division that haunted his native land. An expression of solidarity with all those suffering in the conflict. And a refusal to succumb to the dystopian vision of power that leads inevitably to the desecration of life.[7]

The journey described in this book overturns assumptions that have lodged themselves at the heart of our culture for centuries. Our relationship to nature; our response to struggle; our aspirations for work; our sense of prudence; our commitments to the future: none of these things survive the analysis of the last few chapters in the form allocated to them by capitalism. All of them demand quite fundamental revision.

It's natural to ask how these changes will occur. What can be done right now? Which policies would take us in the right direction? Where are the quick wins, the silver bullets, the double dividends? Where is the satnav to guide us from here to the promised land? The deeper we find ourselves mired in dysfunctionality, the more we struggle to answer these questions. We are back at the crossroads identified in Chapter 3. In our determination to get to Dublin, we rage at the exasperating farmer with her existential prevarications. Yes, I understand that this is not the best place to start. Just point me in the direction of home!

It's easy to sympathize with this urge. But first we need to tackle one last system error haunting capitalism's vision of progress. It bears many similarities to those we have already explored. But it also stands as a distinct impediment to a viable and durable postgrowth society. It concerns power. Without confronting the art of power, our yearning for quick solutions will at best be impotent and at worst a distraction from the need for more fundamental change.

System change

For a short period of time during 2020, a window of almost unthinkable opportunity allowed us to glimpse a radically different political terrain. Policies were enacted that would have seemed unthinkable just weeks before. Governments guaranteed the wages of workers. They issued soft loans and grants to sustain hard-hit businesses. Furlough schemes, rent holidays and suspensions of bankruptcy gave protection to companies and households. Supply chains were reorganized. Production facilities were repurposed. Hospitals were built at lightning speed. Volunteers were deployed. Livelihoods were protected. Communities collaborated.

Perhaps the most extraordinary element in this response was the speed with which governments found the fiscal wherewithal to act. A common meme in the years following the global financial crisis in 2008 was the claim: 'There is no magic money tree.' Everyone could surely understand that the state couldn't just go on racking up debts that would fall on the shoulders of future generations? What would happen to your household if you dared to behave like this?[8]

Most people accepted the argument. It seemed to express a

familiar logic. It became the justification for an austerity that crippled the poorest in society and paved the way for tragedy. But it was profoundly wrong – as a marginalized corner of economics known as 'modern monetary theory' had been saying for more than a decade. Stephanie Kelton's superbly timed book *The Deficit Myth* made the situation abundantly clear. Governments are not households. The sovereign power of government to issue its own currency is curtailed only by inflation – and ideology.[9]

We learned two things from all this. First, that radical change is undeniably possible. Even in the capitalistic West. Second, that incrementalism won't achieve it. The raft of measures introduced in haste to protect populations and safeguard life were not the result of long-winded policy negotiations mired in political ideology. When pragmatism was needed, it was immediately forthcoming. When speed was of the essence, the responses were almost instantaneous. The scale of implementation was not incremental. It was immediate and systemic.

During a brief window of sanity, the ideologies of capitalism were set aside. Government money was no longer a communist plot but an indispensable tool in the fiscal management of calamity. Expediency was the order of the day. Those countries who failed to understand this fared worst in the hideous league tables of Covid-19 mortality. Those who dispensed with dogma early and prioritized health over productivity kept misfortune to an almost unbelievable minimum. The currency of this distinction was measured on the scale of human tragedy.

The pandemic provided an object lesson in the art of the possible. And then, as people's attention began to focus on recovery, there followed a huge flood of proposals to apply the same speed and scale of response to transform society. To address the climate emergency. To counter the devastating loss of species. To protect the integrity of soils and rivers, lakes and oceans. To unravel the damaging impacts of inequality. To deliver essential workers from the precarity of work. To counter the obscenity of rent-seeking behaviours. To free humanity from the materialistic scourge of consumerism. To protect the most vulnerable. To strengthen health systems and improve social care.

To counter obesity. To create education systems fit for purpose and accessible to all. To privilege durability over wasteful convenience. To develop craft. To support creativity. To build a society in which people collaborate in the creation of a durable and meaningful human world.

In short, these proposals sought to build a postgrowth society: free from the failures of capitalism. Because, once again, in all of these areas, it is abundantly clear that incrementalism is not enough. The environmentalist Jonathon Porritt puts the case bluntly in *Hope in Hell*, his unnerving exposé of the failure of governments to respond to the climate emergency. '[T]here is no hope whatsoever in another ten years of incremental change,' he writes. We need to 'stop pretending that leisurely incrementalism is any longer an appropriate response' to the devastating ecological crises that were in part responsible for the pandemic.[10]

When a group of two hundred well-known artists and scientists published a powerful plea for us not to 'return to normal' in the wake of the coronavirus, they ended up making a very similar point. 'The Covid-19 pandemic is a tragedy,' they agreed. But the crisis is 'inviting us to examine what is essential. And what we see is simple: "adjustments" are not enough. The problem is systemic.'[11]

'System change not climate change' had been a rallying cry for those who took to the streets during 2019 to demand climate action. Porritt argues eloquently that if those in power fail in their duty to deliver us from the climate emergency, then the only effective, legitimate response is non-violent civil disobedience. Extinction Rebellion had made this argument explicitly. It was the motivation for their street protests.

In its purest form, it also inhabited the school strikes under the inspirational leadership of Greta Thunberg. 'If solutions within this system are so impossible to find then maybe we should change the system itself,' she told a UN Climate Conference in Katowice in 2018. 'We have not come here to beg world leaders to change. You have ignored us in the past and you will ignore us again. You've run out of excuses and you're running out of time.' But you will not prevail, she suggested, because '[t]he real power belongs to the people.'[12]

The will to power

A conundrum faces us here. Those who want change tend not to be in power. Those who hold power tend not to want change. The possibilities for any kind of change depend on the distribution of power coded into the rules of society. The rules of society lie at the mercy of the state. The mercy of the state depends inherently on its mandate. The mandate forged by western democracy is a very particular one. Political power is uncomfortably tied to the delivery of economic growth.

This association of growth with power is comically illustrated by an encounter I had with a senior adviser to the UK Chancellor of the Exchequer in the months following the publication of *Prosperity without Growth*. I was pleased to have been granted the meeting. The Treasury is definitely one of the most important places to bring forward conversations about a postgrowth economy.

So I laid out the arguments in the book as carefully as I could. The limits to decoupling. The paradox of happiness. The foundations for an economy of care and creativity. The special adviser gave every appearance of listening carefully. At the end, he solemnly asked me just one question. What would it be like for Treasury officials to turn up at G7 meetings knowing that the UK's GDP had slipped down the world rankings?

I was dumbstruck. Not so much by the tenor of the question as by my own naïvety. How could I have missed that the politics of the playground is so evidently still in action, even in the highest echelons of power? Mine is bigger than yours. Might is always right. The will to power, as the philosopher Nietzsche so painfully observed, is a barely conscious urge to dominate, played out against a veneer of civility, masquerading as political progress. In that moment, my confidence in the ability of the state to play any role in averting the entropic slide into chaos didn't exactly evaporate, but it certainly faltered. I remember making my excuses and leaving early.[13]

I can't have entirely given up on the troubling question of developing a postgrowth polity. Otherwise I wouldn't still be teasing away at it. But during that meeting I certainly began to understand what the political scientist Daniel Hausknost calls the 'glass ceiling' of transformation. I witnessed at first hand the limits it places on achieving sustainability. The legitimacy of the social contract forged in the crucible of capitalism is fatally dependent on a false promise: that there will always be more and more for everyone. That promise in its turn is too easily corruptible by the dynamics of political power.[14]

In his wonderfully insightful book on the history of capitalism, *Talking to My Daughter*, the economist (and former Greek Finance Minister) Yanis Varoufakis provides an eloquent and disturbing overview of capitalism's daunting ability to create and legitimize massive asymmetries of wealth and power. It comes, he argues, from the ability of the owners of capital to seize control over the surplus created by the ability of technology to increase labour productivity.[15]

Capturing the surplus relies in its turn on certain key structural dynamics internalized in capitalism. First up is the insatiable process of commoditizing as much of life as possible – at the expense of human values. Adrift from those values, we are drawn relentlessly into consuming surrogates and proxies that feed the system but do little to nourish our souls or alleviate our anxiety.

Next comes a money system that benefits the owners of capital at the expense of the needs of society. Adrift from its social origins, money and debt become tools of oppression, dividing the surplus in proportion to access to the money power. Were the state to have retained (or regained) control of that power, it might conceivably have diminished the extent of the inequality that now predicts capitalism's downfall. But it didn't. Until forced to do so by the tragedy of the pandemic. Finally, these two dynamics would not in themselves be possible were it not for a polity systematically disposed to prioritize the rights of those with power over those of the dispossessed.

The first two of those dynamics admit solutions already intimated in the pages of this book. A life outside of exchange markets is precisely the vision of prosperity offered by less material forms of flourishing. Sovereign money was the most fundamental of the means employed to rescue society from the damaging threat posed by the pandemic. In the hands of a capitalistic state, of course, this ability is insufficient to protect society. Central banks' ability to do 'whatever it takes' to rescue the stock market doesn't in itself ensure that they exercise the same largesse when it comes to protecting the livelihoods of ordinary people, or the stability of the health system, or the integrity of the climate.

Perhaps inevitably, then, if we are to make progress on a post-growth polity, we find ourselves drawn into a re-examination of the assumptions enthroned in the power of the state. Is Thunberg correct to argue that the real power belongs to the people? Is that real power sufficient to create the change she and so many others would like to see in the world – particularly when it must confront the institution-alized power of the state as well as the vested interests of the rich? Is there space for a genuine renewal – a new vision of power fit for purpose in a postgrowth world?

The lotus of compassion

As a young monk in Hué, Thich Nhat Hanh learned that non-at-tachment is the path to enlightenment. But from early on he was uncomfortable with the conservatism inherent in traditional Buddhist teaching. The young boy who'd been inspired by the serenity in the Buddha didn't just covet peace for himself. He demanded from it a response to the suffering around him. In the 1950s, having completed his training, he began to play an active role in the movement to modernize Buddhism and to make it more relevant to the lives and the hardships of ordinary people.

The premise was clear. If the peace sought in monastic retreat was not simply to be a gratuitous pleasure, it must be brought back into the world somehow. It must translate into action. It must stand firm against the suffering of others. Not content with individual content-ment, these young activists came to believe that nonviolent protest – and what Thich Nhat Hanh called compassionate action – was a necessary response to the injustice of war. 'When bombs begin to fall on people,' he said, 'you cannot stay in the meditation hall.' From the soil of suffering grows the lotus of compassion.[16]

Some demonstrations of that principle were dramatic. In the early 1960s, several monks set themselves on fire to protest against the atrocities and injustices of war. Trying to explain these horrendous 'self-immolations' to Westerners at the time, Thich Nhat Hanh described them as acts of love not desperation. But to offer young people in Vietnam a less drastic (and more compassionate) means of protest, he established the School of Youth for Social Service, which trained thousands of young volunteers, both monastic and lay, to relocate refugees and help them rebuild their lives.[17]

Its services were very soon called into action. In 1964, at the height of the conflict, the country was hit by one of the worst floods in living memory. Heavy rains began to fall on central Vietnam during the afternoon of 7 November and continued for six whole days. Homes, and sometimes whole villages, were swept away in the flooding. More than six thousand people lost their lives. The entire country was mobilized in the relief effort. But no one was particularly keen to risk getting caught in the violence still plaguing those regions worst hit by floods.[18]

This was the moment when Thich Nhat Hanh took a small team of his volunteers along the Thu Bon River in seven rowing boats piled high with food and medical provisions. Sometimes trapped in cross-fire, sometimes succumbing to sickness themselves, the volunteers made their way high into the mountains, bringing aid to anyone who needed it, whichever side of the conflict they were on. This sense of unqualified compassion for all living beings was a fundamental precept in what Thich Nhat Hanh was later to call Engaged Buddhism.[19]

It was undoubtedly their common concern for nonviolent protest that drew Thich Nhat Hanh and Martin Luther King so closely together when they met. Thich Nhat Hanh's compassionate action was a close relation to the civil disobedience on which King was building a new social movement. Both men were committed to nonviolent action in response to injustice. What's fascinating is that in arriving at that point, they had travelled along such different paths.

The seeds of disobedience

In April 1963, King was jailed for taking part in a demonstration against racial segregation in Birmingham, Alabama. It was from there that he wrote his famous *Letter from a Birmingham Jail*, appealing to his fellow clergymen to recognize the legitimacy of nonviolent direct action. He drew on Saint Augustine to argue that 'an unjust law is no law at all' and on Saint Thomas Aquinas to explain that we could recognize such laws as those 'not rooted in eternal and natural law'. 'Any law that degrades human personality is unjust,' he wrote. Segregation is unjust because it 'distorts the soul and damages the personality'.[20]

King was deeply influenced by Mahatma Gandhi, who had himself spent plenty of time in jail. 'In my humble opinion,' said Gandhi at one of his trials, 'non-cooperation with evil is as much a duty as is cooperation with good.' From prison in 1906, Gandhi had read the most famous account of civil disobedience – written by the American naturalist Henry Thoreau. It had a profound impact on his thinking. He adopted Thoreau's expression 'civil disobedience' to describe the nonviolent protests that were eventually to lead to the end of the British rule in India.[21]

On the Duty of Civil Disobedience, published in 1849, explains in great detail why Thoreau intended to withhold some of his taxes: because he objected to financing America's war in Mexico and its support for slavery. The essay is a forensic examination of the moral relationship between the state and the individual. Thoreau's concerns are fundamentally the same as those of the extinction rebels and the school strikers who took to the streets across the world during 2019 to protest against the lack of action on climate change. What are the options available to us, he asked himself, when the state no longer represents our moral interests? Civil disobedience was his answer.[22]

At Harvard, Thoreau had read the philosophy of John Locke, whose ideas about the 'social contract' provided the foundations on which our modern notions of government are built. Locke's *Second Treatise of Government*, published in 1689, remains, broadly speaking, the basis for western liberal democracies. The legitimacy of state power, said Locke, rests only on its promise to protect people's rights 'as equals before the sight of God'. Locke's argument starts from the same 'state of nature' that we visited in Chapter 6: that condition which Hobbes so unforgivingly characterized in *Leviathan* as 'a state of war'.[23]

Nothing could have captured the brutal conflict playing out in Vietnam in the 1960s much better than Hobbes' graphic description. The legacy of the Japanese invasion in the Second World War. The insurgency of a communist-inspired nationalism. The power vacuum left when the French colonial regime withdrew from the region. The dividing of a people against itself. The ambitions of the US for control of the region. All of this resembled a horrendous 'war of all against all'.

'If America's war leadership often flaunted its inhumanity,' wrote the historian Max Hastings in his epic account of the war, 'that of North Vietnam matched it cruelty for cruelty.' Vietnam was clearly in a state of war. But this was by no means a state of nature. It was the outcome for an obscene power conflict played out over decades by governments with no legitimacy to act in a theatre thousands of miles from their own democratic mandate. The Vietnam War represented one of the worst failings of legitimate government in human history.[24]

Our concept of power, just like our science, depends fatally on the persuasive influence of metaphor. Hobbes used the narrative of a 'war of all against all' to argue for a form of absolute sovereignty to which all freedoms are subject. Only this degree of power, he claimed, could prevent the state of nature becoming a state of war. In its historical context, this argument was really nothing much more than an unseemly power grab on behalf of an oppressive monarchy, whose political aims (in the English Civil War, for example) had very little in common with the needs or interests of ordinary people.[25]

Locke was, admirably, intent on countering this highly politicized view of the state. His state of nature was a less brutal affair. In fact, he insisted, it is governed by a 'natural law which obliges everyone . . . that being all equal and independent, no one ought to harm another in [their] life, health, liberty, or possessions'.[26]

Crucially, argued Locke, the power vested in government to ensure this outcome is at best a relative one. It is granted by the people for the people, and where necessary it must be taken away again by the people. '[F]or all power given with trust for the attaining of an end, being limited by that end, whenever that end is manifestly neglected, or opposed, the trust must necessarily be forfeited, and the power devolve into the hands of those that gave it.'[27]

Locke's vision of this 'social contract' quite specifically foresaw that, under certain circumstances, and in particular when human legislation stood in poor correspondence to natural law, it was the right and duty of people to oppose the state. Civil disobedience wasn't for Locke the preferred option for achieving that opposition. But in the absence of a foolproof way of ensuring good governance, it was a necessary restraint on a state intent on neglecting the legitimate interest of its citizens.

Thoreau took this view even further. Social progress, he believed, is represented by a gradual transition towards greater and greater respect for individual human rights. 'There will never be a really free and enlightened State,' he suggested, 'until the State comes to recognize the individual as a higher and independent power, from which all its own power and authority is derived.' For the moment, he believed, civil disobedience is essential to oppose moral failings on the part of government. But perhaps we remain in an incomplete state of political progress. 'Is a democracy, such as we know it, the last improvement possible in government?' asked Thoreau, towards the end of his essay. 'I please myself with imagining a State at last which can afford to be just to all.'[28]

This might all seem like a bit of diversion from the task at hand. But my point in tracing the roots of civil disobedience, from King and Gandhi to Locke and Hobbes, is this: that the overwhelming need for civil disobedience we still face today represents not just a failing at the heart of a particular government, but rather an incompleteness in our framing of the state itself. A sometimes-fatal misunderstanding of the art of power. One that stands in desperate need of correction.

A nightmare spectacular

The strange meeting of capitalism and Buddhism on the grounds of civil disobedience hides an even stranger coincidence. Both journeys towards that unsatisfactory resolution to the art of power began in the same recognition of the same underlying conditions of human existence. Conditions already encountered earlier in this book.

Buddhism's 'first noble truth' teaches that suffering is inherent in life. The grounds for that suffering are familiar to us. We have returned to them repeatedly in previous chapters. They arise from our nature as finite beings in a material world. From the moment of our birth to the instant of our death, our lives are framed by these conditions. In many ways, the starting point for Buddhism is the exact same understanding that lies at the heart of capitalism. Life is a harsh struggle for existence. Suffering is inevitable.

The existentialist philosopher Ernest Becker put this understanding in a particularly graphic way. 'Creation is a nightmare spectacular taking place on a planet that has been soaked for hundreds of millions of years in the blood of all its creatures,' he wrote in his classic book *The Denial of Death*. Whatever we do on this planet 'has to be done in the lived truth of the terror of creation, of the grotesque, of the rumble of panic underneath everything. Otherwise it is false.'[29]

This too is metaphor, of course. But it captures an underlying reality not a million miles from the first noble truth. Suffering is all around us. It is a precondition for and an inevitable outcome of life. Capitalism, as we've seen, draws from this same metaphorical well. But from that common source the two ideologies then diverge dramatically.

The journey taken by capitalism is a strange and ultimately paradoxical one. Its base response is to translate the struggle for life into an inevitable competition and to embed this competition into the institutions of culture: the rules of the market, the ethos of business, the norms of consumer society. Not surprisingly, the same metaphor is woven into the fabric of the state. It's at its most obvious in Hobbes, whose *Leviathan* is the convenient remedy for a competitive 'war of all against all'. But it is present too in the Lockean social contract. More by default than by design, perhaps. Yet irredeemably so.

Locke's reasonably inclusive 'life, health, liberty and possessions' has been progressively reduced to the idea that the social contract is a kind of collective insurance policy for the protection of private property. Government becomes the ultimate enforcer of property rights. The result is a vision of the state as an executive club whose main function is to protect the interests of property-owners. And by definition, this convenient elision excludes the interests of the poor, the marginalized and the dispossessed.

Here is a representation of the discontent expressed through today's rising populism. A government pretending concern for the common good but acting as a defender of elites appears worse even than one actively acknowledging the 'war of all against all' and legitimizing barbarism. The slow erosion of decency. The rolling back of social progress. The retreat into xenophobia, racism and sexism. These are as much the consequence of mistrust in the representative power of government as they are of the manipulation of a post-truth media.

But there is worse to follow. This configuration of the state doesn't accommodate the rights of other species. It doesn't allow for the protection of nature. It can never effectively sanction the interests of future generations. It responds to the first noble truth not with a genuine compassion but with a loosely contrived and very limited reciprocal altruism restricted to a subset of the population. No wonder the only moral recourse of the dispossessed is civil disobedience.[30]

Power in this configuration collapses into market or military domination. The metaphorical justification for this limited and dangerous condition is borrowed, when needed, from the competitive logic that is supposed to characterize the natural world. This is the domain of predator and prey. The hunter and the hunted. And the best way for the state to enforce order – either within its boundaries or outside them – is through military might or through economic power.

A fatal conceit

Thich Nhat Hanh observes in *The Art of Power* that what we think of as power in western society is what Buddhists would call cravings: for wealth, property, possessions, status, comfort, sex. And for dominance over others in pursuit of these things. This is such a dysfunctional mythology that the capitalistic state is forced to soften its dark prognosis. Without something more in the way of a reward to offer to those excluded from the ownership of wealth, the social contract would be tethered fatally to an impossible burden: the continual suppression of the rights of the less advantaged.[31]

Here, of course, is precisely where the myth of growth comes in. Its job is to promise that there will always be more and more. Without this promise of eternal accumulation, capitalism cannot function. If we centralize property in the social contract and privilege access to profit over the right to life and health, then civil disobedience becomes the only recourse of the dispossessed. We are left with a state whose legitimacy rests solely on making impossible promises which are entirely incompatible with the state of nature itself.

There is a curious and paradoxical side-effect of this. The dangerous reality of responding to the struggle for existence through a relentless competition for power cannot afford to remain in plain sight. It must be obscured by an intricate veil of pretence that the damage doesn't matter or is insignificant or is elsewhere. Not ours. Becker's 'denial of death' becomes indispensable to the acceptability of capitalism as a social vision.

In a rare moment of honesty, early in the lockdown, then US President Donald Trump made a strange admission. 'I wish we could have our old life back,' he said. 'We had the greatest economy that we've ever had. And we didn't have death.' As the author Zadie Smith pointed out in her intricately woven portrait of life under the 2020 lockdown, death 'is the truth of our existence as a whole, of course, but America has never been philosophically inclined to consider existence as a whole'. Denial is a prerequisite for the game.[32]

One of the sweetest rewards from success in the game is the ability to perfect this denial. A significant portion of the 'winnings' are allocated to social insulation. A hermetically sealed cocoon of comfort and privilege – where the inevitable entropy cascades outwards and downwards, but never really touches our lives. And to those for whom this denial is not affordable, there remains the alluring seduction of a never-satisfied promise. Consumerism's fatal conceit. Modern society is 'drinking and drugging' itself out of awareness, as Becker describes it. Or else shopping, 'which is the same thing'.[33]

Thunberg is correct. There is a 'real power' that rests with the people. But first it must rouse itself from the conditions of its own inertia. Next it must express itself through the ballot box. When that doesn't work, it must take to the streets. Occasionally – perhaps too frequently and always tragically – it may erupt into ever more violent forms of resistance as it did in Vietnam. But none of this is sufficient on its own to deliver the dramatic system change that's called for. It may even lead to yet more dystopian outcomes. Something different is needed.

Constant craving

Buddhism starts from exactly the same place that capitalism does. Suffering is everywhere. And yet it engages in an almost diametrically opposed strategy. The 'second noble truth' asserts that suffering (*dukka*) is the result of craving (*tanhē*). Our restless desire for wealth, fame, sexual advantage and even comfort provides no lasting satisfaction. Our craving for them simply adds more fuel to the fire. And our search for dominion over others in pursuit of them makes matters infinitely worse. This kind of power only intensifies suffering.

The 'frontier capitalism' so prevalent in the forums of Davos is sometimes brutally honest about this reality. 'America First' doesn't care if those outside America thrive or perish. The obscene inequality in financial sector remuneration endlessly celebrates an ethos of narrow self-worth in an openly competitive struggle. The subtleties of the social contract are lost to those who advocate craving as the engine of prosperity. So what if power creates suffering? As long as it's others who suffer.

Buddhism rejects this framing not just as immoral but as imprudent. To be ruled by our cravings is to intensify our suffering. Not only for those excluded from power but even for those who use economic or military power to satisfy them. There is a sense in which we've already seen the reality of this. Even our basic needs for sustenance become polluted in the context of untrammelled desire. It's fascinating to see this insight, which is echoed in the philosophy of Aristotle and Saint Augustine and even in our emergent understandings of neurobiology, embedded in a system of thought two and a half thousand years old.

The response is equally striking. Suffering can only be alleviated, the Buddha insisted, by freeing ourselves from craving. He went on to offer a precise set of instructions on how this seemingly impossible feat might be achieved. Buddhism itself is less a religion than a playbook of practical suggestions on how to live, work, love and even breathe in ways that free us from craving. Power lies not, as capitalism insists, in the endless stimulation of desires achieved only through dominion over others. It lies in our ability not to be ruled by our cravings.

I'm not so naïve as to suggest that the route to a postgrowth polity lies in us all learning to overcome our cravings. No one realized better than Thich Nhat Hanh that the understandings of Buddhism must be adapted for a western world. He devoted much of his life to that task. And even Buddhism doesn't expect its advocates never to experience desire. Craving may be, as the Canadian singer k.d. lang has suggested, an irreducible element in the human condition. Perhaps our 'constant craving' – for wealth, affection, sex, chocolate – is a kind of displaced longing for something deeper. Something indefinable. Something infinite.[34]

Maybe our craving is part of 'life's longing for itself'. Maybe we will never be free of it. It doesn't matter. That's not the point. The point is that the juxtaposition between capitalism and Buddhism offers us a stark and fascinating contrast. Starting from one common position – that suffering is an intrinsic part of life – the two ideologies travel in diametrically opposed directions and reach radically different conclusions. We may not be in a position – or may not wish – to judge which of these conclusions is correct or best or preferable. But we could certainly learn something from an ancient philosophical wisdom to save us from the impasse into which the capitalistic state has driven itself.

Quite clearly that lesson cannot be to confer on the state the task of persuading its citizens to relinquish their cravings. There is nothing so morally suspect as having those in power persuade those with no power to accept the paucity of their condition or to forgo their opportunities in life. But neither can it be that we condone the role of the state as the conveyor of false dreams and broken promises. Or, worse, its function as the principal apologist for a system that deliberately conjures up cravings only to leave them cruelly, perhaps even intentionally, unsatisfied. Purely so as to sustain a corrupt and unjust distribution of privilege.

Governance must mean more than this. It must deliver more than this. 'The care of human life and happiness, and not their destruction, is the first and only task of good government,' wrote Thomas Jefferson in 1809. Taking this as our starting point, we must certainly conclude that the state has a duty to enable – and not to prevent – its citizens in the pursuit of a genuine prosperity: to ensure their ability to pursue healthy and active lives; to facilitate the conditions for psychological and social wellbeing; to develop the ability to find flow; to encourage the creativity that enriches both performer and recipient; to nurture the transcendental work of art; and perhaps even to protect the space within which people are free *not* to crave.[35]

And if these considerations define a role for the state, perhaps they also begin to sketch the form the state must take. Perhaps they reveal desirable characteristics for our state representatives. Maybe Thoreau was right. Maybe we have not yet travelled far enough along the road to democracy. When wealth is a ticket to political power; when elected officials can be influenced by corporate spending; when political position is the passport to monetary gain; then the ideal of a benevolent, unpartisan state has already been irredeemably tarnished by wealth and privilege. Can we truly call this democracy?

Should we regulate the receipt of party funding? Should we require our representatives to take oaths that are accountable in law? Should public servants receive training or pass tests or have proven characteristics before they are allowed to take office? Should their earnings be capped? Should we ask them to renounce material wealth? Should we seek some proof that they possess the particular kind of power that flows from being able to resist the craving for power? Should politicians study economics? Should economists study medicine?

These questions sound outlandish from a liberal perspective. But I believe they should be asked. It's not just that we haven't yet reached the destination of democracy. It's that we have relegated all hope of that prospect to the gutter. We have given up on the idea of an effective, legitimate state at precisely the time when we need it the most.

Real power fulfils its obligations, wrote the Chinese sage Lao Tzu, some two and a half thousand years ago. The Vietnamese monk Thich Nhat Hanh echoed the wisdom of that ancient tradition. Power lies in freeing ourselves from our constant craving, he said. No one suggests this freedom is easy to achieve. But the way towards it is open to everyone. In the ancient Buddhist and Taoist traditions, it's the way itself which brings us power. 'If you have a path to go on, you have power,' wrote Thich Nhat Hanh in the epigraph I used to frame this chapter. 'You can generate this kind of power every moment of your daily life.'[36]

This vision is such a dramatic contrast to our contemporary notions of power that it stands as a fitting monument to the inquiry in this chapter – and indeed in some sense to the book as a whole. Perhaps the very least we should do is require some evidence of this power in our politicians.

The way home

A few days after arriving in America on 1 June 1966, Thich Nhat Hanh presented a peace proposal at a conference in Washington, urging the US to stop bombing Vietnam and start offering aid to both sides in the conflict. In place of war, he said, America should begin the difficult and painstaking work of reconstruction and reconciliation.

On the same day that he made these proposals, the South Vietnamese government declared him a traitor, effectively placing him in exile, thousands of miles from his home. Shortly afterwards, he was forced to leave the US under threat of imprisonment. Thich Nhat Hanh eventually settled in France, where he founded an experimental community known as Plum Village and built it from a small farmstead into a thriving retreat centre. It was to be another thirty-nine years before he was able to return to his homeland.[37]

Reflecting on the experience of suddenly finding himself homeless and stateless at the age of 39, Thich Nhat Hanh recalled waking up in the middle of the night with a sense of panic, not knowing where he was. A recurring dream would often find him back in the temple in Hué, where he first trained as a novice monk. 'I would be climbing a green hill covered with beautiful trees when, halfway to the top, I would wake up and realize that I was in exile,' he recounted. 'I had to breathe in and out and remember what city and country I was in.'

When a severe stroke left him partly paralysed and barely able to speak at the age of 88, it was to the Hué monastery that he returned to spend his remaining days.[38]

Exile had left the younger Thich Nhat Hanh desperate to find a way to get home. But it also led him towards a profound understanding. 'Our true home is the present moment,' he would write almost half a century later. 'Whatever is happening right here, right now.' That is our home. This isn't just an abstract idea, he insisted, but 'a solid reality' that we can learn to experience for ourselves. To set ourselves on the path of reaching this experience is the greatest power that we have. At the end of the day, he explained, there is no way home. 'Home is the way.'[39]

10

Dolphins in Venice

'Hope is the thing with feathers –
that perches in the soul –
and sings the tunes without the words –
and never stops at all.'
Emily Dickinson, ~1861[1]

'That enough's enough
Is enough to know.'
Lao Tzu, ~500 BC[2]

Capitalism is a catalogue of system errors. It has overturned the principle of balance in human health – relentlessly insisting that more is better. It has denigrated care – continually depressing the value of the carer. It has over-stimulated consumer appetites – ruthlessly arousing dissatisfaction. It has accelerated material throughput – dangerously undermining the integrity of the natural world.

Capitalism has overturned the world-building task of work. It has tipped our unending search for security into a relentless and inevitable insecurity. It has transformed investment from a canopy of hope into a dystopian gambling casino. It has systematically privileged the returns to capital over the livelihoods of ordinary people. And in doing all this it has destabilized finance, accelerated inequality and compromised our health.

The starkest lesson of all is that it needn't be like this. With an alacrity that was almost shocking, the coronavirus crisis revealed what capitalism has long denied: that it is possible for government to intervene in the health of society. Dramatically if necessary. To 'furlough' workers. To protect livelihoods. To invest in care. To use the sovereign power over money itself – a power denied for ideological reasons by those who would profit from tragedy – as a legitimate vehicle for change.

In the ruins of capitalism, as I hope to have shown in this book, lie the seeds for a fundamental renewal. More is not always a virtue. Struggle is not the only basis for existence. Competition is not the only response to struggle. Drudgery is not the only reward for labour. Productivity doesn't exhaust the return to work. Investment is not a meaningless accumulation of financial wealth. Denial is not the only response to our own mortality.

These lessons flow from a keen attention to the precepts and the defects of capitalism. They also emerge from the extraordinary social phenomenon that we encountered during the year 2020. That experience was profound for many reasons. Not just for its uniqueness in the lives of those who survived it. But also for the speed with which it transported us out of the structures of capitalism and into a postgrowth world. However short-lived that turns out to be, its lessons will persist for a long time to come.

The thing with feathers

Tuesday, 17 March 2020, St Patrick's Day. It was fifty-two years to the day since Bobby Kennedy had stepped down onto the Kansas tarmac to launch his ill-starred Presidential campaign. Two weeks into Italy's coronavirus lockdown, a strange and wonderful rumour began to circulate on social media. There were signs that nature was already recovering from the onslaught of incessant economic activity. Dolphins had been sighted in the canals of Venice![3]

The next day brought some even more extraordinary news. A group of elephants had wandered into a village in the province of Yunnan, China, drunk themselves silly on corn wine and passed out in a nearby tea field. Both stories went viral. An excitable meme accompanied them on their journey through the virtual universe. The Earth is healing! Nature has pushed the reset button! Sometimes it was accompanied by a more sinister echo: we are the virus. Without us, was the implication, nature will be just fine.[4]

It's reminiscent of a sentiment Lynn Margulis would sometimes express. Fascinated by the length of time bacteria had inhabited the earth, she would speak in glowing terms of their resilience and their creativity. Without them, we wouldn't even be here. Without us, they would be just fine, much as they had been for hundreds of thousands of years before we arrived. Pretty much the only thing they can't do, she said, is talk. But if you listen carefully you can hear them sing. And then she would sing the chorus of an old 1950s song, *Gonna Get Along without Ya Now*. It's entirely possible, of course, that it wasn't the entire human species, but only one or two members of it, that she had in mind while singing it.[5]

A few days after the two stories broke, *National Geographic* magazine published an article debunking them. The reports were false, they revealed. This was just a hoax. Simple as that. Fake news. No dolphin is stupid enough to risk its health in Venetian canal water. Even now.[6]

Readers were furious. For different reasons. 'Wow,' said one. 'This is so like telling your kid "Santa isn't real" right after the child happily sat on Santa's lap in the mall.' Why would you spoil our lives with truth when fantasy is so much more palatable? Others decried the perpetrators: people will do anything to get 'likes', they said. A host of spoof replicas followed. Satirical news outlet *The Onion* published an article claiming that white rhinos had taken over downtown Manhattan. One bright spark relayed the 'earth is healing' meme alongside a post of colourful dolphins cavorting in what he pretended was the Hudson River. The image was in fact a vibrant psychedelic design by the graphic artist Lisa Frank.[7]

Bizarrely, a picture of goats descending on the town of Llandudno in Wales turned out to be genuine. And in Arizona a family of javelinas really did come down from the hills and venture into someone's back yard. There were blue skies in Beijing during a season accustomed mainly to unadulterated smog. A mountain range in the Himalayas was visible for the first time in thirty years from the Indian province of Punjab, 200 kilometres away. Dolphins had actually been sighted, apparently. At a port in Cagliari, Sardinia. Less miraculous. But still unusual. A healing of sorts really was happening somewhere, it seemed.[8]

Lazy news channels first sensationalized the stories themselves and then, peeved at being duped, faithlessly celebrated their debunking. Some made out that all of it was evidence that nobody could be trusted. With everyone confined to their homes, a 'deepfake' conspiracy was stealing the last shred of sanity from overwrought citizens: the ability to distinguish between fact and fiction.[9]

Some of that may well have been going on. Extinction Rebellion notoriously (some might say amusingly) circulated a video of the Belgian premier saying that immediate action is necessary to tackle the climate and environmental crisis. It is, of course. But she didn't actually say it. Sadly. Some of the fake may even have originated from those in high places desperate to spin dark situations to their own advantage. Fake is the currency of confusion. Confusion is the foundation for control.[10]

But when it came to the dolphins. Well. There was a simpler, kinder explanation. The original tweet had been in Italian. And it had been perfectly clear: clean water in Venice; swans in Milan; dolphins in Cagliari. Some of the confusion was a simple mistranslation. Some was hasty repetition. The principal culprit was that most profound of human sentiments. Hope. 'The thing with feathers that perches in the soul.' As the poet Emily Dickinson once called it.[11]

Buried treasure

Lynn Margulis's favourite poet was no stranger to lockdown. Dickinson spent much of her life as a virtual recluse, rarely – and eventually never – leaving the family home in Amherst, Massachusetts. Sometimes referred to locally as 'The Myth', she supposedly confined herself to the upper floor of the Dickinson family home – overlooking Amherst's West Cemetery – dressed in a simple white gown. Rumours circulated that the 'lady in white' conducted conversations with her rare visitors through closed doors.[12]

To be fair, we don't really know how much of this is true. The life of the woman who became one of America's most celebrated poets remains to this day shrouded in enigma. Her literary estate was the focus of an unseemly struggle which has obscured any straightforward understanding of the woman herself. Only ten of her poems were published during her lifetime, all of them anonymously. And before her death in 1886 at the age of 55, she had charged her sister Lavinia with destroying all her papers.

Fortunately for the world, that charge was only partially fulfilled. Days after the funeral, Lavinia discovered a treasure trove in the bottom drawer of a chest in her sister's room. Eight hundred poems organized into forty small notebooks (known as 'fascicles') – each one had been lovingly sewn together by hand. Alongside the fascicles were hundreds of letters, poems and letter-poems – a form peculiar to Dickinson's work. Almost five hundred of these – many of them written in pencil on scraps of paper – were sent as notes to her sister-in-law Susan Huntington Dickinson, the wife of her brother Austin.

The letters and poems to Sue (or Susie or Susan) speak of an extraordinary relationship that defies simplistic characterization. The two women were lifelong companions and confidantes. They had been friends since childhood. They shared a passionate love of poetry. They lived quite literally next door to each other for more than three decades. There is a photo of a well-worn path in the grass between the two houses. They were clearly intensely important to each other.[13]

Strangely, all of this is entirely absent from the first volume of Dickinson's poetry, published four years after her death. There is no mention of Sue at all. The most likely explanation for this is that the woman who took charge of publication, Mabel Loomis Todd, just happened to be Austin's mistress at the time. Expunging all reference to Susan was a good way of writing a rival out of history.

If the evidence is to be believed, Todd even erased Susan's name from some of the original manuscripts, occasionally changing it to 'us' in the context of a letter by erasing the 'S' at the beginning and the 'an' at the end of Susan's name. Talk about rewriting history. It's a difficult thing to pull off for posterity, though. We can never be entirely sure that tomorrow's technology won't uncover yesterday's crimes. More than a century after her death, a resourceful Dickinson scholar named Martha Nell Smith used infra-red light and computer-imaging technology to confirm a deception the essayist John Erskine once described as 'little short of a disgrace to American biography'.[14]

Stranger still is that Todd herself never actually met the poet alive. The first time she saw her was in the open burial casket, where she had been lovingly dressed in white (by Susan), with a bunch of violets at her throat. The convenient narrative of Dickinson as an eccentric disappointed spinster is probably Mabel's doing. Perhaps 'The Myth' was intended as a shield against a more salacious truth. Or perhaps it was designed to inspire readers. Let's be generous. If it was the latter, it worked. *The Poems of Emily Dickinson* emerged to immediate critical acclaim in 1890. The first volume was reprinted eleven times in the first two years.[15]

Since that time, Dickinson's work has never been out of print and her reputation as a writer has soared. Astonishingly, though, it was not until 1955 that her poems were reproduced in full, in the precise form their author intended them. And more than a century passed before the likely nature of Emily's relationship to her sister-in-law dared to be spoken. Even now that view is contested. 'Iridescent, puzzling and explosive' was the *New York Times* verdict on *Open Me Carefully*, a collection of Dickinson's intimate correspondence with her sister-in-law published belatedly in 1998.[16]

One thing is clear from those letters. Emily Dickinson's lockdown experience was nothing like the sad confinement conjured up for the sensitivities of a late nineteenth-century audience by Mabel Todd. The editors of the intimate correspondence are candid about that. 'She knew love, rejection, forgiveness, jealousy, despair, and electric passion,' they write. 'And she lived for years knowing the intense joy and frustration of having a beloved simultaneously nearby, yet not fully within reach.' Reading *Open Me Carefully*, it's hard to dispute that conclusion.[17]

It's a view of Emily's life which is supported by Susan Dickinson's intensely moving obituary for her sister-in-law, written within days of her death. 'Not disappointed with the world, not an invalid until within the last two years, not from any lack of sympathy, not because she was insufficient for mental work or social career,' she wrote. 'But the "mesh of her soul", as [the poet] Browning calls the body, was too rare, and the sacred quiet of her home proved the fit atmosphere for her worth and work.'[18]

Lockdown crazy

I know a few people still reeling from the experience of the coronavirus lockdown who will read references to 'the sacred quiet' of the home with a mixture of disbelief and envy. Not everyone was so fortunate. That much is obvious.

Had capitalism left society in robust health, the damage inflicted by a period of withdrawal from the world might not have been so profound. But it didn't. Precarity in work. Instability in finance. Tension in the body politic. A divided and impoverished society. This much was true, even before the pandemic. In the face of adversity, it would be the rich and the privileged who survived the best, while the frontline workers, those who mattered more than we ever credited them for, populated the tragic statistics of Covid-19. Chronically underpaid and dangerously exposed to the virus, marginalized minorities bore the brunt of the pandemic and suffered most under lockdown.

The poor suffered most. But no one was left entirely unscathed. Almost overnight, as the pandemic spread its dangerous wings, the world faced an unparalleled slowing down of economic and social exchange. Its reality was shocking. Reciprocity is the cornerstone of society. Its civilizing power is one of the key moral arguments marshalled in support of capitalism. Exchange is deemed an irreducible virtue. And yet overnight it became an imminent danger. A more or less unmitigated vice.

'When an unfamiliar world arrives,' asked Zadie Smith in her collection of lockdown essays, 'what does it reveal about the world that came before it?' Structures dissolve. Support systems collapse. Families are separated. Grief goes unconsoled. Tensions rise. Relationships are tested. Unrest accelerates. The United Nations chronicled a 'shadow pandemic' of domestic abuse around the world, with 20% more cases than usual. It was accompanied by a mental health crisis of equally disturbing proportions. Loneliness and frustration. Confusion and sorrow. These were the colours in which so many lives were painted during a year that reconstructed our sense of the world.[19]

The virus held up a mirror to society. The reflection it offered us was shadowy and pale. A ghostlike, barely recognizable façade.

We had not chosen lockdown, as Dickinson did. Nor had modernity equipped us for its privations. The strain was enormous. We were thrown unprepared into a reliance on resources which had lain dormant, underdeveloped and unappreciated, for too long. 'Did a break from society free us from a system that holds us captive, slaves to commerce and media? Or did time outside of the system paralyse us?' asked the novelist Ottessa Moshfegh. 'Are our minds really free?'[20]

The longer you stare in the lockdown mirror, the more its shadowy image resolves into a sharp and discomforting truth. Lockdown was not just an aberration. It was a distillation of the pervasive anxiety at the heart of our lives. We are locked down on planet earth. We are locked down in our material bodies. We are locked down in the confinements of culture and custom. We are locked down in the time allotted to us. We are creatures with an infinite capacity to imagine and to dream. And yet we are prisoners in our own lives.

The busyness of the external world was always just an elaborate subterfuge to distract us from this harsh reality. Laid bare, we could only reel in horror. No wonder we are terrified. No wonder we went lockdown crazy. Our first instinct was to rebel. To break free. To deny. Perhaps that denial is inevitable. But its implications have sometimes been disastrous. The extraordinary coalition of Covid-19 denialism, which brought chaos to the streets at times and made a 'second wave' impossible to avoid, bore witness to the strength of that instinct.

But these were not the only responses to the reality of our new predicament. 'Reactions are mixed even in our own hearts,' admits Zadie Smith. 'But isn't it the case that everybody finds their capabilities returning to them, even if it is only the capacity to mourn what we have lost?'[21]

Nor were these capabilities confined to mourning. We strove valiantly to adapt. Skills long forgotten – or dismissed as irrelevant – were resurrected in haste. Activities deemed worthless acquired new meaning and purpose. Jewels were stumbled on unwittingly. Buried treasures were excavated with care. Relationships were rediscovered. Memories were intensified. Because there was more time for reflection. There was less fear of missing out. Because everyone was missing out. There was a greater attention to the skill of living well on less.

Time was less imposing. Days were less frenetic. We were no longer able to distract ourselves with the endless aim of being somewhere else. Everyday life was honed down through simplicity to its raw, uncompromising essence.

Perhaps surprisingly, just a month into lockdown, a sizeable proportion of the population found themselves wishing that at least some of that would continue. One study revealed that 85% of respondents found things in lockdown they'd really quite like to retain when it ended. Fewer than 10% wanted a complete return to normal. A few months in and the torrent of calls for a new economic normal confirmed this response.[22]

Lockdown had freed our imagination to dream of a better future. To believe in a healthier world. To enjoy things we had forgotten or never knew. Cleaner air. Less traffic. Bluer skies. Fewer contrails. More time for each other. Less pressure to succeed. More kindness to strangers. Less noise. More connection with nature. Less haste. More space for quiet contemplation. Dolphins in Venice. Was it wrong to hope that some of this might prevail?

More than half a century ago, Bobby Kennedy closed his University of Kansas address by quoting the playwright George Bernard Shaw. In his wide-ranging 'evolutionary' play *Back to Methuselah*, Shaw has the legendary serpent explain to a biblical Eve: 'You see things as they are; and you say "Why?" But I dream things that never were; and I say: "Why not?"' Why not? The words belong to the language of visionaries.[23]

Pain which cannot forget

Shortly after that Kansas speech, RFK travelled to Indianapolis for a campaign rally in a predominantly black neighbourhood of the city. It had been organized by John Lewis, a 28-year-old civil rights activist with whom he had been working closely. When Kennedy arrived in the city on the evening of 4 April 1968, he was greeted by a call from the mayor urging him not to attend the rally. Earlier that evening, Martin Luther King had been shot and killed in Memphis. He wouldn't be safe, the mayor said.[24]

'*You* might not want to go there,' Bobby Kennedy answered him. 'But I could go there tonight with my ten children and my pregnant wife and sleep on the street and we'd be perfectly safe.' It was not bravado or arrogance. His long-standing collaboration with Lewis had lent him the credibility and the moral authority to stand in front of a predominantly black crowd who had still not heard the tragic tidings and be the one to break it to them.[25]

He mourned the loss with them, reciting the Greek poet Aeschylus: 'In our sleep, pain which cannot forget falls drop by drop upon the heart until, in our own despair, against our will, comes wisdom,' he said. He empathized with them. 'For those of you who are black and are tempted to be filled with hatred and distrust at the injustice of such an act, against all white people, I can only say that I feel in my own heart the same kind of feeling. I had a member of my family killed . . . he was killed by a white man,' he said. And he pointed the way forwards:

> What we need in the United States is not division; what we need in the United States is not hatred; what we need in the United States is not violence or lawlessness; but love and wisdom, and compassion toward one another, and a feeling of justice toward those who still suffer within our country, whether they be white or they be black.[26]

His audience listened in silence. Applauding occasionally. A gasp of horror had greeted the announcement itself. But the tone of Kennedy's voice elicited sadness and respect. There was no violence. Indianapolis remained calm that night. Elsewhere in the country there were furious riots. Expressions of outrage at the senseless injustice. The summer of 1968 was a summer of turmoil for the entire country. Much as the summer of 2020 was.

Three days after the assassination, the blues singer Nina Simone played the Westbury Music Festival on Long Island, New York. In an emotional highlight of a set dedicated to the memory of King, the band performed a song called *Why? (The King of Love Is Dead)*, which they'd written the day after he died. Just before the end of the song,

Simone broke into a short, improvised commentary on death and loss. It ranges through emotions of anger, despair, grief and hope. A tragic precursor to her own struggle with all of these emotions. Towards the end of the ad lib interlude, her voice is almost breaking as she makes a quiet plea to hold on to the things that matter. Then there's a silence. Into the silence she drops a quiet chord. And very slowly she begins the last refrain. The final line of the song resolves nothing. It's a cry from a broken heart, asking despairingly what's going to happen next.[27]

Let freedom ring

One thing that might have happened next was a shift towards a more compassionate, kinder, more lyrical politics under the guidance of a man who believed implicitly in the possibility of such a thing. Kennedy's vision for an inclusive, egalitarian society imbued with dignity and purpose was exactly what was needed in 1968. It's needed now more than ever. In hindsight, what's striking is how carefully thought through that vision was. The ideas from Kansas, the comfort offered in Indianapolis, the thanks given in California: none of this was idle chatter. It was grounded in deep understanding of the issues and a clear sense of our place in history.

The year before he set out on the campaign trail, Kennedy had drawn together the elements of this vision in a book he called *To Seek a Newer World*. As ever, he drew his inspiration from a poet. In this case, from Tennyson's poem *Ulysses*. There the English poet imagines the eponymous hero about to set out on his last heroic journey:

The lights begin to twinkle from the rocks:
The long day wanes: the slow moon climbs: the deep
Moans round with many voices. Come, my friends,
'Tis not too late to seek a newer world[28]

Two months after King's assassination, the man who might have led America towards that newer world was also slain. But the young black activist who inspired and supported him continued his own path of nonviolent protest against injustice for another fifty-two years. In 1986, John Lewis was elected to Congress to represent Atlanta, a seat to which he was subsequently re-elected sixteen times. He became known to his colleagues as the 'conscience of Congress'. 'When you see something that is not right, not just, not fair, you have a moral obligation to say something,' he argued during the first Trump impeachment vote in December 2019. Congress has 'a mission and a mandate to be on the right side of history', he insisted.[29]

Throughout his life, Lewis bore witness to injustice after injustice inflicted on black people, often by the forces of law and order. Over and again, he called out the hypocrisy of a world preaching progress while the most basic rights of minorities were still being cruelly demolished. Though he lived to the age of 80, he never forgot their names. 'Emmett Till was my George Floyd,' he said after the death of Floyd at the hands of the police on 25 May 2020. 'He was my Rayshard Brooks, Sandra Bland and Breonna Taylor.'[30]

Till was a 14-year-old Chicago kid killed in 1955 by two white men after being accused of making sexual advances towards a white shopkeeper in Money, Mississippi. He had been tortured, shot, wrapped in barbed wire and thrown into the Tallahatchie River. The two men were acquitted of his murder. His accuser later admitted she had lied. At Till's funeral, his mother insisted on an open casket so that people could see what had been done to her son. John Lewis was just 15 at the time.[31]

Sixty-five years later, he survived just long enough to see the rise of the Black Lives Matter movement. This time it would be different, he believed. 'People now understand what the struggle was all about,' he said in an interview on *CBS This Morning*. 'It's another step down a very, very long road toward freedom, justice for all humankind.' Shortly after that interview, on 17 July 2020, he succumbed to the pancreatic cancer with which he'd been diagnosed the year before.[32]

His final words – published on the day of his funeral – were a passionate call to continue the struggle. 'In my life I have done all I can to demonstrate that the way of peace, the way of love and nonviolence is the more excellent way,' he wrote in the *New York Times*. 'Now it is your turn to let freedom ring.'[33]

Ghosts in the mirror

The lockdown mirror is haunted by restless ghosts. Like the cold stones of the bridge at Potter Heigham, they conjure up dark glimpses of the immortal abyss. We can turn away from those spectres. Or we can summon the courage to gaze back at them. That was the choice Emily Dickinson taught us.

Her lockdown strategy had many of the characteristics of our own. Immersion in the household. Socially distanced engagement in her community. Though seldom seen, she would routinely send small gifts to friends or words of sympathy to neighbours in distress. She befriended the local kids, cooking gingerbread for them, lowering it in a basket from her upstairs window. She wrote regularly to more than ninety different correspondents. When her mother became bedridden following a stroke in 1875, Emily nursed her for almost seven years, learning in the process how to love her. 'We were never intimate . . . while she was our Mother,' she wrote. '– but Mines in the same Ground meet by tunneling and when she became our Child, the Affection came.'[34]

For Dickinson, the confrontation with death was a vital one. To acknowledge suffering is the first step towards relieving it. That principle has an echo in the work of Thich Nhat Hanh. He distilled its essence into one of the precepts of Engaged Buddhism. 'Do not avoid contact with suffering or close your eyes before suffering,' he wrote. 'Find ways to be with those who are suffering. By such means, awaken yourself and others to the reality of suffering in the world.'[35]

The tendency to avert our eyes from suffering is the flipside of a society always gauging its success on the barometer of 'more'. It has surprising, mainly negative repercussions, not only for the kindness of our society, but even for our own ability to achieve our full potential, as my colleagues and I discovered in our studies on flow.

We wanted to figure out why some people could experience flow more easily than others. We knew already (Chapter 6) that more materialistic attitudes could undermine that ability. We could also see that being able to apply yourself to a task makes flow easier to come by in the long run. But we couldn't quite connect these things up until we discovered, first, that people who have a greater tendency to avoid undesirable sensations also tend to have weaker self-regulatory resources; and, secondly, that people who express more materialistic attitudes have a greater tendency to avoid undesirables.[36]

Putting these things together, our study suggested that the more materialistic we are, the greater our tendency to avoid undesirables; and this in turn undermines the strength of mind needed to develop our ability to experience flow. By shunning pain, avoiding distress, denying suffering, it seems, we are destroying our own capacity to achieve one of the most fulfilling states of human existence. By being prepared to face the darkness, on the other hand, we free our minds to experience our highest potential.

Emily Dickinson is a fascinating example of this principle. Poetry was her life's work. Lockdown was her writing studio. She deliberately placed her material existence under physical limits. In its confines, she developed a poetry that was deeply entwined with her everyday life. A language through which she communicated her heart to the world. A philosophy that offered a hope that 'sings the tunes without the words. And never stops at all.'[37]

As often as not, her poetry was shot through with a powerful awareness of our mortality: our fear of loss; the inevitability of separation; and the suffering at the core of existence. Unafraid, and determined never to turn away from her subject, she surveyed its intensity with a deliberate, mystical gaze. Her exploration of mortality is steeped in metaphor, her imagery frequently drawn from a deep love of nature. In her poems, death appears as a messenger, a guide, and sometimes even as a friend:

> Because I could not stop for Death –
> He kindly stopped for me –
> The Carriage held but just Ourselves –
> And Immortality.[38]

She used poetry, according to one commentator, as an 'arbiter of immortality'. A way of approaching the mystery of consciousness in a world infused with death. Though it continually informs the world-building task of human work, it's a subject most of us don't seek out in the way that Dickinson did. The contemplation of death is something almost entirely foreign to the denial that inhabits capitalism.[39]

Death was also too much for her at times. As it is for all of us. Her mother died in 1882 and her young nephew, Sue's son Gib, a year later. He was just 8 years old. In the fall of 1884, she complained that 'the Dyings have been too deep for me, and before I could raise my Heart from one, another has come'. Months of ill health followed. But she still occasionally managed to write.[40]

Through the early months of 1886, her condition worsened. Her last letter was a short note to her two younger cousins, Louise and Frances Norcross. It read simply: 'Little Cousins. Called Back. Emily.' On 13 May, she slipped into unconsciousness. By the morning of 15 May, her breathing had become laboured and shallow. 'The day was awful,' wrote her brother Austin in his diary. 'She ceased to breathe that terrible breathing just before the [factory] whistle sounded for six.' It was Susan who washed her body and prepared her for burial.[41]

Enough

Where does this journey end? Where do we find ourselves when lock-down is over? What kind of newer world do we dare to dream? A part of my aim in this book has been to seek insight into the human condition from the ghosts in the mirror. Their wisdom sometimes seems inaccessible to us. They wander Elysian fields far above the plain of mortal existence. But in the foothills of the mountains frequented by the gods run well-trodden paths that even mere mortals may follow.

Beyond the visceral happiness of our raw animal nature lies a profound realization of our own mortality. Its terrifying truth continually informs the narrative of our lives. It emerges with stark clarity in the world-building nature of human work. Our desire for durability propels us into a frenzy of construction. Economic growth, in its essence, is the incarnation of that frenzy. Its aim is no less than to deliver immortality. But in the hands of capitalism, it is destined to fail. Understanding that failure has been one of the aims of this book.

I'm not arguing that work is in vain. On the contrary, I aim to rescue work as a fundamental element in human prosperity. It has the potential to be the site for our most profound experience of the state of flow. And it contributes to our unending need for intimations of immortality. It is in the corruption of work that these rewards are lost. Not in work itself.

Where does the journey end? It doesn't. The work of confronting mortality is never finished. To avoid falling into denial, it must always be anchored in an honest relationship to suffering. But it need never abandon the prospect of hope. This is the message from Emily Dickinson's 'thing with feathers'. We need never relinquish the possibility for human fulfilment. It will never relinquish us.

The material limits to our lives never remotely circumscribe our potential to experience the most intense, the most vibrant, the most unlikely, the most profound of human emotions. Its unlikeliness in an entropic world, as Ludwig Boltzmann pointed out, is only surpassed by the continuity of its presence.

Love – not loneliness – was the redeeming feature of Dickinson's lockdown. Perhaps the same is always true. 'Without it, life is just doing time,' wrote Ottessa Moshfegh. Without it, 'in some form, somewhere in our lives', insisted Zadie Smith, 'there really is only time, and there will always be too much of it'.[42]

In his 1947 novel *The Plague* – a story that might have been written entirely for our times – the Nobel Prize-winning author Albert Camus comes to a similar conclusion. Though the inhabitants of the plague-ridden city returned as swiftly as they dared to the realm of normality and forgetfulness, the survivors 'knew now that if there is one thing one can always yearn for, and sometimes attain, it is human love'.[43]

This reality is lost to capitalism. Our obsession with 'more' relentlessly obscures the fragile balance of the human heart and denigrates the poetry that might return it to us. Of all our activities, wrote Hannah Arendt in *The Human Condition*, 'poetry is closest to thought'.[44]

Shortly before she died, she had returned to the work of her very first lover, Martin Heidegger. He explored a transcendental philosophy in which thought is the gateway to a realm of unlimited, unchanging Being. By retiring from the 'realm of errancy' into the arena of thought, Heidegger supposed, it was possible to relinquish that 'will to [power] which is the source of all disorder in history'.[45]

It is no surprise that Dickinson's poetry has been compared to Heidegger's philosophy. Both of them were searching for something transcendental. Something vital beyond the incessant noise of life. So too, in a slightly different way, was Arendt. 'Every kind of activity, even the processes of mere thought,' she said, 'must culminate in the absolute quiet of contemplation.' That fleeting awareness where we are entirely free may be life's most precious reward.

Reaching it isn't easy. For Thich Nhat Hanh, that's all about technique. The way home begins and ends with the breath, he said. This simplest of all our exchanges is the gateway to unanticipated riches. It's the most fundamental prosperity of all. Its revelations will never exhaust the human propensity for joy. Its simplicity is available to everyone. For as long as we live. For free.

We breathe in, we breathe out.

Sometimes that gift is taken from us forcibly. Eventually we must all relinquish it. But occasionally, in the meantime, its constant consolation is enough to sustain us. Enough to lend us the tranquillity to see beyond our perpetual craving. Enough to offer us a glimpse of a reality far removed from the endless struggle for existence.

'That enough's enough is enough to know,' said the Chinese philosopher Lao Tzu, two and a half thousand years ago. Not to understand this has been capitalism's fatal conceit.

To set ourselves back on the path towards knowing it, as individuals and as a society, emerges as the single most important lesson from this book. The challenge is enormous. But so too is the prize.

Acknowledgements

The cultural is also personal. The day of the California Primary, 4 June 1968, was my 11th birthday. That's why I was still bleary-eyed around 8.30 the next morning (half past midnight in Los Angeles) eating breakfast and preparing for school when the news came through. Old enough to register the horror, too young to understand the implications. But there it was. Right there in bloodless mono-chrome on the small black-and-white TV in our living room. Another senseless shooting. I remember spending the day in a daze of forlorn hope that this time it would end differently. And a numb sense of grief when it didn't. RFK was the first. But all the characters in this book touched my life in various ways. Sometimes personally. Sometimes professionally. Sometimes both. I'm profoundly grateful for the influence they had on me. And for the chance in some small way to honour that debt.

Some years ago, my friend and colleague Jonathon Porritt wrote a book called *The World We Made*. It told the story of the transition to a sustainable society retrospectively, as it were, looking back over time from 2050. During 2019, the playwright Beth Flintoff was tasked with bringing the book to life on stage. She cleverly told the story through multiple characters. Their voices carrying the action forwards. It's a device that clearly inspired the design of this book. I'm grateful to her, producer Becky Burchell, director Sophie Austin, actors Leann O'Kasi, Tom Ross-Williams and Emma Cater, and of course to Jonathon himself, for the opportunity to learn from that project.

Two other particular sources of inspiration for this book are worth mentioning. The first was an unlikely commission from the UK government to write a briefing paper for the 2019 Global Strategic Trends Review: a periodic horizon-scanning exercise to figure out potential threats to geopolitical stability. What interested those who commissioned the piece most was the possibility that one day soon economic growth might forsake us. That report was the incubator for some of the ideas in this book, particularly the arguments in Chapter 2.

The second was a chance encounter with a young corporate strategy manager named Benoît Ost. The day I met him, in early 2018, he'd just very publicly announced that he was leaving his job because he'd read my *Prosperity without Growth* and it had convinced him he was wasting his time. All well and good were it not for the fact that his employers had just invited me to join a sustainability panel to advise them on how to make things better! It was he who persuaded me to try to bring the postgrowth vision to a wider audience. Doing justice to that task was harder than I thought it would be. But when I faltered, the memory of that conversation sustained me.

The list of people I relied on along the way is even longer than my cast of characters. I am particularly grateful for the first-hand accounts of Herman Daly, Kerry Kennedy and Adam Walinsky in relation to the events of 1968, to Gaby Hock and Lucas Rockwood for their insights on the role of the breath in the sympathetic and parasympathetic response, to Gillian Orrow for reminding me of the importance of Lynn Margulis's work, to Peter Sterling for our fascinating exchange on the neurobiology of health, and to Rowan Williams for drawing my attention to the crucial role played in the human condition by our need for security.

Collaborations with my CUSP colleagues have also contributed massively to the development of the ideas in this book. I am indebted to Amy Isham and Birgitta Gatersleben for our studies on the subject of flow; to Kate Burningham, Bronwyn Hayward, Anastasia Loukianov, Sylvia Nissen, Kate Prendergast and Sue Venn for our exploration of people's aspirations for the good life; to Ben Gallant and Simon Mair for our work on work in a postgrowth economy; to Chrissy Corlet Walker and Angela Druckman for our discussions on the challenge of welfare without growth; to Andrew Jackson for our conversations over many years on the subject of finance and money; to Roger Coward and Paul Hanna for our shared journey

Acknowledgements

into contemplative science; and to Malaika Cunningham and Marit Hammond for our shared interest in the role of creativity in a post-growth polity. My long-standing collaboration with Peter Victor on the development of a postgrowth macroeconomics has taken something of a back seat here. But its implications are also visible at times. His support has always mattered.

I'm grateful to the UK Economic and Social Research Council, whose financial support (Grant: ES/M008320/1) for CUSP has been indispensable to all this work. My responsibilities as Director of CUSP have been an enormous privilege. But they would have been almost impossible to fulfil, particularly during the writing of this book, without the expert backing of my two Deputy Directors, Kate Burningham and Fergus Lyon, and the support of our wonderful administrative team: Gemma Birkett, Catherine Hunt and Neula Niland.

Thanks are due to all those at Polity Press who have brought this book to life. I am particularly grateful to Louise Knight for her enthusiastic and sympathetic support for the project, to Justin Dyer for his perceptive and considerate copy-editing and to Inès Boxman for helping me navigate the intricacies of epigraphs.

As ever, I'm grateful to Zac, Till and Lissy Jackson. Not only are they a large part of my motivation for writing anything at all, but in the years since *Prosperity without Growth* was published they've had the good sense to grow into thoughtful, creative adults and the good grace to teach me more than I ever taught them. Each in their own way became confidants in the writing of this book, contributing insights, reflections, moral support, table tennis and sometimes just welcome distractions as I struggled with my own unruliness.

In a similar vein, conversations with my father, Rich Jackson, somehow allowed me to untangle the knots I sometimes tied myself in. Our late-night lockdown telephone calls became a way of measuring both the passage of time and my slow progress on the manuscript.

Finally, I owe the deepest debt of gratitude to my partner, Linda, whose whole-hearted support and unwavering confidence in my ability to carry through the project were often the only reasons I did. Our conversations improved my thinking. Her proof-reading improved my writing. And the time we spent together, savouring the slow revolution of the seasons during the most extraordinary year in living memory, improved my spirit. Endlessly.

Notes

Prologue

1 'On the Pulse of Morning' from ON THE PULSE OF MORNING by Maya Angelou, copyright © 1993 by Maya Angelou. Used by permission of Random House, an imprint and division of Penguin Random House LLC. All rights reserved. This poem was recited by Maya Angelou at the inauguration of US President Bill Clinton, 20 January 1993 (see Angelou 1993). The live performance can be found here: *https://www.youtube.com/watch?v=M9nTt2F0Kdc*.

2 Shakespeare, *The Tempest*, Act 2, Scene 1.

3 Berger 1967, p. 22.

4 History of WEF: *https://www.weforum.org/about/history*. 'All shall be well', from *Revelations of Divine Love* by Julian of Norwich. Online at: *https://www.gutenberg.org/files/52958/52958-h/52958-h. htm*.

5 Merkel at Davos: *https://www.theguardian.com/business/live/2020/ jan/23/davos-2020-javid-merkel-soros-us-brexit-trump-trade-wef- business-live?page=with:block-5e299d708f0879d539efd9c5*. See also: *https://www.bundesregierung.de/breg-en/news/speech-by-federal -chancellor-dr-angela-merkel-at-the-2020-annual-meeting-of-the- world-economic-forum-in-davos-on-23-january-2020-1716620*.

6 Mnuchin: *https://time.com/5770318/steven-mnuchin-greta-thunberg -davos/*.

7 Trump v. Greta: *https://www.cnbc.com/2020/01/21/our-house-is- still-on-fire-greta-thunberg-tells-davos.html*.

8 Less snow in the Alps: *https://time.com/italy-alps-climate-change/*.

9 Sebastian Kurz in Davos: *https://www.weforum.org/events/world- economic-forum-annual-meeting-2020/sessions/a-conversation-with- sebastian-kurz-federal-chancellor-of-austria-db08d177be*.

10 Warmest January: *https://edition.cnn.com/2020/02/13/weather/ warmest-january-noaa-climate-trnd/index.html.* Insider trading: *https://fortune.com/2020/03/20/senators-burr-loeffler-sold-stock-co ronavirus-threat-briefings-in-january/.*

11 Death of Li Wenliang: *https://edition.cnn.com/2020/02/06/asia/ li-wenliang-coronavirus-whistleblower-doctor-dies-intl/index.html.*

12 In picking the subtitle, I was influenced considerably by Wolfgang Streeck's provocative title *How Will Capitalism End?* (Streeck 2016). But I should also pay homage here to Peter Frase's excellent *Four Futures*, which used the same subtitle (Frase 2016).

Chapter 1 The Myth of Growth

1 Greta Thunberg's speech to the UN Conference on Climate Change, September 2019. Online at: *https://www.theguardian.com/ commentisfree/2019/sep/23/world-leaders-generation-climate-break down-greta-thunberg.*

2 Kennedy's speech at the University of Kansas, 18 March 1968: *https://www.jfklibrary.org/learn/about-jfk/the-kennedy-family/robe rt-f-kennedy/robert-f-kennedy-speeches/remarks-at-the-university-of- kansas-march-18-1968.*

3 Details of the day in Kansas from Halberstam 1968, Kennedy 2018, Newfield 1969 and the personal recollections of Kennedy's speechwriter, Adam Walinsky.

4 Kennedy's speech at Kansas State University, 18 March 1968: *https://www.k-state.edu/landon/speakers/robert-kennedy/transcript. html.* 'Happy roar': Newfield 1969, p. 232.

5 This particular anecdote comes from Adam Walinsky's account of that day (personal correspondence). It is also reported in Newfield's (1969, pp. 232–5) account of the trip.

6 Newfield (1969, p, 234) describes RFK's second speech that day as extemporaneous. Walinsky's account of the re-write on the journey from KSU explains why it had this slightly informal quality.

7 Cult phenomenon: *https://www.youtube.com/watch?v=kmkmJk7L Hdk*; *https://www.youtube.com/watch?v=YgLSH-VvwRY.* Scientific

evidence, see, for instance: IPBES 2019; IPCC 2018; Klein 2019; Porritt 2020.

8 The full text of RFK's speech at the University of Kansas can be found in full online (see note 2). A recording of the speech is available on YouTube at: *https://www.youtube.com/watch?v=z7-G3PC_868.*

9 For a more detailed history of the emergence of the GDP, see, for instance: Coyle 2014; Fioramonti 2015; Philipsen 2015.

10 In keeping with the preferences of the day, RFK referred in his speech to the Gross *National* Product, a term which is much less frequently used today, rather than the Gross *Domestic* Product. Formally speaking, the GDP measures the value of goods and services produced within a nation's borders, while the GNP measures the value of goods and services produced by a nation's citizens, whether they live within the national borders or not. There are crucial and important differences between these two measures when it comes to their use as indicators of national progress. Some 'economic miracles' of the last decade (Ireland and Portugal, for example) look a lot less miraculous when the GNP is used in place of the GDP.

   The reference to Whitman's rifle and Speck's knife alludes to the weapons of two infamous serial killers who terrorized America in the summer of 1966. In fact, it places the origins of this section of the speech at an earlier point in time than the Kansas visit – a suspicion confirmed by Walinsky, who remembers it first being used at an event in Salt Lake City, Utah, in 1966. There's no formal record of that first outing.

11 Historical data on GDP and growth rates can be found in the World Bank's World Development Indicators Databank, online at: *https://databank.worldbank.org/source/world-development-indicators.*

12 Critique of growth: d'Alisa et al. 2014; Jackson 2017; Kallis et al. 2020; Raworth 2017; Trebeck and Williams 2019; Victor 2019.

13 On JFK, Carson and Douglas see: *https://www.audubon.org/magazine/may-june-2012/rachel-carson-and-jfk-environmental-tag-team.*

14 See Introduction to Galbraith 1958, p. xi.

15 Schlesinger 1956, p. 10.

16 EU: *https://ec.europa.eu/environment/beyond_gdp/background_en. html.* OECD: *https://www.oecd.org/statistics/measuring-economic-social-progress/.* World Economic Forum: *https://www.weforum. org/agenda/2020/01/gdp-alternatives-growth-change-economic-development/.* Lunatics etc.: see Jackson 2017, p. 21. Prime Ministers: *https://www.gov.uk/government/speeches/pm-speech-on-wellbeing.*

17 For an overview, see Corlet Walker and Jackson 2019. See also: Kubiszewski et al. 2013; *https://treasury.govt.nz/information-and-services/nz-economy/higher-living-standards/our-living-stand ards-framework.*

18 Stiglitz: *https://www.theguardian.com/commentisfree/2019/nov/24/ metrics-gdp-economic-performance-social-progress.*

19 Daly 1968. For a discussion of the paper – and the circumstances of publication – see Victor 2021, Chapter 4.

20 Daly's work was also influenced by his doctoral supervisor, the Romanian-born mathematician Nicholas Georgescu-Roegen, who at that point was preoccupied with the fundamentally 'entropic' nature of the economy as a thermodynamic system. More of that in Chapter 5.

21 Ecological economics: Common and Stagl 2005; Costanza 1991; Daly and Cobb 1989; Daly and Farley 2011; Martinez-Alier 1991. See also the journal *Ecological Economics*: *https://www. journals.elsevier.com/ecological-economics.* Steady state: Daly 1974, pp. 15–16; see also Daly 1977; 2014.

22 Mill 1848, p. 593.

23 Kennedy's shooting, see Newfield 1969, pp. 289–304. See also: *http://jfk.hood.edu/Collection/Weisberg%20Subject%20Index%20 Files/K%20Disk/Kennedy%20Robert%20F%20Assassination%20 Clips/Item%20054.pdf.*

Chapter 2 Who Killed Capitalism?

1 *https://www.nytimes.com/2019/10/14/opinion/benioff-salesforce-capitalism.html.*

2 Translation from an extract from Luxemburg's (1915) Junius Pamphlet in Waters 1970.

3 The expert in question was Anand Menon, Professor of European Politics and Foreign Affairs at Kings College London. He wrote about the experience in a review of 2016 for the UK in a Changing Europe Project, which can be found online at: *http://ukandeu. ac.uk/2016-a-review/#*.

4 On the impact of austerity, see the UN Special Envoy Philip Alston's devastating report on the impacts of poverty in the UK: *https://www.ohchr.org/Documents/Issues/Poverty/EOM_GB_ 16Nov2018.pdf*. Post-truth: Davies 2019; see also: *https://www. nytimes.com/2016/08/24/opinion/campaign-stops/the-age-of-post-truth-politics.html*.

5 *https://www.db.com/company/en/davos--the-world-economic-forum. htm*.

6 Difficult year: *https://www.nytimes.com/2020/01/30/business/ deutsche-bank.html*. Assets: *https://ycharts.com/companies/DB/assets*.

7 See Jackson 2019 for a detailed analysis of these statistics. Updated statistics may be found (for instance) at: *https://data. worldbank.org/indicator/NY.GDP.MKTP.KD.ZG*. See also: *https:// stats.oecd.org/Index.aspx*.

8 See Jackson 2019. See also: *https://www.ft.com/content/1043eec8-e9a7-11e9-a240-3b065ef5fc55*.

9 Collier: *https://www.weforum.org/agenda/2020/01/the-future-of-cap italism-by-paul-collier-an-extract/*; see also Collier 2019. Benioff: *https://www.cnbc.com/2020/01/21/stakeholder-capitalism-has-reach ed-a-tipping-point-says-salesforce-ceo-benioff.html*; see also Benioff's opinion piece for the *New York Times* (note 1). Davos manifesto: *https://www.weforum.org/agenda/2019/12/davos-manifesto-2020-the-universal-purpose-of-a-company-in-the-fourth-industrial-revolution/*.

10 The end of history: Fukuyama 1989 and 1992.

11 Woke capitalism: *https://www.nytimes.com/2020/01/23/opinion/ sunday/davos-2020-capitalism-climate.html*.

12 Summers 2014; see also: *https://www.ft.com/content/87cb15ea-5d1a-11e3-a558-00144feabdco*. New normal: see Galbraith 2014; Jackson 2019; Storm 2017.

13 The term 'secular stagnation' was first coined by Alvin Hansen in his Presidential Address to the American Economic Association in 1938 (Hansen 1939) to describe a situation in which economic fundamentals pointed to serious problems for the growth paradigm; see also Teulings and Baldwin 2014. Goldilocks: see Ford 2015.

14 Collier 2019, p. 4; see also the Collier WEF link in note 9.

15 The business of business: Friedman 1962.

16 Smith 1776, Book I, Chapter XI, Part III.

17 *https://www.ft.com/content/10b7f566-f3fd-11e8-ae55-df4bf40f9d od*. The question of whether we can draw lessons from the past in conceiving a new vision for the future is an important one. We'll return to it at various point in this book. The very least we would have to say here is that any proposals, however successful in a previous era, must also be compatible with the changed conditions in which we seek to employ them anew. Wolf's point is that appealing to a time when they worked before is no guarantee at all that they will work again.

18 'Deficit spending' refers to an increase in government spending beyond its tax revenues. It was the principal policy recommendation of the economist John Maynard Keynes in the wake of the Great Depression of the 1930s and the foundation for Franklin D. Roosevelt's 'New Deal'. 'Stagflation' is the term used to describe simultaneously high levels of both inflation and unemployment. It occurred in particular during the oil crises of the 1970s. I return to the politics of the deficit and of sovereign debt in Chapter 9.

19 Savage indictment: *https://www.dramaonlinelibrary.com/play text-overview?docid=do-9781408169520&tocid=do-97814081695 20-div-00000121*. *Serious Money*: Churchill 1990, p. 88.

20 Exam text: *https://www.ocr.org.uk/Images/260990-caryl-churchill-topic-exploration-pack.pdf*.

21 For a fuller history of these developments, see Jackson 2017, Chapter 2; see also Peston 2017; Turner 2015; Wolf 2015.

22 On inequality, see Jackson 2019; Piketty 2014; Piketty et al. 2016.

23 Summers 2014, p. 68.

24 Unwieldy debt: Felkerson 2011. Austerity: see Stuckler and Basu 2014. Health inequality: Marmot et al. 2020.

25 Communist growth: *https://www.scmp.com/economy/china-econo my/article/3040822/china-2020-gdp-growth-target-be-set-around-6-cent-top.*

26 Marx 1867, Vol. 1, Chapter 24. On 'bad capitalism', see Baumol et al. 2007. On the growth imperative, see Heilbronner 1985. See also Jackson and Victor 2015.

27 *Accumulation of Capital*: Luxemburg 1913. Junius Pamphlet: see Waters 1970.

28 The market in this paragraph really just means the total set of exchanges – the buying and selling of goods and services – across the whole economy.

29 See Goodwin 1967.

30 Summers (2014) has been the most vocal advocate of the argument from demand, which he attributes mainly to loose monetary policy. Gordon (2016) argues that the problem is on the supply side. Early attempts to ascertain the causes of a slowing down in the growth rate (e.g. Kaldor 1966) identify a key element in the dynamic as being the composition of demand as economies mature.

31 See Ayres and Warr 2009; Jackson 2019.

32 Streeck 2016, p. 71; see also: *https://newleftreview.org/issues/II87/ articles/wolfgang-streeck-how-will-capitalism-end.*

Chapter 3 The Limited and the Limitless

1 See Ellen MacArthur's TED Talk: *https://www.ted.com/talks/da me_ellen_macarthur_the_surprising_thing_i_learned_sailing_so lo_around_the_world?language=en.*

2 From Rousseau 1762, Book II.

3 Potter Heigham bridge: *https://www.britainexpress.com/attract ions.htm?attraction=2974.* The Lords Appellant were a group of five nobles who sought to curtail the King's power by accusing his close allies of treason: *https://archives.history.ac.uk/richardII/lords app.html.*

4 The Norfolk Broads: *https://www.broads-authority.gov.uk/.* Bittern: *https://www.theguardian.com/environment/2017/nov/09/bit*

tern-numbers-in-uk-at-record-high-says-rspb; see also: *https://timjack son.org.uk/plays/tj_cry_of_the_bittern/*.

5 *https://www.futureworlds.eu/w/1/a/a8/Predicament_PTI.pdf*; see also Meadows et al. 1972.

6 Reagan: Remarks at Convocation Ceremonies at University of South Carolina, 20 September 1983. Online at: *https://www.pres idency.ucsb.edu/documents/remarks-convocation-ceremonies-the-uni versity-south-carolina-columbia*.

7 For a summary of the debates around green growth and decoupling see Jackson and Victor 2019.

8 Krugman: *https://www.nytimes.com/2014/09/19/opinion/paul-krugman-could-fighting-global-warming-be-cheap-and-free.html*.

9 Relative decoupling refers to a decline in the carbon (or material) intensity of each dollar of output.

10 For the numbers see Jackson 2017, Chapter 5.

11 Carbon emissions during Covid-19: *https://www.independent. co.uk/news/science/coronavirus-environment-co2-emissions-air-pollut ion-lockdown-a9523926.html*.

12 Proponents: see, for instance, *http://newclimateeconomy.report/ 2015/*; see also McAfee 2019.

13 Carroll 1871.

14 *http://www.lathams-potter-heigham.co.uk/historical_lathams.asp*.

15 Wilhelm 1923, p. 231.

16 The translation used here can be found at: *https://chaucer.fas. harvard.edu/pages/knights-tale-0*.

17 God is dead: Nietzsche 1882, Book 3, Section 125. Flattening of cosmology: see Wilber 1996, pp. 16–17.

18 Greta Thunberg's speech to the UN Conference on Climate Change, September 2019. Online at: *https://www.theguardian.com/ commentisfree/2019/sep/23/world-leaders-generation-climate-break down-greta-thunberg*.

19 Teilhard de Chardin 1968, p. 32.

20 'The impossible we do at once; the miraculous takes a little longer' was said to be the motto of the US Army Service Forces during the Second World War. *The New York Times,* 4 November 1945. Cited in: *https://www.bartleby.com/73/1183.html*.

21 Wilber 1996, p. 5.

22 There is no more: see note 1.

23 From Ellen MacArthur's TED Talk: see note 1. On the circular economy see: Jackson 1996; Webster 2016.

24 Shooting the bridge: *https://www.flickr.com/photos/convolvulus/4003179662.*

25 Rousseau: see note 2.

26 Berry: *https://harpers.org/archive/2008/05/faustian-economics/.*

Chapter 4 The Nature of Prosperity

1 Mill 1873.

2 From *Intimations of Immortality from Recollections of Early Childhood*, first published in Wordsworth's *Poems*, in two volumes. The full text is online at: *https://www.poetryfoundation.org/poems/45536/ode-intimations-of-immortality-from-recollections-of-early-childhood.*

3 Saint of rationalism: see Rossi 1970, p. 8.

4 Mill 1873.

5 Mental illness one of the fastest-growing categories, see: *https://www.oecd.org/health/mental-health.htm*. Costs of mental illness and suicide in young people, see: *https://www.who.int/en/news-room/fact-sheets/detail/depression*. Suicide rates in the US, see: *https://www.nimh.nih.gov/health/statistics/suicide.shtml#part_154969.*

6 The source of Mill's story is mostly his own *Autobiography* (Mill 1873). See also Rossi 1970.

7 Mill 1861.

8 See Easterlin 1974; 2013.

9 See Inglehart et al. 2008.

10 See Jackson 2017, Chapter 4 for data and analysis.

11 Data from US General Society Survey. See: *https://www.washingtonpost.com/business/2019/03/22/americans-are-getting-more-miserable-theres-data-prove-it/*. Not all countries show this trend. Data from the World Happiness Survey suggest that for many countries there is some slight improvement in reported happiness over

time: *https://ourworldindata.org/happiness-and-life-satisfaction.*

12 Happiness gaps: deprivation, see: *https://core.ac.uk/reader/2072 94868.* East v. West Germany, see: *https://ourworldindata.org/there-is-a-happiness-gap-between-east-and-west-germany.*

13 On rising inequality, see Piketty 2014; on lower happiness in more unequal societies, see Wilkinson and Pickett 2009; 2018.

14 On the departure of happiness from output, see Easterlin 1974; see also Jackson 2017, Chapter 4. On happiness, see Layard 2005; 2020.

15 Stillinger 1961, p. 184.

16 Stillinger 1961, p. 103.

17 Sen 1984; 1990. There's a slight complexity here as to whether progress should be measured in terms of 'good functioning' or whether it should be measured in terms of 'capabilities'. For a discussion, see Robeyns and van der Veen 2007. Aristotle 2004.

18 For a discussion of the differences between Mill's utilitarianism and Aristotle's *eudaimonia*, see Nussbaum 2004. I see the structural concept of 'balance' as more insightful than the idea of freedom that motivates Sen's articulation of the Aristotelian idea. It does more work for us, it seems to me, in considering the question of what it means to flourish on a finite planet precisely because of Aristotle's sense that virtue lies flanked between two vices of deficiency and excess (see below).

19 See, for example: *https://www.ons.gov.uk/peoplepopulationandcom munity/wellbeing/articles/personalandeconomicwellbeingintheuk/ whatmattersmosttoourlifesatisfaction.*

20 Arendt 1958, p. 108.

21 The work of Martha Nussbaum (2006) is interesting here. A collaborator of Amartya Sen, she has proposed a concrete list of 'central human capabilities' that includes many of these factors.

22 Hierarchy: Maslow 1943. Duality: Maslow 1954.

23 Rat Park: *https://www.brucekalexander.com/articles-speeches/rat-park/148-addiction-the-view-from-rat-park.* The opposite of addiction: Hari 2014; see also: *https://www.ted.com/talks/johann_hari_ everything_you_think_you_know_about_addiction_is_wrong?lang uage=en#t-859481.*

24 Gibran 1923, p. 8.

25 Taylor and Mill: see Rossi 1970, pp. 3–63. Soulmate (*Seelenfreundin*): Hayek 1951, p. 56.

26 As close as possible: Rossi 1970, p. 56. All that is most striking: Rossi 1970, p. 57.

Chapter 5 Of Love and Entropy

1 Shakespeare, *The Tempest*, Act IV, Scene 2.

2 Boltzmann's equation: $S = k \log W$, where S is entropy, k is a constant and W is the probability of the state.

3 The lecture is mentioned in several places, including Broda's (1983) biography of Boltzmann and Blackmore's (1995) account of his later life and philosophy (p. 161).

4 'Available energy' has a formal definition in physics. It means energy that is of a sufficient quality to carry out useful work. Broda (1976) has suggested one such account of the love and entropy lecture. His reconstruction certainly has some of these components. Flamm (1983) describes Boltzmann's fascination with Darwin. Aside from the interpretation in this chapter, my radio drama for BBC Radio 4 offers a fictionalized account, drawing on various documentary sources: *https://timjackson.org.uk/plays/tj_papas_clean_suit/*.

5 I first explored some of these implications in *Material Concerns* (Jackson 1996), which includes more detailed insights into the underlying thermodynamics.

6 The term 'calorie' is commonly used as shorthand for kilocalorie (kcal). It's a measure of the energy content of food: 1 kcal is approximately equal to 4.2 kilojoules.

7 On the link between weight and non-communicable (lifestyle) diseases see: *https://www.who.int/news-room/fact-sheets/detail/obesity-and-overweight*. Recognized risk factor: *https://www.thelancet.com/journals/landia/article/PIIS2213-8587(20)30274-6/fulltext*.

8 The glycaemic index is 'a relative ranking of carbohydrate in foods according to how they affect blood glucose levels. Carbohydrates with a low GI value (55 or less) are more slowly digested, absorbed

and metabolised and cause a lower and slower rise in blood glucose and, therefore usually, insulin levels.' See: *https://www.gisymb ol.com/about-glycemic-index/*. See also: *https://www.hsph.harvard. edu/nutritionsource/carbohydrates/carbohydrates-and-blood-sugar/*.

9 One in five children: *https://www.who.int/nutgrowthdb/jme-2019-key-findings.pdf*. Two-fifths of adults and obesity increase: *https:// www.who.int/news-room/fact-sheets/detail/obesity-and-overweight*. Obesity in children: *https://www.medicalnewstoday.com/articles/ 319710#Childhood-obesity-10-times-higher*; see also: *https://www. cdc.gov/nchs/data/hestat/obesity_child_11_12/obesity_child_11_ 12.htm*. On acceleration of lifestyle diseases and link with obesity: *https://www.telegraph.co.uk/global-health/climate-and-people/ mapped-global-epidemic-lifestyle-disease-charts/*.

10 The map can be found here: *https://assets.publishing.service.gov.uk/ government/uploads/system/uploads/attachment_data/file/296290/ obesity-map-full-hi-res.pdf*.

11 On insufficient levels of physical activity, see, for example, Guthold et al. 2018. Data on physical activity are also available via the World Health Organization's Global Health Observatory, online at: *https://www.who.int/gho/ncd/risk_factors/physical_activi ty/en/*. On rise in fast foods, see: *https://www.franchisehelp.com/ industry-reports/fast-food-industry-analysis-2020-cost-trends/*.

12 Inactivity in young people: *https://www.who.int/gho/ncd/risk_fact ors/physical_activity/en/*.

13 On sugar, see Lustig 2014. see also *Sugar, The Bitter Truth*: *https:// www.youtube.com/watch?v=dBnniua6-oM*.

14 On comorbidity in Covid-19, see Gold et al. 2020; see also: *https://www.cdc.gov/mmwr/volumes/69/wr/mm6913e2.htm?s_cid= mm6913e2_w*. Obesity was a recognized risk factor in the severity of Covid-19 outcomes: *https://www.thelancet.com/journals/landia/ article/PIIS2213-8587(20)30274-6/fulltext*.

15 Impacts of sugar on back and joint pain: *https://www.spinemd. com/vtfc/news/this-just-in-over-consumption-of-sugar-contributes-to-muscle-joint-pain*; Eivazi and Abadi 2012.

16 For more on reward learning, see Sterling 2020. See also: *https:// greattransition.org/publication/why-we-consume*.

17 Eddington 1929, p. 74.
18 Boltzmann's famous entropy law was first published in 1877 (Boltzmann 1877; Flamm 1983). Entropy was first defined by Rudolph Clausius in 1865 (Flamm 1983).
19 The thermodynamics of open, dissipative systems was developed almost a century after the original formulation of the second law, in particular by the Nobel Prize-winning physicist Ilya Prigogine. It builds firmly on Boltzmann's insights into the nature of entropic processes. For an accessible guide to this non-equilibrium thermodynamics, see, for example, Prigogine and Stengers's (1984) book *Order Out of Chaos*. For an exploration of the implications of the second law in terms of irreversibility, see Coveney and Highfield's (1991) *The Arrow of Time*.
20 There are numerous similar formulations of this framing. The original source is believed to be C.P. Snow: *https://en.wikiquote.org/wiki/Thermodynamics*.
21 The sun is also the original source of the available energy locked up centuries ago in our reserves of coal, oil and gas. Free gift from the sun: Georgescu-Roegen 1971, p. 21.
22 Microscopic mist: Georgescu-Roegen 1975, p. 371.
23 Symbolic role of material goods, see: Belk 1988; Belk et al. 1989; Douglas and Isherwood 1996.
24 On the undermining of psychological health, see Armstrong and Jackson 2015; Dittmar et al. 2014; Kasser 2002. When *Can't Buy Me Love* reached the number one spot on the Billboard Hot 100 on 4 April 1964, the Beatles held all five of the top places on the chart: *https://www.beatlesbible.com/songs/cant-buy-me-love/*.
25 See note 1.
26 Broda 1983, p. 33.

Chapter 6 Economics as Storytelling

1 Margulis 1999, p. 9.
2 Sagan 1996, p. 304.
3 For the details of Margulis's story, see, for instance, Sagan 2012 and contributions therein. See also Margulis 1999, p. 19.

4 Margulis, cited in Sapp 2012, p. 59.
5 Narrative economics: Shiller 2019. Draghi, see: *https://www.cusp.ac.uk/themes/aetw/blog-tj_eubef19/*. Pandemic response, see: *https://www.nytimes.com/2020/03/23/business/economy/federal-reserve-how-rescue.html*.
6 McCloskey 1990, p. 5. Rorty 1979, p. 12. McFague 1988, p. 34.
7 Darwin 1859. The alternative title of his famous book *On the Origin of Species by Means of Natural Selection* was 'the preservation of favoured races in the struggle for life'.
8 For a more detailed discussion of this metaphor and its relevance for sustainability, see Jackson 2003. See also Case-Winters 1997; Gale 1972; Roszak 1992. On xenophobia today, see Norris and Inglehart 2019.
9 Darwin 1887, 'My Several Publications'.
10 On Malthus, see, for example: Kallis 2019; Ridley 2015. The idea that life involves suffering was clearly not something he conjured out of thin air. In fact, I want to come back to it at the end of this book. It bears significantly on the inquiry of what prosperity can really mean.
11 Defining poem of the Victorian age: *https://www.bl.uk/collection-items/in-memoriam-ahh-by-alfred-lord-tennyson*. *Temple of Nature*: Darwin 1803, Canto IV.
12 *Leviathan*: Hobbes 1651.
13 Kuhn 1970.
14 Roszak 1992, p. 153.
15 Over-production: see Kenway 1980, p. 25.
16 See Dichter 1964; Jackson 2002; Ridley 1994.
17 See: *https://newint.org/features/2012/05/01/consumer-culture-idealism*.
18 See Douglas 1976; Douglas and Isherwood 1996; Jackson 2006.
19 Williams 1955, pp. 61–2. See also Jackson 2017, Chapter 6.
20 Life without shame: Smith 1776, Book V, Chapter II, Part II. See also Sen 1984, p. 79.
21 See: *https://newint.org/columns/essays/2016/04/01/psycho-spiritual-crisis*.
22 Lebow 1955, p. 7.

23 Richard Dawkins's (1976) account of all this in *The Selfish Gene* – another metaphor drawn from a thoroughly cultural canvas – set out the stall most definitively.

24 Ground-breaking paper: Sagan 1967. Walking communities: *https://science.sciencemag.org/content/252/5004/378.* See also Margulis 1999.

25 Meagher 2020, p. 6.

26 Greed and need: see, for example, Gough 2017 for an interesting analysis of the relationship between heat (climate change), greed and need.

27 Gaia is a tough bitch: *https://www.edge.org/conversation/lynn_margulis-chapter-7-gaia-is-a-tough-bitch.*

28 See Schwartz 1999; 2006.

29 See, for example: *https://www.pbs.org/wnet/nature/the-good-the-bad-and-the-grizzly-what-to-do-if-you-encounter-a-bear/117/.*

30 The sympathetic nervous system is the part of the automatic nervous system in our bodies that responds to perceived danger: *https://www.livescience.com/65446-sympathetic-nervous-system.html.*

31 Sterling 2020, p. 152.

32 The inner game: Gallwey 1975.

33 Flow: Csikszentmihalyi 1990; 2000; 2003. Ecstatic experience: cited in Csikszentmihalyi's TED Talk: *https://www.ted.com/talks/mihaly_csikszentmihalyi_flow_the_secret_to_happiness?language=en.*

34 On the characteristics of flow: Csikszentmihalyi 2000.

35 Heli-skiing and heli-snowboarding (where participants take a flight in a helicopter to a landing site high in the mountains to avoid a tedious ski-lift ascent) are so environmentally damaging that they are banned in some countries. Davos is one of the few European locations where they are possible: *http://www.swissskivacations.com/pages/en/Davos_Skiing___Snowboarding.html#heli-skiing.*

36 Csikszentmihalyi 2003, pp. 94–5. This distinction has clear resonances with Hannah Arendt's distinction between labour and work – see Chapter 7.

37 Low-impact flow: Isham et al. 2018. Materialism and flow: Isham et al. 2020.

38 'On the Origins': Sagan 1967. *Symbiosis in Cell Evolution*: Margulis 1981. Quiet revolution: see Sapp 2012, p. 63; see also: Margulis 1999; *https://vimeo.com/ondemand/symbioticearthhv/303309866.*

39 Margulis 1999, p. 19.

40 See: *https://www.washingtonpost.com/local/obituaries/lynn-margulis-leading-evolutionary-biologist-dies-at-73/2011/11/26/gIQAQ5dezN_story.html.*

41 From Dorion Sagan's (2012, p. 3) introduction to the memorial volume for his mother's life and work.

42 Voyager: *https://voyager.jpl.nasa.gov/golden-record/.*

43 Unruly earth mother/capitalist critics: *https://science.sciencemag.org/content/252/5004/378.* Being right: *https://www.discovermagazine.com/the-sciences/discover-interview-lynn-margulis-says-shes-not-controversial-shes-right.*

44 Tell all the truth: Franklin 1999, #1263; Johnson 1955, #1129; see also: *https://www.poetryfoundation.org/poems/56824/tell-all-the-truth-but-tell-it-slant-1263.*

Chapter 7 The Return to Work

1 Arendt 1958, p. 8.

2 Old Hammond's reply to a question about the incentives for people to work from Morris's *News from Nowhere*: Morris 1890, Chapter 15.

3 *https://www.space.com/11772-president-kennedy-historic-speech-moon-space.html.* See also the wonderful Apollo 11 documentary (dir. Todd Douglas Miller, 2019).

4 Arendt 1958, pp. 1–2.

5 Arendt 1958, pp. 4–5. Emphasis added.

6 Stress in the care sector: for example, Gallagher 2020; see also: *https://www.nytimes.com/2012/05/27/opinion/sunday/lets-be-less-productive.html.*

7 See the report of the Royal Society for the Arts Food, Farming and Countryside Commission, *Our Future in the Land*: *https://www.*

thersa.org/reports/future-land.

8 Precariat: Standing 2011.

9 Arendt 1958, p. 8.

10 Morris 1890. See also Mair et al. 2020 for a deeper discussion of utopian views of work.

11 From 'What Remains? The Language Remains', an interview with Günter Gaus recorded in 1964 and republished in Arendt 2013, p. 17.

12 She recounts this journey in Arendt 2013. See also Young-Bruehl 2004.

13 Arendt 2013, p. 20.

14 *Love and Saint Augustine*: Arendt 1929, p. 11. Reward of labour: Arendt 1958, p. 106. Arendt's view on the visceral happiness of labour is a potentially dangerous one, of course: a little too close perhaps to the *'Arbeit macht frei'* (Work sets you free) of the Nazi concentration camps. But to recognize the rewards of work freely undertaken is not to condone the imposition of hard labour on others.

15 Douglas 1976, p. 207. In fact, Douglas was speaking of the objective of the consumer, but her words are equally relevant to the objective of the worker.

16 Csikszentmihalyi 2003: psychic energy: p. 95; flow and work: p. 99.

17 Csikszentmihalyi 2003, p. 98.

18 The endocrinologist Robert Lustig (2018) argues that these differences are neurochemical. Pleasure (or reward, in his language) is associated with the chemical dopamine; and contentment (fulfilment) with serotonin. Sterling (personal correspondence) argues that we just don't know enough about anything outside the reward learning circuit (dopamine) to be sure of this. Clearly there are huge gaps in our knowledge about the way the human brain functions, which leaves a fascinating space for further exploration of this.

19 Hidden persuaders: Packard 1957.

20 Arendt 1958, p. 133. Lebow 1955, p. 7.

21 Schumacher 1974. The text of the essay, originally written in

1966, may also be found online at: *https://centerforneweconomics. org/publications/buddhist-economics/*. The Buddhist conception of work, outlined in Schumacher's essay, takes the function of work to be threefold: 'to give [us] a chance to utilise and develop [our] faculties; to enable [us] to overcome [our] ego-centredness by joining with other people in a common task; and to bring forth the goods and services needed for a becoming existence'. The resonances with the vision of work in this chapter are strong.

22 Graeber 2018. See also: *https://www.strike.coop/bullshit-jobs/*.

23 The literature on consumer behaviour is particularly telling on these points. See, for instance, the work of Russ Belk and his colleagues: Belk 1988; Belk et al. 1989; Belk et al. 2003. Some of this work suggests that material goods even play a role in a form of spiritual functioning, by embodying aspects of our need for the sacred. Belk (1988) addresses this role. I have also discussed it in various places: see, for example, Jackson 2013.

24 Goods are not goods: Lancaster 1966. Consumer desire: Belk et al. 2003.

25 Arendt 1958, p. 133.

26 Keynes 1930, p. 361. It's interesting to note that many degrowth and postgrowth analyses also assume that the best way to navigate work in a postgrowth economy is to reduce working time. See, for example: Coote and Franklin 2013; D'Alisa et al. 2014; Kallis et al. 2020.

27 Jackson 2017; 2019. See in particular Figure 3 in Jackson 2019.

28 See, for example: Avent 2016; Ford 2015. Numerous examples of this cultural meme have populated science fiction and the popular media at various times over the last half a century or more. For a discussion, see Shiller 2019.

29 Autonomous vehicles: *https://techcrunch.com/2020/07/30/self-drivi ng-startup-argo-ai-hits-7-5-billion-valuation/*. AlphaGo: *https://deep mind.com/research/case-studies/alphago-the-story-so-far*.

30 This phenomenon has a precise name in economics. It's called Baumol's cost disease, after the economist William Baumol who discovered it (Baumol 2012; Baumol and Bowen 1966). His names for the two sectors were the progressive sector and the

stagnant sector. I am deeply grateful to my colleague Ben Gallant at the University of Surrey for coming up with the (slightly) less pejorative terms, fast and slow, which we both much prefer to use. For a more extensive explanation of the Baumol disease and its implications, see Jackson 2017, Chapter 8.

31 Cinderella economy: see Jackson 2017, Chapter 8 for a discussion of this idea.

32 Arendt 1958, pp. 167–8.

33 Young-Bruehl 2004, p. 416.

34 Unthinkable: Heller 2015, p. 109.

35 The story is recounted in Mary McCarthy's 'Editor's Postface' in Arendt 1978, p. 241. The verse from Goethe's Faust (vol. II: Act V, 11404–7) was in German:

> *Könnt' ich Magie von meinem Pfad entfernen,*
> *Die Zaubersprüche ganz und gar verlernen,*
> *Stünd' ich, Natur, vor dir ein Mann allein,*
> *Da wär's der Mühe wert, ein Mensch zu sein.*

The translation here is mine.

Chapter 8 A Canopy of Hope

1 Maathai 2006, p. 289.

2 From *Tao Te Ching* Verse 59. Adapted freely from several translations. See, for example, Le Guin 1997, p. 71 and also: *http:// taoteching.org.uk/*.

3 The details of Wangari's life story are taken mostly from her autobiography (Maathai 2006). The story of her name is in itself a saga of colonialism and gender inequality. Born Wangari Muta, she took on a Christian name, Miriam, at an early age and was expected to use Wangari as a surname. Her father's name (Muta) was dropped. When she became a Catholic, she dropped Miriam and became Mary Jo Wangari. When she married, she reverted to her first name, Wangari, and took on her husband's name Mathai, as a surname. When they divorced, he demanded that

she drop his surname, so she added an 'a' to become Maathai and reinserted her father's surname. For the rest of her life she was Wangari Muta Maathai. For consistency here, and in deference to the name that was most hers, I refer to her for the most part as Wangari.

4 Maathai 2006, p. 45. See also Maathai 2010, Chapter 4.

5 Kennedy airlift: *https://www.jfklibrary.org/learn/about-jfk/jfk-in-his tory/john-f-kennedy-and-the-student-airlift.*

6 By the time she returned, JFK and Tom Mboya were both dead – both victims of an assassin's bullet. Kennedy was 46 and Mboya only 38.

7 'Before the Europeans': Maathai 2006, p. 175.

8 Palm oil and rainforests: *https://www.ran.org/mission-and-values/.* Destruction of the redwoods: *https://www.savetheredwoods.org/abo ut-us/faqs/the-threats-to-the-redwoods/.* Cattle ranching in the Amazon: *https://globalforestatlas.yale.edu/amazon/land-use/cattle-ranching.* Impact on indigenous people: *http://www.ipsnews.net/ 2017/12/indigenous-people-guardians-threatened-forests-brazil/.* Soil erosion:*https://www.worldwildlife.org/threats/soil-erosion-and-degra dation.*

9 For insightful and poignant overviews of these failings, see, for example: Hickel 2018; Klein 2019; Porritt 2020.

10 *Phronesis*: see Aristotle 2004, Book 6. St Augustine on prudence: cited in St Thomas Aquinas, *Summa Theologica, Prudence*. Online at: *https://www.newadvent.org/summa/3047.htm.* On prudence in religion, see: *https://catholicstraightanswers.com/what-is-virtue-and-what-are-the-four-cardinal-virtues/.* On economic prudence, see: Charlier 1996; Vigano 2017. See also: *https://www.adamsmith. org/the-theory-of-moral-sentiments.*

11 See, for instance: *https://www.nationalgallery.org.uk/paintings/titi an-an-allegory-of-prudence.*

12 Pavlov's dogs, see: *https://www.simplypsychology.org/pavlov.html.*

13 Awareness of death in animals: Douglas-Hamilton et al. 2006. The 'worm at the core': Solomon 2015. Anxiety eats up soul: see Jackson 2013.

14 On investment as commitment, see Jackson 2017, Chapter 9.

See also: *https://www.cusp.ac.uk/themes/aetw/wp2/*. Well-known proverb: usually identified as an ancient Greek proverb; but see: *https://www.roger-pearse.com/weblog/2017/08/26/a-society-grows-great-when-old-men-plant-trees-in-whose-shade-they-know-they-shall-never-sit-an-ancient-greek-proverb/comment-page-1/*.

15 Save the land: Maathai 2006, Chapter 5.

16 Maathai 2006, p. 146.

17 Maathai 2006, pp. 146–9.

18 Pray for the judges: Maathai 2006, p. 150.

19 Planting ideas: Maathai, p. 173.

20 Those who came before: Maathai, p. 289.

21 Larry Fink letter: *https://www.blackrock.com/corporate/investor-rela tions/larry-fink-ceo-letter*.

22 Climate finance and finance gap: *https://www.climatepolicyinitia tive.org/publication/global-landscape-of-climate-finance-2019/*. The IPCC's 1.5° scenario aims to restrict global warming to no more than 1.5° Centigrade above the pre-industrial average (IPCC 2018). Investment in biodiversity: Sumaila et al. 2017.

23 Fossil fuel subsidies: *https://www.imf.org/en/Publications/WP/ Issues/2019/05/02/Global-Fossil-Fuel-Subsidies-Remain-Large-An-Update-Based-on-Country-Level-Estimates-46509*.

24 Divest-invest movement: *https://www.divestinvest.org/*.

25 Outperformance of sustainable funds, see, for example: *https:// www.morningstar.com/content/dam/marketing/emea/shared/guides/ ESG_Fund_Performance_2020.pdf*. See also: *https://www.theguar dian.com/money/2020/jun/13/ethical-investments-are-outperform ing-traditional-funds*.

26 Maathai 2010, p. 158.

27 Africa's debt 1970–2002: Maathai 2006, p. 280.

28 On finance flows: Hickel 2018. On Jubilee 2000, see Welby 2016, p. 154. See also: *https://jubileedebt.org.uk/blog/jubilee-2000-anniv ersary-call-photos-memories*. On Covid-19 impacts, see: *https:// www.economist.com/middle-east-and-africa/2020/04/11/africas-debt-crisis-hampers-its-fight-against-covid-19*; see also: *https://www. theguardian.com/business/2020/aug/03/global-debt-crisis-relief-co ronavirus-pandemic*.

29 A stumble: Maathai 2006, p. 164.
30 Impacts of the Green Belt Movement: *https://www.goldmanprize. org/blog/green-belt-movement-wangari-maathai/.*

Chapter 9 The Art of Power

1 From a speech to the UN Climate Change Conference in Katowice, Poland, 15 December 2018. Reproduced in Thunberg 2019.
2 Thich Nhat Hanh 2007, p. 16.
3 The details of Thich Nhat Hanh's life can be found in various places, including his own memoir, *At Home in the World* (Thich Nhat Hanh 2016). See also: *https://plumvillage.org/about/thich- nhat-hanh/biography/.* He recounts his early inspiration in an interview with Oprah Winfrey in 2013: *https://www.youtube.com/ watch?v=NJ9UtuWfs3U.*
4 Vietnam War: Hastings 2018.
5 The source of the war: Thich Nhat Hanh 2016, p. 184.
6 Apostle of peace: *https://plumvillage.org/letter-from-dr-martin-luth er-king-jr-nominating-thich-nhat-hanh-for-the-nobel-peace-prize-in- 1967/.*
7 See: *https://www.mindfulnessbell.org/archive/2016/02/dharma-talk- the-eightfold-path-2.*
8 Magic money tree: *https://www.youtube.com/watch?v=gUtJEfB9 Hi4.* For a biting satirical response making the same point, see: *https://www.youtube.com/watch?v=9oqb6IrLhwA.*
9 *The Deficit Myth*: Kelton 2020.
10 *Hope in Hell*: Porritt 2020, p. 8.
11 Adjustments are not enough: *https://www.lemonde.fr/idees/article/ 2020/05/06/please-let-s-not-go-back-to-normal_6038793_3232. html.*
12 Thunberg 2019 (see note 1).
13 Nietzsche first wrote about the will to power in *Thus Spake Zarathustra* (1883). It was revisited as a theme in *Beyond Good and Evil* (1886). A set of notes on *The Will to Power* was published posthumously: see Nietzsche 1901.

14 Glass ceiling: Hausknost 2020; see also Hausknost and Hammond 2020.

15 *Talking to My Daughter*: Varoufakis 2017.

16 When bombs fall: *https://www.lionsroar.com/in-engaged-buddhism-peace-begins-with-you/*.

17 SYSS: *https://eccemarco.wordpress.com/2016/02/02/mindfulness-in-times-of-war-the-school-of-youth-for-social-service/*.

18 See: *https://saigoneer.com/vietnam-heritage/6505-hoi-an-s-great-flood-of-1964-1#*.

19 Seven boats: *https://www.lionsroar.com/headline-july-2010/*. Engaged Buddhism: *https://www.lionsroar.com/the-fourteen-pre-cepts-of-engaged-buddhism/*.

20 *Letter from a Birmingham Jail*: *https://www.africa.upenn.edu/Articles_Gen/Letter_Birmingham.html*.

21 In my humble opinion: *https://www.crf-usa.org/black-history-month/gandhi-and-civil-disobedience*.

22 Thoreau 1849.

23 On Thoreau's reading of Locke, see Sattelmeyer 1988. Locke's *Second Treatise*: Locke 1689.

24 Hastings 2018. For a review, see: *https://www.nytimes.com/2018/11/20/books/review/max-hastings-vietnam.html*.

25 For a critique, see Kavka 1983.

26 This claim is frequently reduced to the more catchy but less histor-ically accurate: 'life, liberty and property'. Or sometimes of course: life, liberty and the pursuit of happiness. Neither of which quite captures what Locke was searching for in terms of natural law.

27 Locke 1689: natural law – Section 6; conditional power – Section 149.

28 Thoreau 1849, p. 27.

29 Becker 1973, p. 283.

30 It's interesting to note that Locke's natural right to 'freedom', though present in the role of the state, is a highly specialized one: cashed out primarily in terms of the supposed freedoms of the market. Freedoms which are largely inaccessible to those without power and who are inherently vulnerable to the predatory inter-ests of capital.

31 Thich Nhat Hanh 2007, p. 16.

32 Old life back: *https://www.whitehouse.gov/briefings-statements/remarks-president-trump-vice-president-pence-members-coronavirus-task-force-press-briefing-14/*. Lockdown essays: Smith 2020, pp. 11–12.

33 Drinking and drugging: Becker 1973, p. 284.

34 k.d. lang's song *Constant Craving* won a Grammy for best female pop vocal in 1993. She later became a Buddhist and in 2017 described how the song relates to the Buddhist concept of *samsara*: *https://www.theguardian.com/music/2017/sep/26/kd-lang-ben-mink-how-we-made-constant-craving.*

35 The task of good government: Washington 1871, p. 165.

36 Lao Tzu: see Addiss and Lombardo 2007; Le Guin 1997. The power of a path: see note 2.

37 Plum Village and later life: *https://plumvillage.org/about/thich-nhat-hanh/biography/*.

38 A recurring dream: Thich Nhat Hanh 2016.

39 Thich Nhat Hanh 2016, pp. 178–9.

Chapter 10 Dolphins in Venice

1 Emily Dickinson: in Franklin 1999, #314; Johnson 1955, #254; see also: *https://www.poetryfoundation.org/poems/42889/hope-is-the-thing-with-feathers-314.*

2 Lao Tzu: my rendition from various translations, for example: Addiss and Lombardo 2007, #46; Le Guin 1997, p. 56.

3 Dolphins in Venice: *https://twitter.com/LucaVII_/status/12398633 83354224641?s=20.*

4 Elephants in Yunnan: *https://twitter.com/Spilling_The_T/status/1240387988682571776?ref_src=twsrc%5Etfw*. Nature has pushed the reset button: *https://www.telegraph.co.uk/travel/news/coronavirus-nature-environment-swans-venice-clear-skies-china/*; see also: *https://twitter.com/MotherJones/status/1264677705913643011.*

5 Hear them sing: *https://dailycollegian.com/2008/04/detecting-bull-detecting-dna/*. See also: *https://vimeo.com/ondemand/symbiotic earthhv/303309866.*

6 *National Geographic* fake animal stories: *https://www.nationalgeo graphic.co.uk/animals/2020/03/fake-animal-news-abounds-soci al-media-coronavirus-upends-life.*

7 Santa is real: *https://www.nationalgeographic.com/animals/2020/ 03/why-do-people-want-so-badly-to-believe-this-fake-story-is-true/.* White rhinos in New York: *https://www.theonion.com/thousands-of-formerly-endangered-white-rhinos-flood-cit-1842410309.* 'Earth is healing' meme: *https://twitter.com/meesterleesir/status/12493732 49265455104.*

8 Goats in Llandudno: *https://www.facebook.com/JasonManford/pho tos/pcb.10157146434479352/10157146433029352/.* Javelinas in Arizona: *https://www.facebook.com/photo.php?fbid=1022356 9160165902&set=p.10223569160165902&type=3.* Blue skies in Beijing: *https://www.scmp.com/news/china/society/article/3079477/ covid-19-lockdowns-brought-blue-skies-back-china-dont-expect.* Visible from Punjab: *https://edition.cnn.com/travel/article/himalay as-visible-lockdown-india-scli-intl/index.html.*

9 Deepfake: *https://www.dailysabah.com/life/ai-and-deepfake-covid-19-poses-new-challenges-for-detecting-deceptive-tech/news*; see also: *https://apnews.com/86f61f3ffb6173c29bc7db201c10f141?utm_ source=pocket-newtab-global-en-GB.*

10 Belgian premier: *https://www.brusselstimes.com/all-news/belgium-all-news/politics/106320/xr-belgium-posts-deepfake-of-belgian-prem ier-linking-covid-19-with-climate-crisis/.* Confusion in high places: *https://edition.cnn.com/2020/08/05/tech/twitter-trump-restrict/ index.html.*

11 Original tweet: *https://twitter.com/duppli/status/1239491423243 821058.* The thing with feathers: see note 1.

12 Dickinson's life: Sewall 1980; Smith 2002; Wolff 1986.

13 Well-worn path: see Smith 1992.

14 Uncovering deception: *https://www.nytimes.com/1998/11/29/mag azine/beethoven-s-hair-tells-all.html.* Little short of a disgrace: cited in Smith 2002, p. 65.

15 See Wolff 1986, p. 537.

16 All her known poems: Johnson 1955. Letters to Susan: Hart and Smith 1998. *New York Times* review: *https://www.nytimes.com/*

1998/12/13/books/two-belles-of-amherst.html. The love between the two women was first written about in a book of poems from Emily to Susan, published by Susan's daughter Martha in 1914. The possibility that Dickinson and her sister-in-law were lovers is hinted at by several of her biographers but argued for most cogently by Maryland English Professor Martha Nell Smith (Smith 2002).

17 She knew love: Hart and Smith 1998, p. xvii.

18 Hart and Smith 1998, pp. 266–8.

19 Unfamiliar world: Smith 2020, back cover. Shadow pandemic: *https://www.bbc.co.uk/news/av/world-53014211/coronavirus-dom estic-violence-increases-globally-during-lockdown*. Mental health: *https://edition.cnn.com/2020/08/06/health/us-coronavirus-men tal-health-problems-wellness/index.html*; see also Pfefferbaum and North 2020.

20 Moshfegh: *https://www.theguardian.com/commentisfree/2020/apr/ 30/lockdown-novel-self-isolation-coronavirus-pandemic-ottessa-mosh fegh*.

21 Smith 2020, p. 22.

22 Keeping some aspects: *https://www.thersa.org/about-us/media/ 2019/brits-see-cleaner-air-stronger-social-bonds-and-changing-food- habits-amid-lockdown*. Not wanting a return to normal: *https:// www.theguardian.com/world/2020/jun/28/just-6-of-uk-public-want- a-return-to-pre-pandemic-economy?CMP=Share_iOSApp_Other*.

23 *Back to Methuselah*: Shaw 1921, Part I, Act I.

24 Kennedy in Indianapolis: see Kennedy 2018.

25 Perfectly safe: *https://www.theguardian.com/us-news/2020/jul/26/ john-lewis-robert-kennedy-civil-rights*.

26 RFK's remarks on the death of Martin Luther King: *https://www. jfklibrary.org/learn/about-jfk/the-kennedy-family/robert-f-kennedy/ robert-f-kennedy-speeches/statement-on-assassination-of-martin-luth er-king-jr-indianapolis-indiana-april-4-1968*.

27 Nina Simone comments: sadly I can't actually reproduce what she said that day, even though it was completely ad lib, because it later appeared on an album produced by a music company who fought for twenty-five years to secure rights to all her work and finally

achieved it after her husband (and agent) Andrew Stroud died in 2012: *https://www.factmag.com/2015/05/07/sony-battling-nina-simones-estate-over-secret-copyright-deal/.* So now even her words belong to capitalism. But hey, the good news is you can listen to them here for free: *https://www.npr.org/2008/04/06/89418339/why-remembering-nina-simones-tribute-to-the-rev-martin-luther-king-jr?t=1596923892211.*

28 Tennyson, *Ulysses,* online at: *https://www.poetryfoundation.org/poems/45392/ulysses.*

29 Conscience of Congress: *https://www.nytimes.com/2020/07/17/us/john-lewis-dead.html?action=click&module=RelatedLinks&pgtype=Article.*

30 Unforgotten names: *https://www.nytimes.com/2020/07/30/opinion/john-lewis-civil-rights-america.html.*

31 Story of Emmett Till: Tyson 2017.

32 Long, long road: *https://youtu.be/cxJGuHKZcog.*

33 Final words: *https://www.nytimes.com/2020/07/30/opinion/john-lewis-civil-rights-america.html.*

34 Mines in the ground: Habegger 2001, p. 607.

35 Engaged Buddhism: *https://www.lionsroar.com/the-fourteen-precepts-of-engaged-buddhism/.*

36 Isham et al. 2020.

37 See note 1.

38 Because I could not stop: Franklin 1999, #479; Johnson 1955, #712; see also: *https://www.poetryfoundation.org/poems/47652/because-i-could-not-stop-for-death-479.*

39 An arbiter of immortality: Derrick 1983, p. 58; see also Hagenbüchle 1974.

40 Dyings too deep: Habegger 2001, p. 623.

41 The last day: Habegger 2001, p. 627.

42 Without it (Moshfegh): see note 20. Without it (Smith): Smith 2020, p. 24.

43 *The Plague*: Camus 1947, p. 245.

44 Poetry: Arendt 1958, p. 170.

45 Heidegger's transcendental philosophy: Young-Bruehl 2004, p. 474.

References

Addiss, S. and S. Lombardo (trans.) 2007. *Tao Te Ching – Lao Tzu.* Boston and London: Shambhala.

Angelou, M. 1993. *On the Pulse of Morning.* New York: Random House.

Arendt, H. 1929. *Love and Saint Augustine* (ed. J.V. Stock and J.C. Stark). Chicago: University of Chicago Press (reprinted 1966).

Arendt, H. 1958. *The Human Condition.* 2nd edition. Chicago: University of Chicago Press (reprinted 1998).

Arendt, H 1978. *The Life of the Mind.* New York: Harcourt Brace Jovanovich.

Arendt, H. 2013. *The Last Interview – and Other Conversations.* London: Melville House.

Aristotle 2004. *The Nicomachean Ethics* (trans. H. Tredennick and J.A.K. Thompson). London: Penguin.

Armstrong, A. and T. Jackson 2015. The Mindful Consumer: Mindfulness Training and the Escape from Consumerism. Big Ideas Series. London: Friends of the Earth. Online at: *https://tim jackson.org.uk/news_mindful-consumer/.*

Avent, R. 2016. *The Wealth of Humans: Work and Its Absence in the 21st Century.* London: Penguin.

Ayres, R. and B. Warr 2009. *The Economic Growth Engine: How Energy and Work Drive Material Prosperity.* Cheltenham: Edward Elgar.

Baumol, W. 2012. *The Cost Disease: Why Computers Get Cheaper and Health Care Doesn't.* New Haven and London: Yale University Press.

Baumol, W. and W. Bowen 1966. *Performing Arts: The Economic Dilemma.* New York: Twentieth Century Fund.

Baumol, W., R. Litan and C. Schramm 2007. *Good Capitalism, Bad*

Capitalism, and the Economics of Growth and Prosperity. New Haven and London: Yale University Press.

Becker, E. 1973. *The Denial of Death*. New York: Free Press.

Belk, R. 1988. Possessions and the Extended Self. *Journal of Consumer Research* 15: 139–68.

Belk, R., M. Wallendorf and J. Sherry 1989. The Sacred and the Profane in Consumer Behavior: Theodicy on the Odyssey. *Journal of Consumer Research* 16: 1–38.

Belk, R., G. Ger and S. Askegaard 2003. The Fire of Desire: A Multi-Sited Inquiry into Consumer Passion. *Journal of Consumer Research* 30: 325–51.

Berger, P. 1967. *The Sacred Canopy: Elements of a Sociological Theory of Religion*. New York: Anchor Books.

Blackmore, J. 1995. *Ludwig Boltzmann: His Later Life and Philosophy, 1900–1906: Book 1: A Documentary History*. Dordrecht: Springer.

Boltzmann, L. 1877. On the Relationship between the Second Fundamental Theorem of the Mechanical Theory of Heat and Probability Calculations regarding the Conditions for Thermal Equilibrium (trans. K. Sharp and F. Matschinsky). Translated into English: *Entropy* 17(4) (2015): 1971–2009. Online at: *https://doi.org/10.3390/e17041971*.

Broda, E. 1976. Erklärung des Entropiesatzes und der Liebe aus den Prinzipien der Wahrscheinlichkeitsrechnung [An Explanation of the Entropy Law and of Love by Means of Probabilistic Reasoning]. *Physikalische Blätter* 32(8): 337–41. Online at: *https://onlinelibrary.wiley.com/doi/pdf/10.1002/phbl.19760320801*.

Broda, E. 1983. *Ludwig Boltzmann: Man, Physicist, Philosopher* (trans. L. Gray and the author). Woodbridge, CT: Ox Bow Press.

Camus, A. 1947. The Plague (trans. R. Buss). London: Penguin Modern Classics (reprinted 1987).

Carroll, L. 1871. *Through the Looking-Glass*. Online at: *https://www.gutenberg.org/files/12/12-h/12-h.htm*.

Case-Winters, A. 1997. The Question of God in an Age of Science: Constructions of Reality and Ultimate Reality in Theology and Science. *Zygon* 32(3): 351–75.

Charlier, C. 1996. The Notion of Prudence in Smith's *Theory of Moral Sentiments*. *History of Economic Ideas* 4(1/2): 271–97.

Churchill, C. 1990. *Serious Money*. London: Methuen.

Collier, P. 2019. *The Future of Capitalism: Facing the New Anxieties*. London: Penguin.

Common, M. and S. Stagl 2005. *Ecological Economics: An Introduction*. Cambridge: Cambridge University Press.

Coote, A. and J. Franklin (eds) 2013. *Time on Our Side: Why We All Need a Shorter Working Week*. London: New Economics Foundation.

Corlet Walker, C. and T. Jackson 2019. Measuring Progress – Navigating the Options. CUSP Working Paper no. 20. Guildford: Centre for the Understanding of Sustainable Prosperity. Online at: *https://www.cusp.ac.uk/themes/aetw/measuring-prosperity/*.

Costanza, R. 1991. *Ecological Economics: The Science and Management of Sustainability*. Washington, DC: Island Press.

Coveney, P. and R. Highfield 1991. *The Arrow of Time: A Voyage through Science to Solve Time's Greatest Mystery*. London: HarperCollins.

Coyle, D. 2014. *GDP: A Brief but Affectionate History*. Princeton: Princeton University Press.

Csikszentmihalyi, M. 1990. *Flow: The Psychology of Optimal Experience*. New York: Harper & Row.

Csikszentmihalyi, M. 2000. The Costs and Benefits of Consuming. *Journal of Consumer Research* 27(2): 262–72.

Csikszentmihalyi, M. 2003. Materialism and the Evolution of Consciousness. In T. Kasser and A. Kanner (eds), *Psychology and Consumer Culture: The Struggle for a Good Life in a Material World*. Washington, DC: American Psychological Association.

D'Alisa, G., F. Damaria and G. Kallis (eds) 2014. *Degrowth: A Vocabulary for a New Era*. London: Routledge.

Daly, H. 1968. Economics as a Life Science. *Journal of Political Economy* 76(3): 392–406.

Daly, H. 1974. The Economics of the Steady State. *The American Economic Review* 64(2): 15–21.

Daly, H. 1977. *Steady State Economics*. Washington, DC: Island Press.

Daly, H. 2014. *From Uneconomic Growth to Steady State Economics*. Cheltenham: Edward Elgar.

Daly, H. and J. Cobb 1989. *For the Common Good: Redirecting the Economy Toward Community, the Environment, and a Sustainable Future*. Boston: Beacon Press.

Daly, H. and J. Farley 2011. *Ecological Economics: Principles and Applications*. Washington, DC: Island Press.

Darwin, C. 1859. *On the Origin of Species by Means of Natural Selection*. Online at: *https://www.gutenberg.org/files/1228/1228-h/1228-h.htm*.

Darwin, C. 1887. *The Autobiography of Charles Darwin*. Online at: *https://www.gutenberg.org/files/2010/2010-h/2010-h.htm*.

Darwin, E. 1803. *The Temple of Nature*. Online at: *https://www.gutenberg.org/files/26861/26861-h/26861-h.htm*.

Davies, W. 2019. *Nervous States: How Feeling Took Over the World*. New York: Vintage Press.

Dawkins, R. 1976. *The Selfish Gene*. Oxford: Oxford University Press.

Derrick, P. 1983. Emily Dickinson, Martin Heidegger and the Poetry of Dread. *Atlantis* 5(1/2): 55–64.

Dichter, E. 1964. *The Handbook of Consumer Motivations: The Psychology of Consumption*. New York: McGraw-Hill.

Dittmar, H., R. Bond, M. Hurst and T. Kasser 2014. The Relationship between Materialism and Personal Wellbeing – A Meta-Analysis. *Journal of Personal and Social Psychology* 107: 879–924.

Douglas, M. 1976. Relative Poverty, Relative Communication. In A. Halsey (ed.), *Traditions of Social Policy*. Oxford: Basil Blackwell.

Douglas, M. and B. Isherwood 1996. *The World of Goods*. 2nd edition. London: Routledge.

Douglas-Hamilton, I., S. Bhalla, G. Wittemyer and F. Vollrath 2006. Behavioural Reactions of Elephants towards a Dying and Deceased Matriarch. *Applied Animal Behaviour Science* 100(1-2): 87–102. Online at: *https://www.sciencedirect.com/science/article/abs/pii/S0168159106001018*.

Easterlin, R. 1974. Does Economic Growth Improve the Human Lot? Some Empirical Evidence. In P.A. David and M.W. Reder (eds), *Nations and Households in Economic Growth: Essays in Honor of Moses Abramovitz*. New York: Academic Press, Inc..

Easterlin, R. 2013. Happiness and Economic Growth: The Evidence.

Discussion Paper No 7187. Bonn: Institute for the Study of Labour (IZA).

Eddington, A. 1929. *The Nature of the Physical World: The Gifford Lectures 1927.* New York: The Macmillan Company.

Eivazi, M. and L. Abadi 2012. Low Back Pain in Diabetes Mellitus and Importance of Preventive Approach. *Health Promotion Perspectives* 2(1): 80–8. Online at: *https://www.ncbi.nlm.nih.gov/pmc/articles/PMC3963658/*.

Felkerson, J. 2011. $29,000,000,000,000: A Detailed Look at the Fed's Bailout by Funding Facility and Recipient. Levy Economics Institute Working Paper no. 658. New York: Levy Economics Institute. Online at: *http://www.levyinstitute.org/pubs/wp_698.pdf*.

Fioramonti, L. 2015. *The World after GDP: Politics, Business and Society in the Post-Growth era.* Cambridge: Polity.

Flamm, D. 1983. Ludwig Boltzmann and His Influence on Science. *Studies in History and Philosophy of Science A* 14(4): 255–78.

Ford, M. 2015. *The Rise of the Robots.* London: Penguin.

Franklin, R. 1999. *The Poems of Emily Dickinson.* Cambridge, MA: Harvard University Press.

Frase, P. 2016. *Four Futures: Life after Capitalism.* New York: Verso Books.

Friedman, M. 1962. *Capitalism and Freedom.* Chicago: University of Chicago Press.

Fukuyama, F. 1989. The End of History. *The National Interest* 16, 3–18.

Fukuyama, F. 1992. *The End of History and the Last Man.* London: Penguin.

Galbraith, J.K. 1958. *The Affluent Society.* 40th anniversary edition. London: Penguin (reprinted 1998).

Galbraith, J.K. 2014. *The End of Normal: The Great Crisis and the Future of Growth.* New York: Simon & Schuster.

Gale, B. 1972. Darwin and the Concept of a Struggle: A Study of the Extra-Scientific Origins of Scientific Ideas. *Isis* 63: 321–44.

Gallagher, A. 2020. *Slow Ethics and the Art of Care.* Bingley, UK: Emerald Publishing Limited.

Gallwey, T. 1975. *The Inner Game of Tennis: The Ultimate Guide to the Mental Side of Peak Performance.* London: Pan Macmillan (reprinted 2015).

Georgescu-Roegen, N. 1971. *The Entropy Law and the Economic Process.* Cambridge, MA: Harvard University Press.

Georgescu-Roegen, N. 1975. Energy and Economic Myths. *Southern Economic Journal* 41(3): 347–81.

Gibran, K. 1923. *The Prophet.* London: Wordsworth Editions (reprinted 1996).

Gold, M.S., D. Sehayek, S. Gabrielli, X. Zhang, C. McCusker and B. Shoshan 2020. COVID-19 and Comorbidities: A Systematic Review and Meta-Analysis. *Postgraduate Medicine,* 14 July (online first). Online at: *https://www.tandfonline.com/doi/full/10.1080/00325481.2020.1786964.*

Goodwin, R. 1967. A Growth Cycle. In C. Feinstein (ed.), *Socialism, Capitalism and Economic Growth.* Cambridge: Cambridge University Press.

Gordon, R 2016. *The Rise and Fall of American Growth: The US Standard of Living since the Civil War.* Princeton: Princeton University Press.

Gough, I. 2017. *Heat, Greed and Human Need: Climate Change, Capitalism and Sustainable Wellbeing.* Cheltenham: Edward Elgar.

Graeber, D. 2018. *Bullshit Jobs: A Theory.* New York: Simon & Schuster.

Guthold, R., G. Stevens, L. Riley and F. Bull 2018. Worldwide Trends in Insufficient Physical Activity from 2001 to 2016: A Pooled Analysis of 358 Population-Based Surveys with 1.9 Million Participants. *The Lancet Global Health* 6(10): E1077–86. Online at: *https://doi.org/10.1016/S2214-109X(18)30357-7.*

Habegger, A. 2001. *My Wars Are Laid Away in Books: The Life of Emily Dickinson.* New York: Random House.

Hagenbüchle, R. 1974. Precision and Indeterminacy in the Poetry of Emily Dickinson, *Emerson Society Quarterly* 20(1): 33–56. Online at: *https://web.archive.org/web/20160303221225/http://www.hagenbuechle.ch/pdf/precision.pdf.*

Halberstam, D. 1968. *The Unfinished Odyssey of Robert Kennedy.* New York: Open Road Media (reprinted 2013).

Hansen, A. 1939. Economic Progress and Declining Population Growth. *The American Economic Review* 29(1): 1–15.

Hari, J. 2014. *Chasing the Scream: The Search for the Truth about Addiction.* London: Bloomsbury.

Hart, E. and M. Smith (eds) 1998. *Open Me Carefully: Emily Dickinson's Intimate Letters to Susan Huntingdon Dickinson.* Middleton, CT: Wesleyan University Press.

Hastings, M. 2018. *Vietnam: An Epic History of a Divisive War, 1945–1975.* London: William Collins.

Hausknost, D. 2020. The Environmental State and the 'Glass Ceiling' of Transformation. *Environmental Politics* 29(1): 17–37. Online at: *https://doi.org/10.1080/09644016.2019.1680062.*

Hausknost, D. and M. Hammond 2020. Beyond the Environmental State? The Political Prospects of a Sustainability Transformation. Introduction to a special issue of *Environmental Politics* 29(1): 1–16.

Hayek, F. 1951. John Stuart Mill and Harriet Taylor: Their Friendship and Subsequent Marriage. London: Routledge & Kegan Paul.

Heilbronner, R. 1985. *The Nature and Logic of Capitalism.* New York: W.W. Norton and Company.

Heller, A. 2015. *Hannah Arendt: A Life in Dark Times.* New York: New Harvest.

Hickel, J. 2018. *The Divide: A Brief Guide to Global Inequality and Its Solutions.* London: William Heinemann.

Hobbes, T. 1651. *Leviathan.* Online at: *https://www.gutenberg.org/files/3207/3207-h/3207-h.htm.*

Inglehart, R., R. Foa, C. Peterson and C. Welzel 2008. Development, Freedom and Rising Happiness: A Global Perspective 1981–2006. *Perspectives on Psychological Science* 3(4): 264–85.

IPBES 2019. Global Assessment: Policy Makers Summary. Intergovernmental Science-Policy Platform on Biodiversity and Ecosystem Services. Online at: *https://ipbes.net/news/Media-Release-Global-Assessment.*

IPCC 2018. *Special Report Global Warming of 1.5 Degrees.* Geneva: Intergovernmental Panel on Climate Change. Online at: *https://*

*www.ipcc.ch/site/assets/uploads/sites/2/2019/06/SR15_Full_Report_*
High_Res.pdf.

Isham, A., B. Gatersleben and T. Jackson 2018. Flow Activities as a
Route to Living Well with Less. *Environment and Behavior* 51(4):
431–61.

Isham, A., B. Gatersleben and T. Jackson 2020. Materialism and the
Experience of Flow. *Journal of Happiness Studies*, 17 July (online
first). Online at: *https://doi.org/10.1007/s10902-020-00294-w.*

Jackson, T. 1996. *Material Concerns: Pollution, Profit and Quality of
Life*. London: Routledge.

Jackson, T. 2002. Evolutionary Psychology in Ecological Economics:
Consilience, Consumption and Contentment. *Ecological Economics*
41(2): 289–303.

Jackson, T. 2003. Sustainability and the Struggle for Existence: The
Critical Role of Metaphor in Society's Metabolism. *Environmental
Values* 12: 289–316.

Jackson, T. 2006. Consuming Paradise? Towards a Social and
Cultural Psychology of Sustainable Consumption. In T. Jackson
(ed.), *The Earthscan Reader in Sustainable Consumption*. Abingdon,
UK: Earthscan.

Jackson, T. 2013. Escaping the 'Iron Cage' of Consumerism.
Wuppertal Spezial 48: 53–68. Wuppertal: Wuppertal Institute for
Climate, Environment and Energy. Online at: *http://www.sustain
ablelifestyles.ac.uk/sites/default/files/newsdocs/ws48_0.pdf.*

Jackson, T. 2017. *Prosperity without Growth: Foundations for the
Economy of Tomorrow*. London: Routledge.

Jackson, T. 2019. The Post-Growth Challenge: Secular Stagnation,
Inequality and the Limits to Growth. *Ecological Economics* 156:
236–46. Online at: *https://doi.org/10.1016/j.ecolecon.2018.10.010.*

Jackson, T. and P.A. Victor 2015. Does Credit Create a Growth
Imperative? A Quasi-Steady State Economy with Interest-Bearing
Debt. *Ecological Economics* 120: 32–48.

Jackson, T. and P.A. Victor 2019. Unravelling the Case for (and
against) 'Green Growth'. *Science* 366(6468): 950–1.

Johnson, T. (ed.) 1955. *The Complete Poems of Emily Dickinson*.
London: Faber & Faber (reprinted 1976).

Kaldor, N. 1966. *Causes of the Slow Rate of Economic Growth of the United Kingdom: An Inaugural Lecture.* Cambridge: Cambridge University Press.

Kallis, G. 2019. *Limits: Why Malthus Was Wrong and Why Environmentalists Should Care.* Stanford: Stanford University Press.

Kallis, G., S. Paulson, G. D'Alisa and F. Demaria 2020. *The Case for Degrowth.* Cambridge: Polity.

Kasser, T. 2002. *The High Price of Materialism.* Cambridge, MA: MIT Press.

Kavka, G. 1983. Hobbes's War of All against All. *Ethics* 93(2): 291–310.

Kelton, S. 2020. *The Deficit Myth: Modern Monetary Theory and How to Build a Better Economy.* London: John Murray.

Kennedy, K. 2018. *Robert F Kennedy: Ripples of Hope.* New York: Center Street.

Kenway, P. 1980. Marx, Keynes and the Possibility of Crises. *Cambridge Journal of Economics* 4: 23–36.

Keynes, J.M. 1930. Economic Possibilities for Our Grandchildren. In *Essays in Persuasion.* New York: W.W. Norton & Co.

Klein, N. 2019. *On Fire: The (Burning) Case for a Green New Deal.* New York: Simon & Schuster.

Kubiszewski, I., R. Costanza, C. Franco, P. Lawn, J. Talberth, T. Jackson and C. Aylmer 2013. Beyond GDP: Measuring and Achieving Global Genuine Progress. *Ecological Economics* 93: 57–68.

Kuhn, T. 1970. *The Structure of Scientific Revolutions.* 2nd edition. Chicago: University of Chicago Press.

Lancaster, K. 1966. A New Approach to Consumer Theory. *Journal of Political Economy* 174, 132–57.

Layard, R. 2005. *Happiness.* London: Penguin.

Layard, R. 2020. *Can We Be happier? Evidence and Ethics.* London: Pelican.

Le Guin, U. (trans.) 1997. *Lao Tzu: Tao Te Ching – A Book about the Way and the Power of the Way.* Boulder, CO: Shambhala (reprinted 2019).

Lebow, V. 1955. Price Competition in 1955. *Journal of Retailing* 31(1): 5–10.

Locke, J. 1689. *Second Treatise of Government* . Online at: *https://www.gutenberg.org/files/7370/7370-h/7370-h.htm.*

Lustig, R. 2014. *Fat Chance: The Hidden Truth about Sugar, Obesity and Disease.* London: HarperCollins.

Lustig, R. 2018. *The Hacking of the American Mind: The Science behind the Corporate Takeover of Our Bodies and Brains.* London: Penguin Random House.

Luxemburg, R. 1913. *The Accumulation of Capital.* London: Routledge & Kegan Paul (reprinted 1951). Online at: *https://www.marxists.org/archive/luxemburg/1913/accumulation-capital/.*

Maathai, W. 2006. *Unbowed: One Woman's Story.* London: Penguin.

Maathai, W. 2010. *Replenishing the Earth: Spiritual Values for Healing Ourselves and the World.* New York: Doubleday Religion.

Mair, S., A. Druckman and T. Jackson 2020. A Tale of Two Utopias: Work in a Post-Growth World. *Ecological Economics* 173. Online at: *https://doi.org/10.1016/j.ecolecon.2020.106653.*

Margulis, L. 1981. *Symbiosis in Cell Evolution.* New Haven: Yale University Press.

Margulis, L. 1999. *The Symbiotic Planet: A New Look at Evolution.* New York: Basic Books.

Marmot, M., J. Allen, T. Boyce, P. Goldblatt and J. Morrison 2020. Health Equity in England: The Marmot Review 10 Years On. London: Institute of Health Equity. Online at: *http://www.instituteofhealthequity.org/resources-reports/marmot-review-10-years-on.*

Martinez-Alier, J. 1991. *Ecological Economics: Energy, Environment and Society.* Oxford: Wiley-Blackwell.

Marx, K. 1867. *Das Kapital,* Volume One. Chapter 24: Conversion of Surplus-Value into Capital. Online at: *https://www.marxists.org/archive/marx/works/1867-c1/ch24.htm.*

Maslow, A. 1943. A Theory of Human Motivation. *Psychological Review* 50(4): 370–96.

Maslow, A. 1954. *Motivation and Personality.* New York: Harper.

McAfee, A. 2019. *More from Less: The Surprising Story of How We Learned to Prosper Using Fewer Resources – and What Happens Next*. New York: Simon & Schuster.

McCloskey, D.N. 1990. Storytelling in Economics. In C. Nash (ed.), *Narrative in Culture: The Uses of Storytelling in the Sciences, Philosophy and Literature*. London: Routledge.

McFague, S. 1988. *Models of God: Theology for an Ecological, Nuclear Age*. Philadelphia: Fortress Press.

Meadows, D.H., D.L. Meadows, J. Randers and W. Behrens III 1972. *The Limits to Growth: A Report for the Club of Rome's Project on the Predicament of Mankind*. New York: Universe Books.

Meagher, M 2020. *Competition Is Killing Us: How Big Business Is Harming Our Society and Planet – and What to Do about It*. London: Penguin.

Mill, J.S. 1848. *Principles of Political Economy*. Online at: *https://www. gutenberg.org/files/30107/30107-pdf.pdf*.

Mill, J.S. 1861. *Utilitarianism*. Online at: *http://www.gutenberg.org/ files/11224/11224-h/11224-h.htm*.

Mill, J.S. 1873. *Autobiography*. Online at: *http://www.gutenberg.org/ files/10378/10378-h/10378-h.htm#link2HCH0005*.

Morris, W. 1890. *News from Nowhere or an Epoch of Rest: Being Some Chapters from a Utopian Romance*. Online at: *https://www.marxists. org/archive/morris/works/1890/nowhere/index.htm*.

Newfield, J. 1969. *RFK: A Memoir*. New York: Nation Books (reprinted 2003).

Nietzsche, F. 1882. *The Joyful Science*. Online at: *https://www.guten-berg.org/files/52881/52881-h/52881-h.htm*.

Nietzsche, F. 1883. *Thus Spake Zarathustra*. Online at: *https://www. gutenberg.org/files/1998/1998-h/1998-h.htm*.

Nietzsche, F. 1886. *Beyond Good and Evil*. Online at: *https://www. gutenberg.org/files/4363/4363-h/4363-h.htm*.

Nietzsche, F. 1901. *The Will to Power*. Online at: *https://www.guten berg.org/files/52915/52915-h/52915-h.htm*.

Norris, P. and R. Inglehart 2019. *Cultural Backlash: Trump, Brexit and Authoritarian Populism*. Cambridge: Cambridge University Press.

Nussbaum, M. 2004. Mill between Aristotle and Bentham. *Daedalus* 133(2): 60–8.

Nussbaum, M. 2006. *Frontiers of Justice: Disability, Nationality and Policy Design.* Cambridge: Cambridge University Press.

Packard, V. 1957. *The Hidden Persuaders.* New York: I.G. Publishing (reprinted 2007).

Peston, R. 2017. *WTF: What Have We Done? Why Did It Happen? How Do We Take Back Control?* London: Hodder & Stoughton.

Pfefferbaum, B. and C.S. North 2020. Mental Health and the Covid-19 Pandemic. *The New England Journal of Medicine* 383: 510–12, *https://www.nejm.org/doi/full/10.1056/NEJMp2008017.*

Philipsen, D. 2015. *The Little Big Number: How GDP Came to Rule the World and What to Do about It.* Princeton: Princeton University Press.

Piketty, T. 2014. *Capital in the 21st Century* (trans. A. Goldhammer). Cambridge, MA: Harvard University Press.

Piketty, T., E. Saez and G. Zucman 2016. Distributional National Accounts: Methods and Estimates for the United States. NBER Working Paper no. 22945, National Bureau of Economic Research. Online at: *http://www.nber.org/papers/w22945.*

Porritt, J. 2020. *Hope in Hell.* New York: Simon & Schuster.

Prigogine, I. and I. Stengers 1984. *Order Out of Chaos.* New York: Random House.

Raworth, K. 2017. *Doughnut Economics: Seven Ways to Think Like a 21st-Century Economist.* London: Penguin/Random House.

Ridley, M. 1994. *The Red Queen: Sex and the Evolution of Human Nature.* London: Penguin Books.

Ridley, M. 2015. *The Evolution of Everything.* London: Harper Collins.

Robeyns, I. and R. van der Veen 2007. Sustainable Quality of Life: Conceptual Analysis for Policy-Relevant Empirical Specification. Report to the Netherlands Environmental Assessment Agency. Online at: *https://www.pbl.nl/en/publications/Sustainablequalityoflife.*

Rorty, R. 1979. *Philosophy and the Mirror of Nature.* Princeton: Princeton University Press.

Rossi, A. 1970. Sentiment and Intellect: The Story of John Stuart Mill and Harriet Taylor Mill. In A. Rossi (ed.), *Essays on Sex Equality*. Chicago: University of Chicago Press.

Roszak, T. 1992. *The Voice of the Earth: An Exploration of Ecopsychology*. New York: Touchstone.

Rousseau, J.-J. 1762. *Émile*. Online at: *http://www.gutenberg.org/files/5427/5427-h/5427-h.htm#link2H_4_0003*.

Sagan, C. 1996. *The Demon-Haunted World: Science as a Candle in the Dark*. New York: Random House.

Sagan, D. (ed.) 2012. *Lynn Margulis: The Life and Legacy of a Scientific Rebel*. New York: Chelsea Green Publishing.

Sagan, L. 1967. On the Origin of Mitosing Cells. *Journal of Theoretical Biology* 14: 225–74.

Sapp, J. 2012. Too Fantastic for Polite Society: A Brief History of Symbiosis Theory. In D. Sagan (ed.), *Lynn Margulis: The Life and Legacy of a Scientific Rebel*. New York: Chelsea Green Publishing.

Sattelmeyer, R. 1988. *Thoreau's Reading: A Study in Intellectual History with Bibliographical Catalogue*. Princeton: Princeton University Press.

Schlesinger, A. 1956. The Future of Liberalism: The Challenge of Abundance. *The Reporter*, 3 May: 8–11.

Schumacher, E.F. 1974. Buddhist Economics. In *Small Is Beautiful: Economics as If People Mattered*. New York: Harper & Row.

Schwartz, S. 1999. A Theory of Cultural Values and Some Implications for Work. *Applied Psychology* 48(1): 23–47.

Schwartz, S. 2006. Value Orientations: Measurement, Antecedents and Consequences across Nations. In R. Jowell, C. Roberts, R. Fitzgerald and G. Eva (eds), *Measuring Attitudes Cross-Nationally: Lessons from the European Social Survey*. London: Sage.

Sen, A. 1984. The Living Standard. *Oxford Economic Papers* 36: 74–90.

Sen, A. 1990. *Development as Freedom*. Oxford: Oxford University Press.

Sewall, R. 1980. *The Life of Emily Dickinson*. Cambridge, MA: Harvard University Press.

Shaw, G. 1921. *Back to Methuselah: A Metabiological Pentateuch*.

Online at: *http://www.gutenberg.org/files/13084/13084-h/13084-h. htm*.

Shiller, R. 2019. *Narrative Economics: How Stories Go Viral and Drive Major Economic Events*. Princeton: Princeton University Press.

Smith, A. 1776. *An Inquiry into the Nature and Causes of the Wealth of Nations*. Online at: *http://www.gutenberg.org/files/3300/3300-h/3300-h.htm*.

Smith, M. 1992. *Rowing in Eden: Re-Reading Emily Dickinson*. Austin: University of Texas Press.

Smith, M. 2002. Susan and Emily Dickinson: Their Lives, in Letters. In W. Martin (ed.), *Cambridge Companion to Emily Dickinson*. Cambridge: Cambridge University Press.

Smith, Z. 2020. *Intimations: Six Essays*. London: Penguin.

Solomon, S. 2015. *The Worm at the Core: On the Role of Death in Life*. New York: Allen Lane.

Standing, G. 2011. *The Precariat: The New Dangerous Class*. London/New York: Bloomsbury.

Sterling, P. 2020. *What Is Health? Allostasis and the Evolution of Human Design*. Cambridge, MA: MIT Press.

Stillinger, J. 1961. *The Early Draft of John Stuart Mill's Autobiography*. Urbana: University of Illinois Press.

Storm, S. 2017. The New Normal: Demand, Secular Stagnation and the Vanishing Middle-Class. INET Working Paper no. 55, May. Online at: *https://www.ineteconomics.org/uploads/papers/WP_55-Storm-The-New-Normal.pdf*.

Streeck, W. 2016. *How Will Capitalism End? Essays on a Failing System*. London and New York: Verso.

Stuckler, D. and S. Basu 2014. *The Body Economic: Eight Experiments in Economic Recovery from Iceland to Greece*. London: Penguin.

Sumaila, U.R. et al. 2017. Investment to Reverse Biodiversity Loss Is Economically Beneficial. *Current Opinion in Environmental Sustainability* 29: 82–8. Online at: *https://www.sciencedirect.com/science/article/abs/pii/S0168159106001018*.

Summers, L. 2014. US Economic Prospects: Secular Stagnation, Hysteresis, and the Zero Lower Bound. *Business Economics* 49(2): 66–73.

Teilhard de Chardin, P. 1968. *Science and Christ.* New York: Harper & Row.

Teulings, C. and R. Baldwin (eds) 2014. *Secular Stagnation: Facts, Causes and Cures.* London: Centre for Economic Policy Research. Online at: *https://voxeu.org/content/secular-stagnation-facts-causes-and-cures.*

Thich Nhat Hanh 2007. *The Art of Power.* New York: HarperCollins.

Thich Nhat Hanh 2016. *At Home in the World.* London: Penguin.

Thoreau, H. 1849. *On the Duty of Civil Disobedience.* Online at: *https://www.ibiblio.org/ebooks/Thoreau/Civil%20Disobedience.pdf.*

Thunberg, G. 2019. *No One Is Too Small to Make a Difference.* London: Penguin.

Trebeck, K. and J. Williams 2019. *The Economics of Arrival: Ideas for a Grown-Up Economy.* Bristol: Policy Press.

Turner, A. 2015. *Between Debt and the Devil: Money, Credit and Fixing Global Finance.* Princeton: Princeton University Press.

Tyson, T. 2017. *The Blood of Emmett Till.* New York: Simon & Schuster.

Varoufakis, Y. 2017. *Talking to My Daughter: A Brief History of Capitalism.* London: Penguin.

Victor, P.A. 2019. *Managing without Growth: Slower by Design, Not Disaster.* 2nd edition. Cheltenham: Edward Elgar.

Victor, P.A. 2021. *Herman Daly's Economics for a Full World: His Life and Ideas* (forthcoming). London: Routledge.

Vigano, E. 2017. Not Just an Inferior Virtue, Nor Self-Interest: Adam Smith on Prudence. *Journal of Scottish Philosophy* 15(1): 125–43.

Washington, H. (ed.) 1871. *The Writings of Thomas Jefferson, Vol. 8.* Charleston, SC: Nabu Press (reprinted 2010).

Waters, M.-A. (ed.) 1970. *Rosa Luxemburg Speaks.* London: Pathfinder Books.

Webster, K. 2016. *The Circular Economy: A Wealth of Flows.* Cowes: Ellen McArthur Foundation Publishing.

Welby, J. 2016. *Dethroning Mammon: Making Money Serve Grace.* London: Bloomsbury.

Wilber, K. 1996. *A Brief History of Everything.* Revised edition. Boston: Shambala (2000).

Wilhelm, R. (trans.) 1923. *I Ching or Book of Changes*. London: Arkana (reprinted 1989).

Wilkinson, R. and K. Pickett 2009. *The Spirit Level: Why Equality Is Better for Everyone*. New York: Bloomsbury Press.

Wilkinson, R. and K. Pickett 2018. *The Inner Level: How More Equal Societies Reduce Stress, Restore Sanity and Improve Everyone's Wellbeing*. New York: Allen Lane.

Williams, T. 1955. *Cat on a Hot Tin Roof*. In *Cat on a Hot Tin Roof and Other Plays*. London: Penguin (reprinted 1998).

Wolf, M. 2015. *The Shifts and the Shocks: What We've Learned – and Have Still to Learn – from the Financial Crisis*. London: Penguin.

Wolff, C. 1986. *Emily Dickinson*. New York: Alfred A Knopf.

Young-Bruehl, E. 2004. *Hannah Arendt: For Love of the World*. New Haven: Yale University Press.

Index

Index